SAILING
ON FRIDAY

Merchantman wheelhouse, *Socony Mobilube,* circa 1940. Courtesy of Mobil Corporation

SAILING ON FRIDAY

The Perilous Voyage of America's Merchant Marine

JOHN A. BUTLER

BRASSEY'S
Washington • London

Editorial Offices: Order Department:
22841 Quicksilver Drive   P.O. Box 960
Dulles, VA 20166   Herndon, VA 20172

Brassey's books are available at special discounts for bulk purchases for sales promotions, premiums, fund-raising, or educational use.

Library of Congress Cataloging-in-Publication Data
Butler, John A., 1927–
    Sailing on Friday : the perilous voyage of America's merchant marine / John A.
Butler. — 1st ed.
        p.   cm.
    Includes bibliographical references and index.
    ISBN 1-57488-124-8 (alk. paper cloth)
    1. Merchant marine—United States—History. I. Title.
VK23.B88   1997
387.5'0973—dc21   97-20850
                                                        CIP

1-57488-299-6 (alk. paper paperback)

Designed by Margaret Nelling Schmidt, Appalachian Prepress

10 9 8 7 6 5 4 3 2 1

Printed in the United States of America

For Elinor, pilot and mate

Contents

Illustrations

Preface

Superstitious sailors, and few are not to some degree, have long believed that if they set sail on Friday something would go wrong and that misfortune almost certainly would befall them if that day was also the thirteenth of the month. Yet probably more ships leave port on Friday than on any other day of the week. A merchant ship earns money only while under way, so it makes sense for the captain to put to sea before a weekend to keep otherwise idle crew members occupied in productive work.

There is little correlation between day of departure and outcome of the voyage. All ships take at least one bad journey in their lifetime, either to the bottom of the sea or to the breaker's yard. But during a ship's life countless mariners depart on Friday and return home safe, having enjoyed brilliant sunrises from the decks, carved wakes across deep water in all its moods, perhaps made history or planted seeds of adventure in their own lives that blossomed into memorable tales, many retaining an element of truth, and exulted in the nostalgia of a colorful past. Discard the superstition, but look for the reality behind it.

Fateful concern might better apply to the 220-year history of America's merchant marine. Something has indeed gone wrong in the nation that twice was the world's greatest maritime power. A voyage through the story of our merchant service, a search perhaps for a more empirical "Friday," is worthwhile if for no other reason than to affirm or disprove the belief that our seagoing future is doomed. The story is as glorious and as stormy as the waters on which it took place. Shipowners, sea captains, crews, and the federal government have demonstrated a perverse ability to make inept decisions and pluck disaster from every success. We must not dwell on results if we are to find our Friday, but look instead for antecedents. There is much to be related about two centuries of seafaring—enough to make a tale of epic dimension. In my research I found limited interest in boardroom intrigues, which have increased with the growing complexity of the industry. I was drawn instead to study the effects that investors' and executives' decisions had on mariners and shoreside workers—on those who played more active roles. This is a yarn best told from sea level, from the letters, journals, and books of the ones who took part. Many mariners were writers. Richard Henry Dana, Samuel Samuels, and Raphael Semmes come to mind. More writers—Charles Dickens, Samuel Eliot Morison, John McPhee, among the more appealing—became mariners and wrote well of their experience. I have drawn on their works and scores of others, joining them together in a narrative of broader scope than that of their combined works. Additionally, I have relied on information from the *American Biographical Dictionary* and from obituaries, journals, and newspaper articles going back nearly 150 years.

You will find no scholarly historical perspective here. The text is not annotated. My purpose is to make history attractive. To quote Morison in his preface to *The Maritime History of Massachusetts,* "having written these pages for your enjoyment, I have not burdened them with citations; but, having discovered much sunken historical treasure, and taken of it but sparingly, I have added some sailing directions and soundings thereto in a bibliography." There should be enough material included here to set the scholar off on a detailed study of sources. The texts and articles listed by chapter at the end identify useful writings about each period. Frequent citations of a book reflect its broader scope of years, not the importance of its content. Many books listed are themselves unannotated secondary sources, most with splendid bibliographies. The reader is encouraged to explore any topic of unusual interest as one would chart an estuary. A search for more detail can be a nautical adventure in itself.

Unlike many sea tales, my narrative avoids the anthropomorphic assignment of femininity to ships, except in direct quotes. The use of "she" or "her" in reference to a ship, even with a name like *George* or *President Harrison,* is quite acceptable coming from those who have lived, adventured, and perhaps risked life and limb on board. Many ships are vital to my report, but having had no intimacy with them, I must treat them not as personal elements of my life but as objects in an interesting story. Some ships are so revered that dropping the preceding article from their names, as sailors are wont to do, is a mark of respect that I support.

No history of the American merchant marine can ignore its European counterparts. Rarely has the United States taken the lead; far more often it has followed Great Britain and France. If I pay little tribute to the great European advances, it is in the interest of brevity. I hope I have avoided an overly patriotic slant and acknowledged the significant elements in a chronicle that is truly worldwide. Excluded from my account, except where peripherally contributing, are the whalers and fisheries; also omitted, although they may have played a significant part, are the mercantile but illegal activities of piracy, slave transport, smuggling, and rum-running. Each deserves a story of its own, but I leave that for another day down by the docks.

The range of years accompanying each chapter heading provides a framework. But definitive events do not organize themselves into tidy calendar cells. They have been placed in the periods best suited to them at the cost of looking backward, and sometimes forward, from the specified time. The chapter divisions reflect shifting fortunes—periods of growth, decline, or significant change, as short as three years or as long as thirty-six.

The remarkable tale of the American merchant marine is at risk of becoming obscure. Most of its segments are kept alive in the rich treasures of scores of maritime museums and libraries. To the maritime archivists, librarians, and curators I owe thanks for their cooperation with my efforts to tie things together. The following people are noteworthy for their help: Kathy Flynn at the Peabody Essex Museum in Salem; Claudia McFall at the Mariners' Museum, Newport News; Ann Carver House, librarian of the splendid Steamship Historical Society Collection in the Langsdale Library of the University of Baltimore; and Bob Barney, U.S. Coast Guard historian.

I am also grateful to the unnamed librarians and archivists at the James Duncan Phillips Library of the Essex Institute; the G. W. Blunt White Library at Mystic Seaport; the Library of Congress, Naval Historical Center, Navy Department Library, and National Archives in Washington, D.C.; the Marine

Museum of the Great Lakes in Kingston, Ontario; the Bland Library at Kings Point; and the Hurley Library at the Massachusetts Maritime Academy. The staff of Maryland's Montgomery County Department of Public Libraries, as always, patiently guided my research efforts.

For information generously shared, recognition must be accorded to James Stevenson, historian of the American Merchant Marine Veterans; Bill Wilkinson, retired from the Mariners' Museum and still well connected with maritime sources; Paul Ledvina, Mobil Corporation archivist; LJ Evans of the Public Information Office, Exxon Valdez Oil Spill Trustee Council; Gail Perkins of the Maritime Administration; William McQuaide of the American Bureau of Shipping; and Captain Jeff Monroe of the MassPort Maritime Division.

One very worthwhile source of information was the Internet Maritime History List (Marine History Information Exchange Group), managed by Maurice D. Smith, curator of the Marine Museum of the Great Lakes. The list has more than four hundred subscribers around the world, many of whom suggested useful texts and were themselves splendid sources of information. I am grateful to Chris Arvidson, Lars Bruzelius, Stan Crapo, Joan Druett, Jane Fitzpatrick, Kevin Foster, Morgiana Halley, Trevor Kenchinton, Brooks Rowlett, and Jack Schmidt, all knowledgeable MARHST-L subscribers. They reside as far away as Sweden and as close as a few miles along the Capital Beltway, but it was the information highway that brought them to my aid. Day or night, I could pose a question or seek confirmation of some obscure fact and, within hours, have one or more useful responses at hand.

Some mariners and shipowners, upon learning of my project, became enthusiastic supporters. Rear Adm. Leroy Alexanderson, USNR (Ret.), a master mariner and commodore of United States Lines, shared memories of life in that shipping company with a spirit that seems not to have dwindled through a half century spent at sea. John Morris III, president of Red River Shipping Corporation, proudly related the story of his successful American-flagged, modern-day shipping company. Joe Fernon of BOAT/U.S. gave a useful demonstration of the global positioning system. Bruce Malenfant, captain of MV *Eagle,* demonstrated the intricacies of collision avoidance systems. Becky Fitzgerald, mother of a mariner, and my own daughter Stephanie, a Chesapeake sailor, introduced me to two of the three people I interviewed for the epilogue. Bob Scott, whom I've met only through e-mail, came forth as the third. To all, my heartfelt thanks.

Don McKeon and Kathleen Graham, Brassey's editors, encouraged me in getting my material through every stage. Copy editor and fact-checker Martha

Yager was meticulous in her painstaking effort to polish the text—a demanding task, appreciated only in its absence. Finally, I am grateful to my lifetime mate Elinor for her patience in listening to tales told too many times but well refined by the questions she has raised. What she may have considered an exercise in futility was in fact invaluable aid.

John A. Butler
39°03'08" N, 77°10'48" W

Chapter 1

MERCHANT PRINCES: 1776–1790

Resplendent in its rising, a midwinter sun silvered the western Atlantic's crests as they rolled onto the rockbound coast of Massachusetts. Low eastern light reached over Marblehead's dark promontories, gilded an array of islands protecting Salem harbor, and sent beams across a lengthy pier jutting straight from the shore, its planks glistening with dew. Masts of ships moored alongside sliced the light into stripes that slanted across rough clapboard warehouses positioned along the pier. Poised on a rise near the waterfront stood a countinghouse, its red brick aglow in the morning sun. Beyond the facade's windows, the sun's brilliance warmed a walnut-paneled room, where a man and a young lad stood before a table covered with charts. Held down with pewter disks, the broad sheets of heavy paper were British-engraved diagrams of the West Indies, the North Sea, and the Orient, and uppermost, a hand-etched world map divided diagonally by the east coast of North America. At midpoint on that shoreline the small New England seaport of Salem sparkled like a gem, lines radiating from there toward every quadrant, across the Atlantic to Gibraltar, eastward and up to the Baltic, southeast to Cape Town, south to Martinique, Panama, and Cape Horn. The two continents of the Western Hemisphere were framed in ocean passages, courses stretching leftward across the Pacific from Spanish California to the Philippines and Canton, courses curving through the

1

islands of the Orient to Malacca, and on the far right lines slicing westward across the Indian Ocean to tiny Ile de France (Mauritius). The center point of that assemblage of far-reaching routes was marked by a small circle, minutely labeled "Derby Wharf."

This was the world of Elias Hasket Derby, a world peopled by courageous sailors, ambitious adventurers, and canny traders with a profound understanding of luxury markets and foreign interests. The charts lying under the map grew from close to three hundred years of maritime development, starting with the Spanish explorations of the West Indies, followed by the establishment of trade routes from Spain and England to the colonies along the North American coast, and from there to the Baltic and the Orient. Derby and his eighteen-year-old namesake discussed the fur trade in semitropical Canton. The senior's decisions could add to the worldwide fame of this seaport while enhancing the renowned Derby enterprise. The year was 1784, a time of worrisome economic letdown after the War of Independence. The new republic had a ragtag navy and, except for a few ships owned by traders like the Derbys, the merchant fleet of the former colonies was in disarray. It was from New England's surviving vessels that the American merchant marine would emerge. It could surge like a spring tide, or it could diminish to a rivulet among world maritime powers. In time, both fates would befall it.

The thirty-five-year Derby "dynasty," from halcyon start through the glory years to ultimate dissolution, anticipated in miniature the tidal fluctuations of American seafaring history. This still unfinished story is a boisterous and colorful one, as turbulent as the seas on which it has transpired. It is rich with accomplishment and failure, and threaded with continuing hopes.

The progenitor was Richard Derby, born in Salem in 1712, departing from there only for seagoing periods when his mariner's skills were needed. At twenty-four, not uncommonly young for the task, he took command of the sloop *Ranger* to engage in trade with the Spanish West Indies. It was customary for captains to share in the profits of voyages, and Derby, quick to recognize financial opportunities, was a savvy capitalist—The phrase "shrewd as a Yankee trader" was inspired by people of his ilk. By the time he was forty and owner of at least one vessel, he retired from the sea to run an oceangoing mercantile business from the shallow waters of his home port.

More than 150 years of deepwater trading in the new land preceded Derby, marked with Captain John Smith's 1614 delivery of a shipload of fish to England and Spain, that six-month venture netting the explorer 1,500 pounds. Nor was

Smith the first, for his interest had been attracted by the stories of earlier unnamed traders. The shores of the seventeenth-century colonies bristled with maritime activity. By 1627 coastal traffic between Plymouth Colony and New Netherland (Manhattan) had grown to the point where the possibility of short-ening the route by cutting a canal across the marshy portion of Cape Cod was considered. Within Boston harbor, by 1631 a sailing ferry was operating between Charlestown and Chelsea, across the mouth of the Mystic River, while upstream the first colonial trading bark was under construction. Builders of houses, ships, and the casks and barrels to be stowed therein found timber plen-tiful. By 1635 seaports had risen along nearly every tidal river in Massachusetts, Rhode Island, and Connecticut, with ships building in each. Seventeenth-century traders transported New England lumber to the West Indies in exchange for sugar carried to Medford and Newport, where it was distilled into rum and that in turn shipped to France and Africa. The African trade gave rise to the piti-less Middle Passage, the transport of slaves to the West Indies to work the sugar fields, where they were traded for the cane they cut. Southern tobacco was loaded on empty slave ships in Jamestown and Charleston to be exchanged for European manufactured goods. At the turn of the century, tobacco planters were the wealthiest economic group in the colonies, followed by the merchants of Boston. The timber trade was excellent in Massachusetts, forests spreading to within a few miles of the seaports. Gloucester, in 1706, had more than thirty lumber sloops traveling to the West Indies with precut barrel staves, knocked-down boxes, and raw lumber.

Richard Derby prospered while looking with concern on the increasing number of restrictions placed by the mother country on colonial commerce. Merchant traders, under the British thumb, wanted open seas, the freedom to carry goods on their own ships between any nonbelligerent ports free of re-straint. But Derby found opportunity in the tensions that arose from the citi-zens' desire for luxury goods, including East Indian tea, under terms that didn't impinge on their liberty.

A shipment of tea owned by the East India Company arrived in Boston in November 1773 on three British-chartered cargo vessels. The hated British Tea Act gave the East India Company the right to transship tea from England with-out payment of duty. Cargo was to be taxed to the colonial merchants upon receipt, a proposal certain to rile citizenry from Massachusetts to South Car-olina. The *Dartmouth,* owned by Joseph Rotch and Sons of Bedford Village (later New Bedford), passed through customs and moored off Long Wharf.

Duty was due within twenty days to avoid seizure of the tea in default. The people, who saw conformity with the Tea Act as submission to "slavery" and the act itself as reprehensible, refused payment of the duty. Rotch (the name rhymes with "poach") had a load of whale oil to put aboard and wanted the tea unloaded along with his other cargo. The consignees wanted the tea unloaded and warehoused while they waited for directives from the East India Company. Colonial governor Thomas Hutchinson wanted it unloaded to prove that the tax was collectible. The Boston Committee, an unofficial group led by brewer and political activist Samuel Adams, wanting tea without tax, tried to stir up the authorities to get the act repealed. To no avail. On November 29, the day after the *Dartmouth*'s arrival, and again the next day, five thousand people gathered at Old South Meeting Hall to discuss the issue. Meanwhile the ship was forced to move to Griffin's Wharf, while the crowd decided what to do next. Send the tea back to England, they said. But Governor Hutchinson held that the duty was due in any case because the tea had passed customs. Aggravating the situation, two more tea ships—John Rowes's *Eleanor* and William Rotch's *Beaver*—arrived and tied up alongside the *Dartmouth*. The days were running out, and the governor refused to issue a pass for the *Dartmouth* to sail beyond the Castle Island customs point. Rotch stated he would not return the tea, knowing that to attempt it would expose his vessel to the gunfire of English ships patrolling the port. He wanted to be rid of the tea and get on with his shipping. Then, just before time ran out, a crowd quietly gathered in the dark along the quay. They watched as fifty men dressed like Mohawks boarded the three ships. Doing no damage to the vessels, they hoisted 340 casks on deck, smashed them open, and dumped ninety thousand pounds of tea, valued at 10,000 pounds sterling, into the harbor. By morning the tea had floated in soggy brown clumps as far as Dorchester Neck.

Abigail Adams described tea as "the weed of slavery." The weed sprouted into armed resistance and then blossomed into a declaration of independence from the feckless King George and the arrogant British Parliament. Toward the end of January, faced with reports of the affair, the authorities called Rotch and Postmaster Ben Franklin to London as witnesses. There, Franklin was viciously reviled. What brought the colonists to the edge of rebellion was Parliament's reaction to the tea dumping by issuing new restrictions, the first and worst of these "Intolerable Acts" being the closing of the port of Boston. The port extended from just south of Salem across Boston Bay and around Cape Cod, and included the whaling port of Nantucket. The Americans would do without their tea until they had won their freedom.

1-1. Medal cast in honor of schooner *Quero*, Society of the American Revolution. COURTESY, PEABODY ESSEX MUSEUM, SALEM, MASS.

In Salem, tucked between Boston and Gloucester on the North Shore of Massachusetts Bay, two hours closer than Boston to the ocean route to England, Richard Derby started preparing his ships for hostilities as the year progressed. His son John, eldest of three children, had taken command of the fast schooner *Quero*, which Richard later offered for service to the Provincial Congress. When news of the battles of Lexington and Concord reached him in April 1775, he dispatched the *Quero* to London with affidavits stating that British soldiers had initiated what became a colonial rebellion. The news reached Parliament before the official report from the British commander could be delivered.

With John at sea, Richard turned his business affairs over to the family's acknowledged financial manager, his second son, Elias Hasket. Born in 1739, at twenty-two Elias had wooed and wedded Elizabeth Crowninshield, the spoiled daughter of John Crowninshield, founder of a rival shipping house. That marriage, and later the marriage of Elias's sister Mary to George Crowninshield, brought together two of the leading fleet operators in the colonies.

Elias Hasket Derby was well suited to his position. Unique among merchant princes in never having gone to sea, he managed his affairs with a Midas touch. It was difficult to do business with him on equal terms. Possessing a rare eye disorder called heterochromia, in the midst of negotiations he could smile affably across a desk, his brown right eye warmly encouraging agreement while the blue left eye cast a stare chilling enough to unsettle the coolest observer. Unlike many of Salem's wealthiest gentry who entered into the stormy politics of the period, Elias preferred to work out of his father's brick mansion overlooking Derby Wharf, his interests focused on the growth of the Derby fleet. When the War of Independence cut off most of the colonies' West Indian and European trade, Elias, seeing little future if the rebellion were crushed, encouraged his father to give freely of the Derby fortune to support the Continental Army. He fitted out the senior Derby's ships as privateers, put up the surety, and obtained the necessary papers and agreements whereby the booty of a privateer's successful enemy encounters accrued to the shipowner. He then set out to hire skillful and courageous men as sea captains, granting them large shares in their ventures.

The difference between vessels carrying letters of marque and those commissioned as privateers was vague, but clearer in the early days of the breakaway nation than it would be later. The extent of armament may have made the difference. A merchant ship with modest armament might carry a letter of marque, that is, a letter of permission to undertake battle with the enemy's lesser-armed cargo carriers on behalf of the government. With more gun carriages and less cargo-carrying capacity, a privately owned vessel could pass for a naval warship and become a privateer, welcomed by the sparse Revolutionary navy. However they were identified, the sailors of these private ships were little more than licensed pirates. Before war's end the house of Derby put eighty such vessels under its own flag, and they traded as they could while fighting to capture whatever the enemy put afloat. Thus Elias Hasket Derby rose in tandem with George Washington to become the father of the American merchant marine.

Richard Derby died in 1783. By the end of the war, through marriage, shrewd politics, inheritance, and a share in the plunder of battle, his son was poised to become America's wealthiest citizen. Now, one year after the war, he stood with his elder son, Elias Hasket Jr., to assess their future.

Thomas Godfrey's 1731 invention of the sextant in Philadelphia improved the precision of land triangulation and high-noon latitude determination. But without accurate seagoing timepieces the sextant did nothing for resolution of longitude. A nautical almanac was published in 1767, seven years after the Royal

Society recognized Yorkshire carpenter John Harrison for his development of a seagoing clock able to sustain its rate for several weeks under the rigors of ocean sailing. But owners wouldn't equip their ships with the costly Harrison clocks, and sea captains remained content to run down latitudes. (Less expensive and sturdier chronometers became available from France and England after the war, more appealing to the captains, who had to pay for them with their own funds.) Course and distance tracking from a known latitude remained the favored way to set the final courses to a port. Heaving a deep-sea lead helped mariners find the continental shelf and ease through fog into a known channel. It took five or more men to accomplish the task. One stood on the high spritsail yard holding the long lead weight, armed on the bottom with tallow and suspended over the water, the attached line leading down to another man poised on the cat-head with the line in a coil. A third man hung out from the fore chains, another in the waist, and still another at the main chains, each holding a coiled segment, eighty or more fathoms in all. Upon command the lead was swung forward of the bow and let drop, and the line payed off from each hand, fore to aft, until it came to the mate tending the final coils near the taffrail. If the line slackened, the mark at the water was called out; if not, "Eighty fathoms and no bottom!" The trailing line was snatched into a block, and three men heaved in and coiled it for another cast. When the lead found bottom, the mate examined the tallow for what it had collected. Its makeup was a certain indicator of location along the Atlantic coast—clean, white sand on Georges Bank, white sand mixed with shells off Cape Cod, dark sand around Nantucket, thick black mud off Block Island and southward.

Derby sea captains became known for superb seamanship, although they cared little for the intricacies of mathematical navigation. They were further relieved of the business aspects of trading by a Derby innovation, "supercargoes" responsible for handling the exchange of goods carried in Derby bottoms. The supercargoes' knowledge of foreign commerce matched the nautical skills of the captains. After a period at Harvard, some years in his father's countinghouse, navigation training, and time at sea as clerk to Captain Jonathan Archer, Elias Hasket Jr. became supercargo of the Derby brig *Rose,* traveling to the West Indies. The *Rose* was in effect a training ship, often the first command for Derby captains. In the opinion of Derby supercargoes, paraphrasing the words of the Psalmist, those who did business on great waters saw the works of the Lord fulfilled in the growth of the Derby enterprise.

The ships' crews were more interested in the wonders of foreign shores. Recruited mostly from New England farms, these youths readily accepted the hardships of a sailor's life in return for a reasonable living and travel to places few landsmen had ever heard mentioned. Some, but not many, came from the northeast fishing fleet. Fishing was a much different trade. Men comfortable in a dory, hauling a net or handing a cod line, usually were not inclined to lay up to the yards of taller vessels, clambering out on footropes to furl topsails. Nor did they like the discipline and long voyages of the fledgling navy or the merchant service. But the relatively high wages and deepwater adventures of ocean seafaring were enough to draw the lads from the plow to the foredeck. Many first went to sea at the age of thirteen or fourteen. Men in their early twenties predominated; those over thirty were rare. There were a only few foreigners and not more than one or two blacks on most ships, free men sailing usually as cooks or stewards. Most eighteenth-century seamen were schooled well enough to draw up a manifest or post a log; some could find a ship's position at sea by dead reckoning. After one or two voyages a capable lad might be rated as a petty officer or mate by meeting loosely defined standards subject to the master's whims. During the eighteenth century several of these youths sailed long enough to get commands of their own and later took their savings to retire, resume farming, or engage in a trade.

Communications between the colonies and the mother country continued apace, despite the obstacles presented by war. With the end of hostilities in 1783, the enterprising William Rotch's *Bedford* of Nantucket set sail for England. Rotch arrived in London on February 3, prior to Parliament's declaration of peace, to find that without a commercial treaty American traders were still at the mercy of the hated Navigation Acts. The *Bedford* returned to Nantucket on April 15, 1783, the first ship to bring back news of the Declaration of Peace, which was to be signed as the Treaty of Paris the following September. Anxious to expand trade, each state took up its own cause. Although this resulted in destructive competition, the staunch New England merchants resisted government intervention in maritime affairs. The need for federal legislation, while reluctantly recognized by the citizenry, would not be met until after the Federal Era.

American shipbuilders had long been known as skilled craftsmen. At the outbreak of the war, 30 percent of the British merchant fleet came from colonial shipyards, purchased at prices as much as 40 percent lower than those of vessels built in English yards. Philadelphia and Boston continued as the top two shipbuilding ports when work resumed after the war, while the practical New Englanders continued to build the smaller ships they favored. Vessels of less than five hundred tons fit better into the sea, they felt; that is, they cost less to build and could accommodate full cargoes with smaller crews. This theory was confirmed by the brief career of the ship *Massachusetts* of nearly eight hundred tons' burden, at that time the largest ever delivered from an American yard. The ship was built in 1789 in Quincy, modeled on a British East Indiaman and staffed like one. It sailed in the following year on its first and only American voyage, with a general cargo intended to be traded in Batavia to pay for goods to be sought in Canton. The trip took longer than anticipated; several weeks were lost when the ship missed Java Head because of faulty navigation. In Dutch-held Batavia an unloading permit was refused, and the ship continued to Canton with goods that turned out to be unsalable. Time, together with the size of the investment in ship and cargo, eroded any potential for profit. To cut the losses Samuel Shaw of Boston, supercargo of the *Massachusetts* and one of its principal investors, sold the ship to the Danish East India Company for $65,000 and a lasting prejudice against large vessels. To assemble the hulls and masts of the smaller ships required only a half-dozen carpenters and a blacksmith; later a sailmaker, riggers, and a boatswain could complete the outfitting. (The designer and master builder of a ship, who was often the financier as well, was known as a "shipwright." All others were classified as "mechanics" regardless of specialty.) The smaller ships could operate with smaller crews—another incentive to limit tonnage. Generally, for every fifteen tons of deadweight one man was needed for the crew, with an officer for every five seamen. A five-hundred-tonner might carry thirty to thirty-five men, a cook, and a clerk or supercargo reporting to the master. Small and fast became the rule for a better return on investment.

The postwar panic that emerged in the new nation found American shipbuilding at its lowest point thus far. Trade routes were in need of reestablishment, and foreign competition was taking much of the trade that existed from vessels like the Derby privateers *Astrea* and *Grand Turk*. Samuel Shaw announced that he would go aboard the *Empress of China* in New York as supercargo to help financiers in New York and Philadelphia open the Orient to regular trade. Meanwhile, the fifty-five-ton sloop *Harriet* had departed from Hingham on Boston's South Shore carrying a load of ginseng for the Orient. It stopped at the Cape of Good Hope, and finding there an opportunity to trade it for a cargo of tea worth three times as much, the captain exercised his option to return home with a quick profit.

The dilemma facing the Derbys—one destined to plague American merchantmen in every peacetime period over the next two centuries—amounted to a lack of trading goods. The new nation was agrarian, able to consume most of what it grew except for southern tobacco and cotton. Imagination and industry were needed to resolve the trade imbalance. Ginseng, pulled from the forests of New England, was in high demand in the Orient. The curious yellow roots shaped like tiny human dolls were long believed to have medicinal value and to be an aphrodisiac, grand for impotence. The Chinese variety grew only in Manchuria, and the Derbys knew they would be able to trade all the ginseng they could carry for Cantonese tea. But the roots would not fill their holds. Other cargoes in equal demand were needed. Boston and Philadelphia merchants were making a profit from pelts gathered by the Indians of the Northwest. Perhaps the New Englanders could trade makeshift tools of cheap manufacture for fur, load pelts for the Orient above the ginseng, and bring back cases of tea, bales of silk, crates of porcelain—luxury goods in high demand. From the exchange of simple colonial handcrafts for much-needed tea, top-quality China teapots and dinnerware, and elegant silk to dress the ladies pouring the tea, the potential for financial returns loomed large. The English would be bested at their own trade.

The shrewd Derbys foresaw quick profits in the Baltic, to be generated by outfitting their own ships. The *Light Horse* headed for St. Petersburg with a load of West Indian sugar. Hemp was the return cargo, in demand by the Salem, Charlestown, and Plymouth ropewalks. Salem's rope-making facilities were open to the air. The frugal Yankees saw no sense in building long, covered sheds to protect material that would spend the rest of its life exposed to the elements. Profits from that venture were reinvested in the tea trade. Ile de France, an isolated island in the Indian Ocean, had recently opened to commerce as a tea source.

By 1786 the *Grand Turk,* the senior Derby's favorite ship, had returned from the Cape of Good Hope with news of the island tea port and was ready for the long haul via the Indian Ocean to the Far East. Elias Jr., trained well to respect his father's capital and standards of profit, would travel with the ship to establish a trading center on the mid-ocean isle and expand further the Derby enterprises.

Life was hard on extended voyages. Common seamen were subject to corporal punishment on both naval and merchant ships, the captain supreme on both, the bosun with belaying pin and a rope's end "starter" ready at hand. Flogging, common in England's naval and merchant fleets, carried over with lesser frequency to the U.S. vessels. A century after the formation of the American democracy, Raphael Semmes put into words what has been known from the

1-2. Derby brig *Grand Turk,* from *Hutchinson's Navigation,* 1777. Courtesy, Peabody Essex Museum

first days of sail: "Democracies do very well for the land, but monarchies, and pretty absolute monarchies at that, are the only successful governments for the sea." His words, published in *The Confederate Raider* Alabama, hold true today.

Salt horse was the seamen's standard fare—brine-soaked beef or pork, typically served with unleavened dry biscuits called hardtack, which were often ridden with weevils. Sailors became so accustomed to the menu they would suffer no variant. Beer was a staple, as was watered rum on some ships (on others it was curtailed by fundamentalist owners). On special days a wad of boiled dough, called duff, covered with molasses and often spiced with raisins, finished off the meal. Captain Cook's report to the Royal Society on the importance of antiscorbutic vegetables in time reduced the incidence of scurvy on long voyages. A half century would elapse before cause and cure were widely known. Beyond sources of citrus and leafy vegetables, a concoction called scouse, the dried-out sludge of reduced roots and greens, boiled in fresh water with the briny beef and thickened with hardtack, helped alleviate the disease. Livestock was often kept aboard, the waists of many vessels converted to miniature barn-yards before the ships left port, with goats for milk, chickens for eggs and meat. The animals weren't always destined for slaughter, subject as they were to storms and starvation.

Adventurous sailors, fretful under harsh living conditions and attracted to the idyllic life of the South Seas, could be tempted to leave their vessels under-manned in remote ports. Shipowners and masters had long required the sign-ing of contracts outlining terms of performance between seamen and master. There was little consistency in the articles of agreement during the Federal Era. Standardization awaited the convening of the First Congress of the United States, when the nation's first maritime laws were enacted.

While prevailing winds were respected in laying out ocean passages, little attention was paid to the effects of ocean currents. For forty years Ben Franklin wondered why westbound transatlantic crossings took predictably longer than eastbound. In 1770, as colonial postmaster responsible for rapid delivery of mail to and from the mother country, he exercised his interest in matters "philosophic" and commissioned the engraving of a chart outlining the known courses of North Atlantic currents. It was based on the recorded observations of Nantucket whalers over decades of whale-hunting at the currents' edges. Most merchantmen had ignored the available information. In 1785, at the age of seventy-nine, the much-traveled Franklin, on one of his longest passages across the Atlantic, continued adding notes to his "Maritime Observations" on the peculiarities of what he called the Gulf Stream. He knew even of the higher temperature of the waters within its boundaries. Mariners paid a bit more attention, cursing the opposing blue waters as they headed south in the favor-able northeast trade winds. In the Pacific the Kuroshio would remain unknown for years.

The *Empress of China* returned to New York from the Orient, and Samuel Shaw reported a 25 percent profit for the one-year voyage. Two years after the discussion between father and son in the Derby countinghouse, the Derby ship *Grand Turk* departed for the Far East under Captain Ebenezer West. Elias Jr., well seasoned at age twenty, left with it for a long tour as supercargo and agent, stopping at Ile de France, Bombay, Madras, and Calcutta. The *Grand Turk* continued eastward to become the first New England vessel to bring the Ameri-can flag into the port of Canton. It joined the *Hope,* out of New York, and thanks to Shaw's preliminary work, established a tea and silk trading center in

Canton before returning to Salem in March 1787. By the time the Derby scion arrived home on the last day of 1790, his Cantonese and East Indian trading activities had netted the enterprise $100,000, an astonishing profit at the time. "King" Derby's dynasty was passing to the next generation.

Yet the Derbys as merchants faced new, strong competition. Trade routes dictated export and import cargoes. Although commerce with the West Indies improved and the *Grand Turk* buoyed Salem's activities, Massachusetts failed to regain its prewar trade levels. The Salem and Boston merchants held different views about voyages to the far side of the world. Salem vessels were not involved in the fur trade, heading instead for the Cape of Good Hope and from there to the East Indies to trade in tea and spices. Boston ships followed the route around Cape Horn to the land of the Oregon tribe of natives and thence to the Orient, where they established a fur trade between the North American coast and the northern coast of China. Seaports, and the fleets within them, stagnated or grew according to how well the merchants met the needs of the consumers.

Six months after the *Grand Turk* returned from its Canton voyage, two vessels departed together from Boston for Cape Horn and America's little-known northwest coast—the ship *Columbia* under John Kendrick and the ninety-ton sloop *Lady Washington* under Robert Gray. Gray, the de facto leader of the venture, was fascinated by the possibilities of a trade link between the unexploited Oregonian coast and Canton. Kendrick chose to investigate opportunities in the newly charted Sandwich Islands. The two captains exchanged vessels, and Gray took the *Columbia* across the Pacific with Vancouver furs. Upon its return to Boston in the summer of 1790, the *Columbia* received a thirteen-gun salute as the first American ship to have sailed around the world. The focus of New England shipping shifted southward as ships got bigger and carried more profitable cargoes. Many of Salem's ships when fully laden carried enough draft that they were obliged to anchor offshore in their home port and lighter their goods to and from shore on barges pulled across the water by eight-oared longboats. Often vessels of lesser draft sat alongside the dock on mudflats until lifted off by rising tides.

Yankee traders generated worldwide interest in the maritime potential of the new nation. Its location within temperate latitudes accommodated long-established European trade routes through all seasons. Shipowners in New York and Hampton Roads, two of the finest natural harbors in the world, awakened to the new opportunities as New England was about to stake a claim to the continent's western ports. ("Hampton Roads" is the collective name for Hampton harbor and the adjacent ports of Newport News and Norfolk. Norfolk ultimately became the port of entry.) Nearly every Atlantic waterside community, supported by the abundance of natural resources available near the coast, became engaged in vigorous international commerce through a combination of shipbuilding, trade, and ocean transport. Bold merchants, fearless sea captains, and astute supercargoes had carried the American flag to the Baltic, the Indian Ocean, and the Orient. Elias Hasket Derby Jr., seventeen when his grandfather died, his skills proven after four years under his father's tutelage, was ready to raise the Derby flag over piers around the world. In 1799, when he departed on his next voyage to the Orient aboard the *Mount Vernon,* he could not have expected that he would never see his father again.

Chapter 2

SHIFTING WINDS:
1790–1810

For the new nation's maritime interests it was not a case of putting to sea on an ebb tide with a quartering breeze. It was more like coming safely out of a squall, right on course, to have the wind settle on dead ahead. Fortune had its complexities in approaches to uncharted waters. After the loss of the North American colonies, the British turned their sights to the Pacific, focusing their attention on trade in the Dutch East Indies, locale of the *Massachusetts's* misadventures. Within five years British competitors were shipping Alaskan furs to China in exchange for tea, having put some thirty-five ships into the activity. Captain James Cook's return to England from his first exploration opened the great ocean to worldwide shipping. Good health was not easy to maintain at sea on long voyages, as Cook had observed. Aware of the potential for the spread of diseases such as smallpox through foreign trade, major seaports instituted quarantines and pratique (no admittance without clean bills of health)—this some eight years prior to Jenner's development of a smallpox vaccine. The broad Pacific, associated often with the loss of crew members through scurvy and desertion, called for larger crews, larger ships, larger investments. American seafarers were undaunted by its demands.

The Federal Era approached its end with the formation of the First Congress. In its initial session in 1789, after three years of contention between the states, the legislature established federal control of tariffs and created the U.S. Customs Service. As one of the nation's first regulatory agencies, the Customs Service took on an array of responsibilities that stretched far beyond the collection of duties. It enforced quarantine and health laws, funded health care for sick and disabled seamen, maintained trade statistics, oversaw the operation of lighthouses, and handled sea searches and rescues. Its surveyors attended to the standards and usage of weights and measures, and the measurement and certification of registered vessels.

In its second session the following year, Congress enacted the nation's first maritime laws, which standardized the articles of agreement between masters and seamen. With wording based on the kinds of individual contracts then current, the articles favored the interests of shipowners, remained vague on the specification of voyage destinations and durations, defined in more detail the minimum requirements for victualling and medical care, and preserved the master's supremacy at sea. With this act, the forces of commerce, the federal government, and the merchant marine became entwined like loosely stranded rope.

The assessment of tariffs to be collected by the Revenue Service required clearer definitions of tonnage terms. The term "tuns burthen" in use at the time of the Boston Tea Party was no longer useful. It derived from the older system of measuring a ship's capacity in wine barrels, double barrels (tuns), and triples or tierces. Such terminology signified little for the measurement of bulk and packaged goods and was inadequate for the calculation of fees and harbor dues. British law in 1789, adopted by Americans with minor modification, defined "tonnage" as internal capacity in terms of volume, a function of hull measurement. Gross (register or documented) tonnage was defined as the total internal capacity in units of one hundred cubic feet, the common designation of merchant ship size; net register tonnage was the gross tonnage minus the space without earning capacity. "Displacement," a measure of weight, was and is determined by the volume of water displaced by a vessel, which varies with the different weights of sea and fresh water (respectively, 64 and 62.5 pounds per cubic foot). Americans defined a ton as 2,240 pounds. "Deadweight," the difference in weight between an empty vessel and the ship fully loaded, was well named, as too great a difference could be deadly to the crew. The extent of loading remained subject to the notions of each ship's captain for nearly a century more.

"Make 'em boxy," said the shipwrights. "Speed is for the privateers—aren't you in the business to carry cargo?" And so they took maximum advantage of the gross hull measurements of keel length, beam, and draft. "Make 'em fast," said the merchants. "He who gets there first gets the most." They specified sleek, deep-keeled vessels. The compromise meant making ships bigger overall, and that called for more sailors in the crew and more supplies to be carried. Every vessel was a collection of compromises. American ships with a full cargo or committed to a scheduled departure didn't hesitate to sail shorthanded if necessary. When they arrived in British ports the captains often recruited British seamen to fill out their crews. The locals were happy to sign aboard for higher American wages, although not perhaps as high as their American shipmates. The British Navy, undermanned during the Napoleanic Wars, pursued with extraordinary vigor its customary practice of boarding suspect vessels to retrieve British citizens and impress them into its own fleet. Citizenship was difficult to prove among illiterate sailors, and more than a few Americans found themselves unwillingly taken aboard British fighting ships. In response, in 1796 Congress introduced Seaman's Protection Certificates (SPCs), the earliest shipping papers, to identify merchant seamen as U.S. citizens and protect them from impressment. In effect the SPCs stated that American ships were floating extensions of their country's sovereign territory. With consular support the SPCs served as visaed passports in foreign countries.

On May 12, 1792, Robert Gray, master and now part owner of the *Columbia,* stood on deck peering to port through a long brass telescope, searching North America's northwest coast for native villages with pelts to trade. The 212-ton ship was on a second world-circling voyage, sailing south from the island first reported by Captain Cook, now being surveyed by George Vancouver. (The island was later named for Vancouver. Gray and Vancouver were contemporary west coast explorers. On November 14, 1792, Vancouver became the first Englishman to enter San Francisco Bay.) Days before, Gray had discovered and proudly named Grays Harbor, but rejected the possibility of its being the estuary of the legendary River of the West. (Spanish and English mariners, including Vancouver, had spoken of such an estuary but failed to explore or define it.) Gray had been sailing along the mountainous coastline, some of its peaks close to half a mile high and seeming to rise directly from the water. A cleft in the rolling green line of forest came into his view and he called for a change of course, hauling wind to bring the ship closer to shore. There he saw, quivering in his lens, a wide harbor guarded by a long, sandy bar stretching northwest from the coast, with a forbidding line of foaming breakers between his ship and the harbor's entrance. Gray was curious and called for the crew to reduce sail. He had them lower a pinnace and sent it ahead toward the seething surf. On the *Columbia* leadsmen were put to the chains, calling out the diminishing depth with each cast. At three and a half fathoms, the two vessels passed over the bar as water swirled wildly around them. (The bar remains treacherous to this day.) Inside they discovered an entrance protected by two long sand spits, the pass turning northeast into a stream so generous that water close by the sea was found to be drinkable. Under a fair wind the ship proceeded upstream some fifteen miles—five leagues from the entrance, according to John Boit Jr., the seventeen-year-old mate. Indians followed along the shore and came off from the beach in canoes laden with dried salmon and furs. Gray's vessels moored near a large Indian village to trade copper, cloth, and iron nails for the furs they would bring to China. Robert Gray realized that he had discovered the sought-after river, which he named Columbia for the vessel that brought him there. His discovery later served as the basis for America's claim to the Oregon Territory. Upon his return to Boston in 1793, word of his discovery having preceded him, he received an eleven-gun salute as the *Columbia* anchored off Long Wharf. Gray's report and the success of his second venture were enough to draw American shipping activity from Salem's shallow harbor down the coast to Boston, to the shipbuilding facilities of Philadelphia, and to the increasingly active port of New York. By 1805, sixty-eight American ships from Philadelphia and New York had taken over the Pacific fur trade, ranging the West Coast from the Mexican provinces to the Aleutian shores, and nearly twice as numerous as the British fur-carrying vessels.

Beginning in 1792, Great Britain—and many British merchant ships—became embroiled in a series of wars with France. To the neutral Americans this offered splendid shipping opportunities between Europe and the West Indies, in markets the British merchants had controlled. Maritime wealth poured into every U.S. port despite contention with the British on the free transport of goods between nations. Boston used the money to erect a new, Bulfinch-designed pier and to mark the President Roads channel with buoys where it passed through the rockbound approach to its harbor. New York enjoyed a similar surge in wealth, growing from a population of thirty-three thousand in 1790 to seventy-five thousand in 1805. Even minor ports like Plymouth and New Bedford, which had given up competing with Salem and Boston, revived. Thomas Jefferson felt he could peacefully advance American power by closing U.S. markets to the warring European nations and extracting political and economic concessions from them. He hoped to accomplish this through the Embargo Act of 1807, forbidding clearance from U.S. ports for American flag vessels headed for foreign destinations. Coastal and foreign trade became separated since inter-state trade continued. Shipowners were furious at the loss of their overseas markets; seamen found themselves without work; heavily invested shipbuilders could not complete what stood on their ways. Coastal shipping required the posting of bonds, tying up capital as surety that cargoes remained within the United States. The embargo, one of Thomas Jefferson's poorest actions, incurred the rancor of the nation's maritime interests.

The embargo was defended by the Salem family of Crowninshields, Repub-licans in their politics despite marriage alliances with the Federalist Derbys. The Republicans had sided with the French in the Napoleanic Wars, while the Federalists had sided with the British. Jefferson's election in 1800 marked the decline of Federalism, and the Crowninshields capitalized on it. For decades, Salem's merchant class had pooled capital and power through political associa-tion, loosely defined partnerships, and intricate marital connections, sometimes between first and second cousins. It is difficult to sort out the relationships, ashore or at sea. Derbys and Crowninshields sailed on each other's vessels, underwrote each other's voyages, and when it was fiscally expedient, married into each other's families. Yet the two families remained intensely competitive. As their wealth increased, they became more inclined to set aside their gentility and display mutual animosity. For years Derby Wharf was the longest in the har-bor. Then the Crowninshields built India (later Crowninshield) Wharf, dwarf-ing the famous Derby pier. In 1796 "King" Derby sued, claiming the new structure projected too far into the channel and was silting up his own pier. The court forced the Crowninshields to shorten their wharf by twelve feet. At that length it was still the longest of Salem's more than thirty wharves. (However, Derby Wharf regained its preeminence in 1806, when it was extended to more than double its prior length.)

As "King" Derby's affluence increased, his wife's ostentatious desires grew with it. Elizabeth convinced her husband to contract with Salem's master archi-tect to complete a plan begun by Charles Bulfinch for a mansion to match the Derby's new level of prosperity and social prominence. The result was a three-story Federal-style building, which took five years to complete, on grounds that occupied an entire block along the Salem waterfront. The Derbys would not enjoy it for long. In 1799, shortly after moving in, the two died within a few months of each other. Upon settlement the estate comprised at least forty vessels owned wholly or in part, a quarter of Salem's shipping tonnage, Derby Wharf, warehouses, a distillery, shops, a farm outside Salem, and the grandiose mansion. All of this was assessed at more than $1 million, making Elias Hasket Derby

America's first millionaire. Bitter feelings continued between the two families, to such an extent that no Crowninshield attended the funeral of Elizabeth Crowninshield Derby, the sister of George Crowninshield Jr. and wife of Elias Hasket Derby. George Crowninshield Sr. and his five sons were never popular in Salem, despite their remarkable seafaring, business, and political careers.

The fortunes of both families waxed into the nineteenth century and the last years of Salem's golden age. Elias Jr.'s agencies, particularly the one on Ile de France, established the dominance of the house of Derby in the Indian Ocean. His voyage into the Mediterranean on the *Mount Vernon* during the Napoleonic Wars, while it involved several risky encounters with the French, added another $100,000 to the Derby coffers. He came home to find his parents deceased and himself heir to a larger share of their estate than either of his siblings. This set off further family battles, further erosion of the Derby fortune (already considerably depleted by his mother's extravagance), and a cloud of gossip among his Salem neighbors. In an effort to recoup, after the *Mount Vernon* returned from a stint of privateering, he took it on a final voyage to Brazil and England. The voyage was a costly failure and contributed to the end of the house of Derby.

Meanwhile, the five Crowninshield sons—students of navigation at twelve, seafarers at fifteen, and vessel commanders at twenty—continued to prosper. The slender and handsome Jacob took several Crowninshield ships under his command. His most spectacular accomplishment was the delivery, via the armed ship *America* in 1795, of the first live elephant ever seen in the United States. He purchased it in Ile de France for $450, charged admission to see it perform, and eventually sold it for $10,000. Jacob became ex officio director of the Crowninshield shipping firm, founder and president of the Merchants Bank, and absentee secretary of the navy. He died while in office as a Massachusetts congressman.

George Jr., short, strong, and a lifetime bachelor, was the most colorful of the Crowninshield brothers. A courageous seaman, at the age of thirty-four he came ashore to serve as nominal head of his father's firm, a position he occupied from 1800 until the firm was dissolved fifteen years later on the death of George Sr. If not the first American yachtsman, George Jr. was the showiest in those years—flashy in dress, with a reputation that would endure for a century. After his retirement he commissioned the construction of *Cleopatra's Barge,* an elaborate brig modeled on the fast privateer *America IV,* and took it on a Mediterranean pleasure cruise shortly before his own sudden death. His "toy" was later sold to the king of the Sandwich Islands for use as a royal barge.

It was William Gray of Salem (apparently no relation to fur trader Robert

Gray of Boston) who would eclipse that port's maritime fame. Eleven years younger than Richard Derby's son Elias, Gray apprenticed in the Derby countinghouse and was active in privateering during the Revolution. In the midst of the war at the age of twenty-eight he left the Derby enterprise to start his own business. In classic Salem fashion he began trading in the Mediterranean, then expanded to India and China, acquiring outright ownership of at least forty-seven vessels before moving to Boston. In his lifetime Gray would hold part or full interest in 181 vessels.

William Gray supported the Jeffersonian embargo and for that reason was ostracized in Salem. Independent, honest, and then owner of the largest fleet of vessels in the United States, a true patriot, Gray's defense of the president caused his Salem associates to accuse him of profiteering from his preembargo stock. He was excluded from local maritime interests and lost his social standing. In 1809, after Jefferson, on his last day in office, signed the repeal of the embargo, Gray moved thirty-six ships to Boston. One lasting effect of the embargo was that the nation's smaller ports were put out of business; because of their limited resources, they were unable to sustain themselves and keep their river mouths dredged until renewed maritime activity might help them recover. Even Salem was faced with that threat, and Gray may have sensed that its ventures had peaked. When he moved, Gray's assets were valued at more than $3 million, and his finest hour was yet to come.

Maritime prosperity benefited all involved. Wages grew during the Federalist period, and by the turn of the century seagoing pay rates exceeded those on shore. Companies set wages according to trade routes, voyages to the Baltic and Orient paying the highest. Ship's boys earned $8 to $10 a month, ordinary seamen $14 to $17, "able-bodieds" (A-Bs) $18 per month. The term "ship's boy" is a proper title, not an indicator of age. Boys, if for some reason they did not progress, could be in their forties. Promotion came through experience and the display of learned skills according to a well-defined list—everything from knotting and splicing to furling and reefing sail in the upper yards, steering, sounding, and keeping a log. Should an A-B move to another ship, a history of leadership and cooperation might win him a position as a petty officer—bosun, carpenter, or quartermaster—with earnings of $24 per month. Sailors were responsible for their own clothing, and slop chest charges at high profit to the owners could consume $100 to $150 over a two-year voyage.

To become an officer took schooling, and every seaport had its private schools of navigation. In 1809 Salem's Cushing & Appleton School offered "lessons in the pathfinding art, fundamentals of geometry, algebra, and how to maintain a logbook." Officers had to be competent in dead reckoning, taking a latitude, and working up a day's run, and responsible enough to stand a watch. They had to know how to stow cargo for proper trim, order the setting or reefing of sail, and maintain discipline among the crew. Mates were paid $27 to $30 a month in addition to a percentage of the voyage's net proceeds (varying from 1 to 5 percent), and were allocated "privilege" or a portion of return cargo space for their own ventures. The master received a similar base wage—$30 to $35 a month, but 5 to 8 percent of the net proceeds and a larger privilege for use on the return passage. Hard work in driving a vessel and skilled entrepreneurship on one or two successful voyages produced some wealthy young men, many still in their early thirties.

The men in the fo'c'sle knew ample hardships and privations along with the routine perils of the sea. It was the lure of foreign ports that drew them to multiple voyages. Seaman or officer, the calling was dangerous, and disease, particularly in the tropics, was widespread. The Cape Horn passage was frightful, the Roaring Forties around Africa no better. Medical care, usually in the hands of the captain, amounted to little more than the dispensation of nostrums. The blessing of good health came from a regular diet, sobriety, and a stable life in fresh sea air.

Good seamanship was taken for granted among men in their mid-twenties who had spent close to half their lives afloat, but off-soundings navigation remained a mysterious art. Throughout the eighteenth century, seamen kept time by half-hourly turns of a sandglass. If the skipper carried a watch, it was for his own interest, its accuracy always suspect. "Make it noon," the captain would say, putting down his octant after observing the sun reach its zenith, crossing the local meridian. At that midday point, a fresh sandglass was set in place and from there all watches were scheduled. (The octant, often made of hardwood, sometimes with an attached ivory vernier to refine angular measurements to minutes of arc, remained in use to the end of the century. Its arc was one eighth of a circle, or 45 degrees, with double reflecting mirrors able to measure angles up to 90 degrees.) After noting the sun's maximum altitude for the day, the captain could determine a precise latitude. Brass sextants that extended angular measurements to obtuse angles aided in landmark triangulation. Engraved charts were expensive and unreliable, being based on unorganized soundings compiled over decades with little correction, and lacked notation on compass variations.

The man who brought the musty art of navigation flying like a full-rigged ship into the nineteenth century was Nathaniel Bowditch, from his youth one of Salem's most highly regarded citizens. His father, Habakkuk Bowditch, a sea captain down on his luck, apprenticed twelve-year-old Nathaniel to a ship's chandler, who instructed him in algebra. Slight of build and narrow of jaw, Nathaniel had a large head, perhaps a sign of his extraordinary versatility. A voracious student, the lad came across a private library captured by a local privateer and taught himself Latin by his seventeenth birthday. He later studied other languages, becoming particularly proficient in French. On his own he acquired knowledge in mathematics, navigation, and astronomy. He went to sea in his early twenties and made four voyages as ship's writer and supercargo. Aboard the *Astrea,* on his second voyage, he learned the arcane and difficult practice of taking lunar sights to determine longitude without a chronometer. Based on the moon's phases and its angular distance from the sun, the technique takes skill because any observational errors are magnified in the calculation. An observational sextant error of 5 minutes (one twelfth of a degree of an arc) results in an error of 2.5 degrees of longitude; at the equator this would be 150 miles, more than a typical day's run. Bowditch passed his knowledge on to twelve seamen, commanding the respect of skipper and sailor alike. Later, he and his brother William were called upon to revise and correct J. H. Moore's *New Practical Navigator,* printed in 1799. Moore's text, the first American navigation guide, was poorly organized and filled with errors. William died after the publication of Moore's second edition, which was not fully corrected, but by then Nathaniel was taken up with the challenge. When the third edition was found to be still rife with errors (eight thousand in all), Bowditch resolved to write his own book. He did so with the express intention of including nothing in it that he could not teach the crew of the vessel on which he then sailed as supercargo. The product of his effort was the *New American Practical Navigator,* published in Newburyport in 1802. (In 1996 the federal government sold the copyright it held since 1868 to a commercial publisher. More than 900,000 copies of updated derivatives had been printed in seventy-five editions.) From that time, the claim to have sailed with Nathaniel Bowditch was the ultimate assurance of a mate's berth.

Bowditch proved the reliability of his navigational theories on his final voyage as part owner and master of the *Putnam.* On December 24, 1803, returning from Sumatra with a load of pepper, he successfully entered rockbound Salem harbor in a northeast blizzard without having made a single landfall prior to his arrival. In 1806 he published a large-scale chart of that harbor based on surveys and soundings taken by another sea captain and the Reverend

William Bentley (pastor of Salem's Unitarian East Church and Elias Derby's eulogist). Bowditch declined offers of professorial positions at Harvard, West Point, and the University of Virginia. Instead, he became an insurance actuary and later, the secretary and president of the East India Marine Society, a professional guild of sea captains, which included Jacob Crowninshield. Learned mathematician and astronomer that he was, Bowditch was constrained by the limitations of science in his day. There remained a gaping hole in navigational knowledge that would not be filled for three more decades.

The winds of change blew throughout the maritime world during the first decade of the 1800s. By the turn of the century French vessels were looked upon as the finest, although both French and English packet ships carried most of the transatlantic mail. In 1783, with the fifteen-minute voyage of the experimental *Pyroscaphe,* the French became the first to navigate under steam power. Although the experiment was considered unsuccessful, it inspired development in the New World. American inventor John Fitch built a steam-powered, six-oar vessel that showed little improvement over the *Pyroscaphe.* Then, doggedly learning from his first trial, he demonstrated an operational paddle-driven steam vessel on the Delaware River in 1787 and won recognition as the first American inventor of the steamboat. Fitch operated two boats of his own design on a regular ferry service while unsuccessfully seeking funding to correct their shortcomings. His efforts were eclipsed by those of several other inventors, and the despondent Fitch committed suicide.

It was Robert Fulton who achieved fame as inventor of the steamboat. An American Leonardo, Fulton was a gunsmith during the War of Independence, a painter well known in Europe, and an engineer and inventor. He designed and had built a hull to accommodate a commercially available steam engine and produced a steam-driven paddle-wheeler in 1807. His September round trip between New York and Albany won him a Hudson River monopoly on its commercial shipping operation. Fulton called his invention the *North River Steamboat,* but in popular usage it was called *Clermont* for the name of the Hudson River estate of his financial backer, Robert Livingston. In 1809 the first steamers appeared on the St. Lawrence River and Lake Champlain, and the age of smoke and steam puffed into the waterways.

Steamboats were well suited to freshwater rivers and lakes. They could be controlled better than sailing vessels when headed upstream or in narrow waters with adverse winds, and fueling ports were never far away. However, various limitations of the early steamboats made them impractical for ocean

2-1. Fulton's *North River Steamboat*, a.k.a. *Clermont*, 1809. PRINTS AND PHOTOGRAPHS DIVISION, LIBRARY OF CONGRESS

traders. The New England shipbuilders looked instead for new designs in sail-powered vessels, swifter than their old two- to four-knot ships with box-shaped hulls. They turned to the Chesapeake Bay watermen, who were building long, narrow bows that cut better into choppy seas, and raked masts for increased stiffness in carrying large sails. The New England yards began to adapt their tubby, cargo-carrying hulls to Baltimore's clipper designs.

Another innovation of the period was the oceanic weather chart. To support the needs of insurers in evaluating losses due to storms, the U.S. Weather Service adapted British admiral Sir Francis Beaufort's 1805 wind-velocity scale to a table of wind forces and speed, from calm to hurricane-grade (0 to 12). Logbook entries had done little to belie the attitudes of "drivers"—sea captains who felt that traveling under reduced sail threatened their reputations for courage and accomplishment. In time, the Weather Service's meticulously kept records found an interested agent for the production of oceanic weather charts, to the benefit of all—shippers, sailors, and captains alike.

Seeking new export markets, twenty-two-year-old Frederick Tudor, son of a Massachusetts ice merchant, saw opportunity in climate differences and in

1805 experimentally shipped pond ice to the Caribbean. Through Yankee per-sistence he overcame his first failure, a midsummer attempt to deliver winter-harvested blocks from his Saugus ice house to Martinique. He learned to preserve eighteen-inch cubes cut during spells of deep cold by shipping them in double-sheathed hulls filled with pine sawdust. In six years he built a tidy ice trade in the tropics, even extending it to Calcutta in his most famous shipment. Ice proved a timely new foreign market. The Pacific fur trade brought tea, silks, and porcelain from the Orient, spurring commercial growth in Boston, Philadel-phia, and Baltimore. The luxury merchants then poured their funds into the steam-powered production of textiles and shoes. These goods, of more interest in the West than in the Far East, created new markets and expanded the seaports' inland economies.

In 1803 the Louisiana Purchase gave the nation a coastline on the Gulf of Mexico. (Florida was not yet a part of the United States.) With full access to the Mississippi River, extended intercoastal shipping became possible. Ameri-can shores, both the original ones and those newly acquired, had never been adequately charted, a circumstance of marginal interest to the hardy mariners, accustomed to lore and leadline when approaching from the sea. In 1807, when shipping was confined to the coasts by the Jeffersonian embargo, the U.S. Coast Survey was established to survey and plot the nation's shores. Forty years passed before the usefulness of the project was recognized.

By 1810 the American merchant marine stood poised to enter its greatest period of growth. The nation's deepwater ports flourished while sturdy Ameri-can fleets prospered in worldwide ventures. Design improvements helped ship-pers achieve their main goal, speed of passage. The feared alliance of government and commercial interests proved more encouraging than inhibiting to the ocean traders. Nothing short of war could curtail the expansion of American foreign trade.

Chapter 3

A MARITIME PRESENCE:
1810–1815

Robert Fulton's *Steamboat* reduced the New York to Albany passage from something over two days to thirty hours. The need for shore-to-shore tacking against headwinds on the broad Hudson River was virtually eliminated. The decks remained level, or nearly so—the vessel still carried sails fore and aft for stability and reserve power. Yet with all the advantages introduced by steamboating, there remained ample room for improvement. Provisioning for passengers and crew on a two-day run included the loading of forty cords of hardwood for fuel at each end of the route. The initial steamboat experiments used stout, deep-keeled converted schooners, their valuable midships cargo space given up for machinery and fuel bunkers. Fulton avoided that problem by starting with the steam engine and designing his vessel around it, with living quarters and cargo space removed from the noise and vibrations of the main plant. The boilers—rectangular boxes made of costly copper-plate, with bolted seams—leaked steam, bubbled, dribbled, and lost pressure. (Rolled iron for the formation of cylindrical boilers was not yet available.) Water burbling through horizontal tubes over simple fireboxes developed a pressure of only about twelve pounds per square inch, hardly enough to lift the big piston and vertical metal connecting-rod in the earliest engines. The heavy cast-iron fore-and-aft walking beam that converted the engine's reciprocating motion to rotation at the drive shaft was lodged above the superstructure, high enough to raise the ship's center of gravity and cause a perilous roll in choppy waters. Smoke poured from a tall stack between the masts and spread a layer of soot and ash downwind, often across the benches on the afterdeck.

As fuel burned off, a steamer's hull and its side-wheels rose higher above the water, necessitating large-diameter wheels to keep the driving chord below the surface. Nonfeathering paddles encountered energy-wasting resistance at the blades' entry and exit, a problem that Fulton was quick to correct on his *Steamboat.* If the boat had a narrow hull, a list caused by crosswinds would lower one set of paddles and raise its counterpart, making an offset rudder angle necessary to hold a straight course at slower speeds.

Not every seaman engaged in stoking the fire could manage the gauges and valves that regulated the flow of water and steam. An error could cause pressure to be lost or worse, to increase to the point of rupture. Qualified steam engineers, on the other hand, knew little of navigational needs or of the importance of responding quickly to bell signals delivered from the quarterdeck, such as signals to reduce pressure and shift the drive mechanism out of gear or into reverse. The lubrication of moving parts was an hourly requirement, the clearing of ashes nearly so. New types of maritime laborers came aboard—engineers, oilers and wipers, firemen and stokers—organized in regular watches like their counterparts on deck.

For all of that, the trip between New York and Albany was faster and in enough demand that Fulton was able to charge an exorbitant one-way rate of $7. His Hudson River steamboat monopoly was due in large part to his partnership with inventor and New York politician Robert E. Livingston. In association with others, the two proposed to establish similar steamboat operations in the intracoastal waters from Albany to Charleston, and in the Ohio and the just-gained Mississippi Rivers from New Orleans to Natchez. The steam vessel *New Orleans,* built at a cost of $40,000, became the first to ply the Mississippi when it embarked on March 17, 1811, with a complement of three officers and six men. The planned routes from Albany and New York to Trenton and from New Orleans to Natchez had been established when the War of 1812 began and the remaining plans cancelled.

After the French Revolution tensions emerged on both sides of the Atlantic. In an attempt to keep foreign shippers from carrying goods between France, Spain, and their possessions in the West Indies, Great Britain reinstituted its pre-

Revolution rule forbidding trade to neutrals in wartime without first touching at British ports. The British threatened to seize vessels that attempted the direct routes between the specified European ports. American shippers evaded capture by including American ports in their itineraries until a British court ruled that this did not circumvent the rules. In 1805 Great Britain increased its seizure of American ships in an attempt to stem the American circumventions. This added to the Americans' resentment about impressments undertaken by the British navy during the last years of the eighteenth century. Just how many citizens were impressed before the War of 1812 is unclear. The Madison administration made exaggerated claims, and shipowners like William Gray, who reported small losses of his sailors, issued vehement denials. In any case, enough men were taken to become a major cause of hostilities.

The next year England established a blockade along the European coast while Napoleon's fleet blockaded the British Isles, exposing American merchant ships to confiscation in both areas. Jefferson's failed embargo was an attempt to ease the stress peacefully. It was followed by other unsuccessful nonintercourse acts, which Congress passed in the hope of breaking down the trade restrictions both countries had imposed on American shippers. Then Napoleon convinced Madison to impose an act specifying nonintercourse with Great Britain. The hapless victims of all this international gamesmanship were the American merchant shippers, blocked from entering lucrative seaports where no state of war existed, their neutral rights infringed by threats of impressment and seizure.

Meanwhile, American frontiersmen, uninterested in the troubles across the Atlantic, looked upon the land around the Great Lakes with some degree of desire. Southerners wanted to round out the nation's possessions in the southeast by winning west Florida from the Spanish. Great Britain was suspected of arming and provoking Native Americans to form a confederacy that would oppose the American presence. Westerners hoped a resolution of these issues would stem from the expulsion of the British from Canada and a U.S. takeover of the territory surrounding the Great Lakes. Avarice from every angle led to an American declaration of war against Great Britain on June 18, 1812, in the name of "free trade and sailors' rights." Curiously, trade with England continued surreptitiously during the early part of the war through foreign registry of American ships or the indulgence of blockading squadrons—until both sides got serious. Then, most of the hostile action took place off American shores. Within eighteen months Congress halted all ocean shipping, even along the coast.

3-1. Letter of Marque issued by James Madison, 1812. COURTESY, PEABODY ESSEX MUSEUM

It was a wretched war that achieved little for either side. The forty-four-gun frigate, USS *Constitution,* launched in 1799, was financed by a subscription loan of $136,500 from Boston merchants. But the impoverished U.S. Navy could not afford to send it to sea. It took the wealthy patriot William Gray, then of Boston, to pay for its outfitting from his own pocket and make it ready for battle. The proud vessel soon met with the British *Guerrière,* defeating it in August 1812. Later in the year it bested the *Java* in midocean. Salem's idle merchant ships were once again converted to privateers. Some five hundred privateers and vessels with letters of marque were fitted out in coastal harbors from Salem to Baltimore. It appeared that anyone with a musket and a long-boat could carry a letter of marque and set out into the fray. The Derbys sent the *Grand Turk* and the *Mount Vernon.* The Crowninshields' *America IV,* at 473 tons one of America's largest merchantmen, was among the most successful. Modified with solid oak sides, it hoisted a grand array of sails that could produce speeds up to thirteen knots. Twenty-four guns were shipped and a crew of

150 put aboard. During the war *America IV* took twenty-six British ships as prizes, which were sold for more than $1 million. Privateering shallow-draft Baltimore clippers, fast and maneuverable, were a common sight along the coast. But within a year the number of free-ranging vessels, many underarmed, was greatly reduced in the face of British naval superiority. At war's end both sides had lost as much tonnage as they had won.

New Englanders, never in strong support of the war, talked of secession. The Americans lost battles at Detroit and on the Niagara River but achieved some success on Lake Erie. Meanwhile, British warships worked their way up Chesapeake Bay and burned Washington before finally being restrained at Fort McHenry in the approach to Baltimore. With no decisive victory on either side, negotiations took place over a period of several months and concluded at last with the 1814 Treaty of Ghent. No changes in neutrality rights or impressment procedures were achieved. As in the previous war, the American merchant marine was devastated. The spoils of battle again accrued to a few privateersmen with wealth, capable crews, and the courage to risk both. The smaller harbors lost their livelihoods as shipbuilding centers and ports for foreign trade. The open sea now awaited only the mighty.

Salem's dominance neared its end. By 1815 it had lost two thirds of its fleet and harbored just fifty-seven vessels. Pacific commerce was lost to the British, who had sustained and expanded it during the American blockade. *America IV* languished at its pier for lack of trade. Builders considered the bluff-bowed Indiamen too slow and focused on the sprightlier Chesapeake designs. A group of Salem carpenters, without work because of the war, set out to build a clipper-styled privateer, the *George,* but failed to complete it before the war ended. They sold it to the man who single-handedly would keep trade to the East Indies alive: Joseph Peabody, a Revolutionary War privateersman, sea captain, and merchant. Peabody owned sixty-three vessels wholly or in part during his lifetime and employed some seven thousand seamen, training many of them aboard the *George.* Forty-five men from the *George's* working crews became masters, thirty-five of them promoted by Peabody; and twenty-six others graduated to mate. The *George's* twenty-one fast runs to Calcutta set the standard for the next generation of sailing traders, to survive long after oceangoing steam vessels became feasible.

Experimentation with steam had continued through the war on the Midwestern lakes and rivers. Horizontal-thrust engines were found to lower a vessel's center of gravity and increase its stability, though at the expense of cargo space.

These engines were more popular with the British than the Americans, who resisted the conversion of even more earning capacity. Improved boiler assemblies allowed higher pressures, more power. Stern-wheelers were tried on the Mississippi. In a country as large as the United States, economic development depended on ease of transport everywhere—over mountains, along rivers, and across the sea. It cost as much to carry goods thirty miles inland from a major port as it did to bring them from across the Atlantic. Transatlantic trade exceeded interstate commerce, which was inhibited by the lack of roads and the difficulty of upstream navigation. The most practical way to ship goods from Cincinnati to New York was by downstream barge to New Orleans, then over salt water along the Gulf and Atlantic coasts—a seven-week trip.

If the United States gained anything from the war, it was a new spirit of nationalism. In spite of curtailed overseas commerce and internal dissension that tolled the bell for Federalism, the nation had established a maritime presence and proved that its people could rally in defense of open seas and free trade around the world. On that foundation the United States became a major maritime power.

Chapter 4

HOUSE FLAGS:
1815–1838

Circumstance again favored the venturesome. From Massachusetts to Virginia, communities grew along the fall line wherever a mill was
poised close to a river's head of navigation. An industrial belt between seaports
and croplands spread into the Piedmont, drawing laborers from shipboard and
farm. Europe's overpopulated cities and failed farms drove Irish and Germans
with all their possessions to the immigration docks. On the American coastland
the newcomers found work, and if their new country didn't offer wealth it gave
unlimited hope. Goods started to move across the land, and the wharves of
East Coast ports bustled with loaded horse-drawn carts. Inland, rutted dirt
roads were tarred and graveled and locked canals dug to accommodate barge
traffic. Westward, immigrant farmers found opportunity in undeveloped territories where they could grow grain for the Eastern market.

By 1816 Boston Light had burned at the Atlantic's edge off and on for a
century while the nation's saltwater activities expanded. (The British blew it up
in 1776, but for most of this period America's first lighthouse kept its welcoming beacon in operation.) On inland waters the merchant marine paralleled the
growth in size and sophistication of its ocean counterpart even while limited by
geography. Technical development surged ahead after the first steamer appeared
on Lake Erie. A converted conventional schooner with high paddle-wheels on

the sides, built around 1816 in Buffalo, it was a novelty vessel more suited to passenger transport than commercial freight. Its name, *Walk-in-the-Water,* was the translation of a term Native Americans had applied to the strange craft. It burned as much as forty cords of hardwood steaming from Buffalo to Detroit, but fares were low and the operation was profitable. Bituminous coal, a difficult fuel to handle, would not be considered a suitable replacement for wood until ten years later. In 1826 the development of shipboard mechanically powered forced-draft furnaces made coal a more compact, cost-effective fuel than wood. Within four years improved gratings permitted the replacement of bituminous coal with anthracite, bringing even further improvements. On the New York–Albany run twenty tons of anthracite, costing about $100, replaced forty cords of hardwood costing $240, and occupied one fifth of the space. Anthracite burned so hot that the passenger cabins near the fireroom became unbearable, but it produced higher steam pressures when used with the new, more advanced boilers.

When a canal linking Lake Erie with the Hudson River was proposed in 1809, Thomas Jefferson considered the idea to be "a little short of madness." Faced with a similar proposal, President Madison declared that federal funding would be unconstitutional since it would favor a single state. Finally, New York Governor DeWitt Clinton raised $7 million within the state to link Buffalo, which faced the Canadian shore across Lake Erie, with the Hudson River at Troy, a few miles north of Albany. The first shovelful of dirt was lifted in Rome on the Fourth of July, 1817, and laborers started digging in both directions. Irish immigrants, upon arrival in New York, were recruited to do most of the work. They toiled in twelve-hour days at 37 cents an hour to complete the canal within eight years. The result was 350 miles of testimony to the power of back-bending labor with pick and shovel. Four feet deep and forty wide, the canal was no technical wonder. Rather, it was an example of traditional engineering used to good effect: aqueducts crossed gorges, and eighty-three locks climbed from the confluence of the Mohawk and Hudson Rivers up 564 feet to Lake Erie. Travel between Buffalo and New York by horseback could take a month; on the Erie Canal it took less than a week. Mule-drawn barges navigated the entire length of the canal, reducing the cost to ship a ton of grain across the state from $100 to $10.

The rapids of the St. Lawrence River were only for the adventurous. By 1832 the Welland Canal could accommodate vessels less than one hundred feet long and could lift them through its locks up the Niagara Escarpment. Following this route, small ships began to arrive on the Great Lakes from Europe. Most of these voyages were uneconomical, however, and for decades, barge transshipment on the Erie Canal continued to be the main method for moving transatlantic cargo to the lakes. Manhattan's piers began to thrive with American produce destined for export, most of it on American bottoms.

In the port of New York nothing caught the interest of cagey shippers more than the canvas and leather packets of mail routinely shipped across the Atlantic. For more than a century the British Post Office had arranged scheduled mail transport to the American East Coast. The French introduced postal connections between Havre and New York after the American War of Independence. Mail packets occupied little space, earned high freight rates, and enabled a ship to operate as a common carrier—that is, to transport several consignments of goods owned by others, thereby reducing the shipper's financial risk. The term "packet ship" came to refer to any common carrier that was fast and intended to operate on schedule, whatever its cargo. A permanent cleavage was thereby introduced between ownership of vessel and of cargo. Shipowners could negotiate long-term mail contracts with the federal government with little subsequent regulatory interference. The mail carriers could then draw on the steady supply of nonseasonal cargoes that accumulated regularly on the docks. With frequent departures, express cargoes and passengers would round out the shipments, assuring profitability. The main transatlantic destination was the port of Liverpool on England's west coast, closer to New York than London by 224 miles and connected by inland canals to the English industrial area.

Four New York textile importers, Quakers like many shipping financiers, examined their purses, conferred on available vessels that would suit their purpose—fast-sailers, somewhat larger than those being built in New England—and contracted jointly to buy four local ships. In October 1817 they announced that a line of packet-carriers would offer regularly scheduled sailings between New York and Liverpool. The practice of posting a fixed departure date and then sailing coastwise close to the date, with or without full cargo, was not new. Spring and fall sailings across the Atlantic were routinely scheduled, but it was revolutionary to pin transatlantic departures to calendar dates on a regular basis. Advertisements in the New York *Commercial Advertiser* and *Evening Post* listed the vessels *Amity, Courier, Pacific,* and *James Monroe* and stated "it is the intention of the owners that one of these vessels shall sail from New York on the 5th, and one from Liverpool on the 1st of every month." Skeptics scoffed, but passengers and shippers of perishable cargoes soon flocked to the booking desks.

The crew of the *Pacific,* owned by Isaac Wright and Francis Thompson, had plied the New York–Liverpool route before the War of 1812 and knew the Mersey River's difficult approaches well. The *Courier* was scheduled to initiate the service from Liverpool on January 1, 1818, but its start was inauspiciously delayed by four days. In New York, on January 5 at the advertised hour of ten in the morning, the largest of the four ships, the *James Monroe* (424 tons; James Watkinson, master), cleared its slip and headed to sea. When its fore-topsail was set it bore a large black disk painted on the canvas, a trademark of the firm, which then called itself the Old Line. The Quakers—Benjamin Marshall, Isaac Wright, and Francis and Jeremiah Thompson—were well pleased as they saw off seven passengers, a small packet of mail, and a cargo of apples, flour, ashes, and cotton. All four men were related by blood or marriage; Jeremiah, born in York-shire, England, was the nominal head of the American firm.

During the Old Line's first two years of operation, a period of reduced for-eign trade, its vessels often sailed with unfilled cargo space; yet they took the edge over their nonscheduled competitors. Eastbound passages averaged 22 to 25 days, westbound 33 to 48 days. Each ship made three round trips annually, with ample layover time at both ends for refitting, provisioning, and the collec-tion of forward cargo. The ships became known for reliability in service, first-class passenger comfort, and low steerage fares. (The term "steerage" initially referred to berth space low and aft, near the rudder post. Later it referred to compartments beneath the waterline, typically near the machinery space.) The *Pacific* had fourteen first-class cabins adjacent to the main saloon, a narrow cen-tral room, forty feet by fourteen, embellished at the end with an arch supported by pillars with embedded tilework. The Old Line, later and better known as the Black Ball Line, prospered. Its square riggers became familiar on both sides of the Atlantic, sailing on schedule for the next sixty years, with the house flag, a black ball on a crimson background, flying from the mastheads.

The agrarian South settled into an easygoing, comfortable trade with England. Cotton was shipped to British mills; woven goods returned. Tobacco remained a European staple. In 1819 Spain ceded its Florida territory, making the coastline of the United States continuous from the Canadian border to western Louisiana. That same year, a steam-assisted packet ship was completed in New York, financed as a speculation by the Savannah Steamship Com-pany. Named *Savannah,* it was a small ship of about three hundred tons, hermaphrodite-rigged (that is, square-rigged on the fore and main masts, fore-and-aft-rigged on the mizzenmast), with collapsible side paddles. An angular midships smokestack on a swivel above the wood-burning fireroom diverted some of the soot from the sails to leeward. The ship departed from Savannah for Liverpool on May 22 under the command of Moses Rogers, the man who had constructed its engine. Its mission was to prove steam's advantage in ocean passenger service. The owners hoped to sell the vessel to Russian investors for operation in the Baltic. It carried no passengers on the first voyage and ran its steam plant for little more than ninety hours during the month-long voyage. The *Savannah* proved uneconomical and was never sold, but it left its mark on history. Its departure date became identified as National Maritime Day in recognition of that first voyage. For twenty years no other American steamer crossed the Atlantic, and during that period very few European steamships went into transatlantic service. It was clear that the seagoing steamships were premature.

Oak was the timber of choice for oceangoing hulls, and live oak was valued for its natural curves in shaping the riblike frames and sharp-angled knees. No other wood could take the strains of a winter crossing as well. Live oak is heavy—when dried it weighs some 25 percent more than its white oak counterpart. Taken from great, spreading trees with trunks wider than a man can span, the limbs yield a hard-grained wood ideal for the framework of a hull, where strength is most needed. Actually a species of beech, live oak seems to thrive in proximity to the Gulf Stream; it is found along America's southeastern coasts, from just south of the Chesapeake to the Gulf of Mexico. It was troublesome to transport the wood over the considerable distance to New England's shipyards, and iron was found to be a useful substitute. The wedding of oak and iron in the hulls of ships for the new scheduled-shipping lines hastened their construction, and iron became as significant to shipbuilders as steam. The first composite ships had keels of elm, wood-straked hulls, and oaken frames joined to the deck beams by iron knees. Iron was later forged into keels and stems, and eventually made up the ship's entire framework. Builders favored sturdy iron structures when they began building clippers designed to carry more sail for greater speed. The *Albion*, built in 1819 for Black Ball, was that company's first composite ship. Iron foundries began to appear alongside shipyards, striving to replace strakes of oak with iron plate and to combine riveting with carpentry.

Economic recovery in 1822 brought competition on the North Atlantic for the Black Ball owners when a new line offered a similar monthly schedule of staggered departure dates. In response, Black Ball doubled the frequency of its sailings. Two more lines between New York and Liverpool were inaugurated, then two between New York and Havre. These were profitable times for all, but no vessels were as well fitted out with passenger accommodations as were the

Black Ballers. First-class passengers enjoyed superior food delivered fresh from an on-deck barnyard: milk from a cow tethered on top of the main hatch, eggs from a chicken coop in the longboat, mutton and pork from animals slaughtered at sea. Immigrants sailed at small cost in crowded quarters, supplying their own bedding, food, and cooking utensils, and when the seas permitted, sharing the air on deck with the livestock.

In 1829 the elderly Francis Thompson, his business still expanding, brought in a nephew to take over. That nephew, in turn, was joined by two of his own nephews. Isaac Wright had a son who was also involved in the Black Ball's affairs. At some point the evolving company acquired the curious new name Samuel Thompson's Nephew & Company. The Quakers were canny, clanny, and not without levity.

The New York packets were so successful that similar services arose in other ports. Philadelphia produced the Cope Line in 1822 and the New Line in 1824. Boston launched the White Star Line, New York the Black Star Line, one of the most famous. Edward Knight Collins of Cape Cod had already made a reputation as a commission agent in the cotton market when he turned to the management of packet ships. His initial ventures took him to Charleston and to New Orleans, where he gained control of a shipping line. He moved permanently to New York in 1836 and founded the Dramatic Line (with ships named after famous actors) for runs from New York to various English ports. The shipping industry was flourishing, but its growing fleets and changing technologies were not without difficulties. The troubles brought more government intervention, and Collins was poised to capitalize on it.

Shipyards, long accustomed to a steady supply of skilled shipwrights and carpenters, faced a difficult transition to iron and steam. Laborers had to be retrained as ironworkers and engine mechanics. The demand for those who chose to stay in the old trades diminished. Some yards were forced out of business, and the inevitable layoffs were accompanyied by labor unrest, a new phenomenon in the land of opportunity. The most successful builders were those who had the capital to handle both wood and iron, both canvas and coal, and the flexibility to invest funds where needed. Boston, New York, Philadelphia, Baltimore, and Hampton Roads became shipbuilding centers—a significant segment of industry in the northern half of the nation.

The Atlantic crossing of the *Savannah* and the introduction of iron in shipbuilding brought changes in ship design. The new oceangoing steamships had broad, stable hulls designed for large coal-fired engines and sturdy paddlewheels suited to ocean navigation. But the technical problems first encountered

4-1. SS *Savannah,* first steamship to cross the Atlantic. Courtesy of Steamship Historical Society, University of Baltimore Library

in riverboats extended to ocean travel. Deeply loaded at the start of a voyage,
the steamships rose out of the water as coal burned off, causing the paddle-
wheels to lose effectiveness. Seaborne crosswinds buried the leeward paddles in
the waves while the windward paddles thrashed air. The concern in oceangoing
vessels was not just the need to create a counterbalancing rudder motion, as on
the riverboats, but the possibility that in rolling seas strong variable stresses on
the drive shaft would cause it to break, rendering the engine useless. Another
problem was that the stern-wheelers couldn't deliver enough thrust to produce
the desired speed. Screw propulsion had been considered since the late eighteenth century, but a reasonable turning speed required more power than early
steam engines could deliver. After 1819 rolled iron corrected that shortcoming,
and western riverboats took the lead in its use. The iron was shaped into large,
cylindrical water-tube boilers that could raise steam pressure as high as forty
pounds per square inch. When the steam was fed to double-expansion (two-
cylinder) engines its efficiency was multiplied. While inland steamship lines
retained their colorful side- and stern-wheelers, Atlantic shippers installed propellers on harbor tugs and some of the packet boats. The Swede John Ericsson

is credited with the first successful application of the screw propeller to ship design, based on work he did in England sometime before 1836. Highly regarded as an engineer, he contracted to design a screw-propelled ship. His first challenge was to overcome the leakage introduced into wooden hulls by vibrations caused by the screws. Ericsson, more a technical facilitator than an inventor, saw iron as the solution. In 1839 his *Robert F. Stockton* became the first American commercial, propeller-driven vessel, and the first iron-hulled ship, to cross the Atlantic. Ericsson's work impressed the navy's shipbuilding bureau, where he was hired to design warships. His USS *Princeton* was the world's first steam-powered warship; later in the century another Ericsson-designed warship, the USS *Monitor,* would revolutionize the conduct of ocean warfare.

In the meantime, the steam-driven packets were beset with problems. Screw propulsion sometimes imparted a corkscrew motion to the ship. The usual solution was to place the screw inside flat plate stabilizers. Increasing the number of propeller blades from two to four or more also seemed to help, as did smaller pitch and increased rate of revolution. The use of coal created another navigation problem. Needed in large supply for crossings that took three to five weeks, the coal was subject to shifting that could alter the trim of the vessel. Furthermore, coal was difficult to replenish in many of the smaller ports. This created a need for multiple bunkers with adequate capacity to service the vessel between coaling ports. Even boiler water caused problems. Seawater was used at first, although known to be corrosive and to encrust tubing with salt. The unavailability of fresh water was a major problem on long ocean passages. It was some time before recirculating steam condensers, cooled by ocean water, came into use. Qualified mechanics and replacement parts were available only in the few seaports that produced steam engines. This limited the number of ports of call for the ocean steamers.

The upshot was that steamships had a limited range of operation, whereas a sailing vessel could go anywhere: it carried its own replacement canvas, cordage, and spars, and its crew included craftsmen to do the repairs. It could stay at sea indefinitely, often under extreme conditions, a self-sufficient floating world. There were ample reasons to continue the development of the sailing vessel—its ability to round either of the South Atlantic capes being foremost. In 1820 Nathaniel Palmer, in command of the brig *Hero,* found the Antarctic peninsula, a discovery that so excited him he returned the following year aboard the *James Monroe* to explore further the land that would later be named for him. That was work for a windjammer.

Early in the century, Cape Codder William Sturgis, a sea captain long attracted to mercantile opportunities on the West Coast, formed a partnership with Boston merchant John Bryant to trade common dry goods for the pelts of Pacific sea otters. After the War of 1812, Bryant and Sturgis reopened the abandoned California fur trade and looked for other goods useful to New Englanders. In January 1822, their ship *Sachem* departed Boston for the Mexican provinces and picked up a cargo of hides destined for the Brockton shoe companies. Within six years the company Bryant & Sturgis was shipping two thirds of California's imports, including return cargoes of shoes made from California hides. It was this trade route that turned the California economy away from Orient-bound fur and toward northeast-bound leather. It also provided the strange employment of the first man to protest in print the merchant seaman's harsh life and take up the cause for reform.

Intense demand for fast transport generated a new breed of sea captain— fearless, hard-driving, and fierce in the use of power. These skippers took pride in being called "drivers," not without the owners' admiration. They gathered petty officers about them, known to their crews as "bucko mates" and "bully boys," men who were quick with the metal fist and rope's end in rousing sailors to action. Seamen on the fast ships were often a mixed lot, many gathered from among the vagrants of New York and Liverpool—destitute laborers, short on employment for whatever reasons, known on the waterfront as "packet rats." The man-killing schedules of the packet boats, which typically kept all sails aloft even in the most appalling weather, enforced speeds twice those of the plodding ocean traders. In the leaky and airless fo'c'sle where the crew ate, slept, and stowed their gear, the cramped living quarters were wet and thick with the nauseating smells of damp bedding, unwashed bodies, and slopping bilges. The packet rats hustled to the challenges, though often at the cost of life or limb. In dockside taverns it was said that signing on to a packet ship was taking a ticket on a blood boat. It was little different among the "hide-droghers" who sailed around the Horn.

Richard Henry Dana Jr. withdrew from Harvard at the age of nineteen because of an illness that had ruined his eyesight. Against the advice of Nathaniel Bowditch's son, he refused a cabin berth and signed on to the brig *Pilgrim* for a two-year voyage as a common sailor before the mast. The adventurous Dana knew what he wanted. He had applied for a seaman's berth to J. Ingersall Bowditch, part owner and supercargo of the ship *Japan*. Young Bowditch thought it improper for a Cambridge gentleman like Dana to ship in the forecastle and

4-2. Spars and rigging of a ship, *The Seaman's Friend,* 1841. Prints and Photographs Division, Library of Congress

called his father into the discussion. Nathaniel, forgetting that he himself had sailed as a ship's boy, agreed with his son. Dana refused their offer of a cabin passage and walked the Boston waterfront to find lesser employment. At the office of Bryant & Sturgis he found work aboard the brig *Pilgrim,* bound around Cape Horn for a cargo of California hides. Richard Dana's voyage produced a literary classic that called public attention to the brutal life of merchant sailors. *Two Years Before the Mast,* Dana's only publication except for a sailor's handbook, *The Seaman's Friend,* made him famous. This was also the first printed report on California before it became a territory of the United States. Dana described California as a primitive land thinly populated by multiple classes of Mexican rancheros and serf-like "Indians" who did most of the manual labor.

The *Pilgrim* got under way from Boston on August 14, 1834, under the command of Frank Thompson. At sea, the master wields absolute power over all who have signed articles, is accountable to no one but the owners for the performance of his vessel, stands no watch, eats alone, and comes and goes on deck as he pleases. His use of authority determines the behavior of the crew and the ultimate success or failure of the voyage. Thompson was moody and sadistic, a tyrannical commander, and an inept seaman. His ship departed with a crew of fourteen: two mates, three idlers (non-watch-standers—a carpenter, cook, and steward), six A-Bs, two ordinaries, of whom Dana was one, and a boy of ten or twelve. During the trip one A-B was lost overboard, one jumped ship after being demoted from second mate, and one sickly former accountant was made ship's clerk; the two short-handed watches made do.

The *Pilgrim's* chief mate, though a capable sailor, was a slack and ineffective leader. That trait irritated the captain, who more than once preempted the mate's role. The second mate on such a ship is no more than a petty officer who furnishes the supplies from the boatswain's locker, does sailor's work, and even goes aloft with the watch. In return for being assigned a berth in the cabin, he is expected to exercise some degree of responsible leadership in his tasks. But the *Pilgrim's* second mate was an idle and worthless individual, and only half a sailor. When the captain caught him sleeping on watch he broke the man to fo'c'sle duty. While it was permissible, with cause, to remove any crew member from duty, it was doubtful that the captain had the right to put an officer before the mast. One of the A-Bs, a bright and industrious lad, was appointed as replacement, reducing the strength of the watches but easing somewhat the tensions in the afterguard. This was not enough, however, to curb Captain Thompson's disposition.

In 1835, while the *Pilgrim* was on the West Coast, Congress passed legislation prohibiting beating, wounding, or physical punishment by a master or mate, "if without justifiable cause"—an unfortunately weak provision. Flogging, albeit a legal form of punishment, was used rarely by all but the most inhumane captains; it was not specifically forbidden until 1850. In midvoyage there was little opportunity for the crew to become aware of the law or to seek its protection, and Captain Thompson was not subject to it under articles signed prior to its enactment. While the *Pilgrim* was at anchor on the West Coast, Thompson had two foremast men spread-eagled at the main shrouds for punishment, with little beyond his own unharnessed temper to provoke him to such an extreme. The offense in both cases: talking back to the captain. Thompson rolled up his sleeves, took a rope in hand, and flogged each of the offenders, all the while shouting, according to Dana, "If you want to know what I flog you for, I'll tell you. It's because I like to do it!—because I like to do it!—It suits me! That's what I do it for." One of the men prayed in agony. "Don't call on Jesus Christ," yelled Thompson. "He can't help you. Call on Frank Thompson! He's the man! He can help you! Jesus Christ can't help you now! . . . I'll make you toe the mark, every soul of you, or I'll flog you all, fore and aft, from the boy up! You've got a driver over you! Yes, a slave-driver,—a nigger-driver!" After the two men were cut down, he made them put on their shirts and row him ashore. There was no American consul in any of the Mexican ports. The men had no recourse.

There were other incidents on the voyage. As keeper of the medicine chest, the captain refused care to more than one sick crew member. He ineptly maneuvered the brig to crash into another in an anchorage. While on the coast, under orders from the owners, he exchanged commands with the captain of the *Alert,* which was to return home earlier. Dana and another ordinary were also shifted to the *Alert,* leaving the *Pilgrim* undermanned. Thompson at first tried to deny what Dana already knew—that the owners had requested Dana's early return. The two transferred *Pilgrim* sailors were made to pay two *Alert* sailors to replace them on their old ship; Dana forfeited six months' wages out of his account. On the return voyage Thompson gave his own black steward half a dozen strokes with a rope's end. He was also known to have withheld food out of meanness, there being ample supplies aboard.

Old Captain "Bill" Sturgis knew his way about ships, having sailed from the age of sixteen and come up through the hawse-hole to become master of his own ship at twenty-one. In a later command he fended off the attack of sixteen East Indian pirate junks, protecting $300,000 of specie he had aboard. Upon the *Alert*'s return to Boston, Sturgis somehow got word of Frank Thompson's behavior, and Thompson never again sailed on a Bryant & Sturgis ship. The *Alert,* the first of the two vessels to arrive, carried a cargo of forty thousand hides, which sold at $1.50 to $2.00 each, the captain receiving 1 percent of the gross by agreement. Learning of Dana's forced agreement to "buy" his replacement, the owners covered the payment, a total of $72.

Dana recorded the story of his voyage under Captain Thompson objectively and without emotion. His book describes the life of a merchant sailor much as it would have been under any skipper. The crew signed articles, but the qualifications for ratings seemed arbitrary. Experience determined berthing status. Dana and another ordinary were put in steerage, where they slept not in bunks but on top of coils of rope, spare sails, and other ship's stores. Later they were overjoyed to negotiate relocation to the forecastle, where the air was often so foul that the single overhead lamp could work up no more than a weak blue flame. There at least they lived with fellow crew members, removed from the watchful eyes of the captain and his mates.

Sailors earned $12 a month, minus slop chest charges for whatever clothing they drew. Idle time, what little they had, was often spent mending and patching. The crew stood watch-and-watch under the "all hands" system, four hours on duty, four off, with all hands turned to during the afternoon watch on every day but Sunday. Some ships got Saturday afternoon free of all-hands work, but not any of Captain Thompson's commands. Evening dog watches caused assignments to shift, so that one worked either ten or eighteen hours in a twenty-four-hour period—or more when it was necessary to change sail or replace broken spars or rigging, or when heavy weather called for the duties of all hands.

On the California coast the sailors were put to work "droghing" hides—carrying the heavy slabs on their heads out to four-oared boats that waited beyond the breaking surf, then rowing three miles to the anchored ship. With a full load the trip could take two hours. The hides had to be stowed twice: after their first delivery on board in the form of uncured rawhide they were returned to shore at collection points to be cured by scraping, pickling, and drying, and then redelivered by the same tedious method. The half-dozen foremast hands, along with some Sandwich Island Kanakas, were assigned this work in various harbors along the southern California coast for close to a year. For them—wet and cold at the water's edge, baked in the summer sun, dusty and flea-bitten in the ship's fetid hold—the return trip around the Horn in the depth of winter became something to welcome.

There was work to be done aloft under all conditions: handing and reefing in wind and storm; worming, parcelling, slushing, and tarring down the rigging when the weather was calm enough to permit it. It was not unknown to spend an hour and a half on the yards in icy sleet, hauling in and securing sail, the lee scuppers under water all the while. Furling frozen canvas is comparable to folding sheet metal. While grappling with the canvas the men are assailed at the head and arms by loose, ice-encrusted lines. Before doubling the Cape the *Alert* traveled for two weeks in the depths of the southern winter, laying to in blustering easterlies, dodging field ice and giant bergs, running on beam ends in gale-whipped quartering seas. No one on deck stood idle during daylight. Replacement spars and rigging, heavy blocks and tackle, had to be hauled into place while the scuppers ran with breaking seas. In clear weather there were decks to holystone and cable to scrape, both odious tasks never complete.

The *Alert*'s crew suffered from scurvy on its homeward voyage. On the West Coast they had had the benefit of California's fertile farms with fruits and vegetables in plentiful supply. During the last weeks of loading hides they ate beefsteak three times a day. But fresh provisions ran out before the middle of the five-month journey back to Boston. The debilitating illness appeared while the ship was in the South Atlantic. Two sailors became unable to work, one so weak he was confined to his bunk, powerless to move his scabby limbs, his eyes sunken, his breath rotten. When he could no longer handle the daily fare of salt horse, his shipmates thought he had but a day or two to live. They knew the symptoms of scurvy and its cure, but all were vague as to its cause. It was attributed to excess consumption of salt, grease, and fat, to uncleanliness, and, as if such could be achieved under a driver, laziness. All the men developed an intense urge for vegetables of any variety—one of the first symptoms of the lack of the vitamins they supply. Fortunately, south of the Bermudas the ship passed within hailing distance of a brig out of Plymouth, and the crew procured a boatload of onions. Every manjack ate them raw, like apples. The onions were diced and boiled down into a soup for the sickly ones to take a teaspoon at a time. In ten days, after a steady diet of potato and onion stew, both men were up and climbing the rigging, the worst of the disease behind them. The *Alert* came on soundings with a crew healthy enough to tidy it up for arrival in Boston.

What manner of man was drawn to seafaring—not the adventurers who made one voyage and quit, but seamen who returned aboard trip after trip, despite the hardships? Sons of the best families went to sea, learned the trade, and were proud to accept the risks of the harsh life for pay that might exceed what could be earned ashore. They were young and robust when they took up the seagoing life. Regular living (in-port behavior excepted) and a working environment that in most circumstances was free of contagious diseases kept sailors generally healthy, less in need of medical attention than landsmen. Medical care was unavailable, and they adjusted to its absence—ignored bruises, toothache, and temporary pain. They often recovered from infections and even from minor fractures on their own and without comment. It was a matter of pride for the nineteenth-century sailor that he stand among his shipmates appearing fearless and unperturbed by threats to life and limb. He became calloused to the daily dangers, poised on the cathead over breaking seas and an unsecured anchor, stretching the footropes above the foretop, or fending off flailing lines and swinging blocks and falls. The bosun's rope ends stung and were forgotten.

If one disease was endemic among seamen, it was alcoholism. Perhaps the type of personality drawn to the sea was prone to overindulgence. Perhaps sailors drank to block out the miseries and discomforts of the seafaring life or the boredom of long days and nights at sea. Some couldn't handle the spells of shoreside freedom interspersed with dull and disciplined periods at sea. Drunkenness was more common in port, "ardent spirits" being rationed aboard if available at all.

If the typical sailor was not originally inclined to be asocial, he soon became so. He had no choice of shipmates. Destined to work with the same people for long periods, living with them in confined quarters, the sailor developed a guarded approach. His understanding of the attitudes, strengths, and weaknesses of the crew unfolded slowly despite the lack of privacy. Sailors were tolerant by default. From their first day at sea they worked with mixed races and nationalities, accepted it as a matter of course, found it stimulating; most wouldn't have wanted to sail in a crew that was all alike. In that they differed from their naval counterparts. Sometimes sailors shared no common language apart from the common jargon of the ship. Visiting lands their homebound associates had never heard of, dependent for support from strangers representing different cultures, seamen took tolerance for granted.

Shoreside liberty was brief, yet the time spent in port was longer by far than it would be a century later. Time ashore was often spent with little companionship, the loneliness in its own way enhancing the sailor's brief sense of freedom. In London, Bremen, or Canton he rarely saw what travelers call "the sights." Time permitted no travel far from the ship—a walk through the edges of the seaport, a bartered exchange for curios, a visit to a tavern or bordello were the extent of his limited life ashore.

Sailors were apt to be sexually liberal. They categorized sexual activity— like eating, sleeping, bathing, and grooming—as a normal human need, to be discreetly satisfied with little discussion. The tendency was to be morally neutral. Removed from the customary strictures of society in a routine without religious support, sailors relied on the faith that came from within or from youthful conditioning. Fear didn't engender it—the captain or bosun was more to be feared than God. Yet sailors retained an innate sense of morality, shaped by circumstances but ever alert to injustice, as became evident later in the century when their dissatisfaction with working conditions grew. Apart from fleshly indulgences in port, temporary escapes into alcohol, or fits of uncontrolled rage after long periods at sea, sailors deviated little from normal standards. They trusted shipmates with their lives if not their money, but had little faith in those ashore. Most of their few possessions remained unlocked in the crowded quarters in which they lived, but were easily taken from them, ashore.

Seamen were and still are narrow in worldview. Cut off from all events on land, they are focused so intently on the ship that they lose interest in the doings of ordinary society. They are inclined to collect and enlarge on maritime tales, which represent in total what constitutes their life. Although they see more of the world than most landsmen, their knowledge of foreign countries tends to be limited. Lacking landsmen's culture, sailors mix better with fellow seamen than with any others, whether at sea or ashore, and often continue in this way to the end of their lives. This may explain why most societies don't welcome sailors more than a few blocks beyond the waterfront.

Conditions on the transatlantic routes were no worse for men in the forecastle than for the poorer passengers below decks. The European migration of impoverished Irish, English, and Germans introduced a new trade. Emigrant liners packed aboard hundreds more people than were carried by the fast packets on their westbound trips. Five hundred to eight hundred travelers would be crowded into steerage under dreadful conditions, bringing their own food aboard with whatever belongings they had. They were provided nothing more than water from a common bucket and access to a cook-stove and slop pails. Vermin-infested straw made up their bedding, in a hold which stank of rotting food, vomit, and excrement. The horrid environment produced general malaise, chills, and fever among the occupants, some of whom were ill before coming aboard. When rampant skin eruptions and hot rashes signaled "ship fever," or typhus, it was apt to spread wildly. Typhus was unwelcome to owners and ship

4-3. *Ann McKim* of Baltimore, first American clipper. COURTESY OF THE MARINERS' MUSEUM, NEWPORT NEWS, VIRGINIA

masters more for the delays it would cause upon entering port than for the on-board deaths that were certain to occur. In 1819 Congress legislated against steerage overcrowding, but the wording of the new statutes was too weak to curb the awful conditions to any extent. The nightmare of the ocean passage to America lingered long in the memory of the new arrivals.

Steamship technology, the surging tide of immigration, and new international incentives further expanded American maritime activities. In 1829, coincident with construction of a network of railroads and amid much controversy, Chesapeake Bay and the Delaware River were connected by a locked waterway called the C & D Canal, which cut through marshy land. The canal brought Baltimore four hundred sea miles closer to the northern ports. In a move to keep southern cotton flowing to British mills, the British Parliament passed the Navigation Acts of 1830, which accorded special privileges to American vessels. By 1840 most raw cotton that moved across the Atlantic did so on American bottoms, and southern ports flourished. Baltimore took a stride forward in shipbuilding, capitalizing on the fame of its fast privateers. One of these, the *Ann McKim,* is widely recognized as the prototype American clipper. It was launched in the Baltimore shipyard of Kennard & Williamson in 1833 and named by the owner, Isaac McKim, for his wife. At 493 tons and 143 feet in length, it was the largest ship in the U.S. merchant fleet. Elegantly built on the lines of earlier Baltimore privateers, *Ann McKim*'s raked masts, wedge-shaped stern, and long afterdrag defined the clipper style. Its fame accompanied it to the Pacific, where it voyaged to and from the Orient until McKim's death in 1837. Dana and his shipmates twice looked for it while on the West Coast. Despite its bluff bows, the *Ann McKim* was swift. Its speed inspired further improvements in ship design, which were applied in the building of scores of clippers—always, it seemed, in the name of faster passages.

This period of growth brought with it other maritime innovations of little note but long-lasting effect. In 1837 the Fall River Line's *King Philip* made the first use of a steam whistle. Installed to add panache to the passenger steamer, in time the device was widely adopted and became a safety requirement. For some time, the haphazard operation of passenger-carrying steamboats had been recognized as a threat to personal safety. Unsafe midships fireboxes in wooden vessels, smokestacks discharging embers aloft to light on sails and cabin tops, boilers and tubing near bursting with high steam pressure—all combined to make steamboats hazardous. In 1838 Congress introduced the Steamship Inspection Act, one of America's first laws calling for the examination and supervision of private enterprise on behalf of the general welfare. To assure some degree of passenger safety, the law set minimum standards of operation for steam passenger vessels and required regular inspection of those within its jurisdiction.

In 1837 a New England sea captain, Thomas Sumner, made a simple observation that vastly improved the practice of celestial navigation. Sumner filled the gap in Bowditch's exposition of the science when he published a description of his own method in "A New Method of Finding a Ship's Position at Sea." He pointed out that any particular altitude observation of a celestial body (based on its sextant angle above the horizon) locates the observer on an imaginary circle on the earth's surface, the bottom of a cone whose center lay directly under the body at the time. If the exact position of the celestial body is known, the earthly circumference of the cone becomes a line of position. If such a circle is of sufficient diameter—that is, if the angle of measured altitude is smaller than 85 degrees—the circle's arc can be represented as a straight line (known as a Sumner line) on a chart covering the observer's vicinity. Two or three observations on different bodies provide an intersection that fixes the observer's position accurately on the ocean. (If the body is nearly overhead, the circle diminishes enough that the arc must be represented as a curve of small radius. In that case, since each line is actually a segment of a circle, two points of intersection are derived from two observations, one of which is likely to be some distance from the observer's estimated position. However, three properly determined arcs intersect at only one point.) In Sumner's day, tables were available showing the earthly coordinates of the sun, visible planets, and major stars in their daily revolutions as a function of precise time. Chronometers soon became popular on board ship, accompanied by expanded nautical almanacs. Sumner's discovery changed the practice of astronomical science forever; its principles apply as well to satellites and electronic methods of navigation.

One scientific discovery of the period was long delayed in its application, for no other reason than the federal government's laggard bureaucracy. In 1822 Augustin Fresnel, a French physicist, perfected a lens that would revolutionize lighthouses worldwide by refracting and intensifying their lights. The Fresnel lens was well known in America by 1837, a time when the country's lighthouses were in deplorable condition. Lighthouse towers were badly constructed and often poorly positioned. Lanterns were dim and not regularly lit. They sometimes failed to revolve, producing incorrect signals. Lightships, or "lightboats," as they were called at the time, were in equally poor condition and were not always attended as expected; captains and crews were known to depart from them for extended periods.

The First Congress made the U.S. Treasury's Customs Service responsible for the nation's aids to navigation. Alexander Hamilton, first secretary of the treasury, administered the lighthouses until 1792. Responsibility was then passed around like a football, first to the commissioner of revenue, then back to the next secretary of the treasury, again to the commissioner of revenue, and finally, in 1820, to the fifth auditor of the Treasury. None of these people had maritime backgrounds; they were bookkeepers, more concerned with the nation's financial accounts. Stephen Pleasonton, the fifth auditor, had clerks who oversaw the lighthouse establishment but were allowed to make only minor decisions; he approved all expenses.

From time to time Congress heard distressing reports about the lighthouse service. In 1837 when the Treasury Department requested authorization for a number of new lights, Congress looked for assurance that the nation's needs were being properly met and appointed a naval commission to examine the sites of the requested lights. The commission found that thirty-one of the proposed lights were unnecessary. Congress then called for a broader investigation. In its act of June 7, 1838, it divided the nation's shores into six districts on the Atlantic and two on the Great Lakes. Each district had a naval officer assigned to it who was to report on the current state of affairs and select additional sites. There followed fourteen years of inspections, anguish at the findings, and half-hearted and wasteful attempts at corrections amid political wrestling and a rising tide of complaints. Until the shameful situation could be rectified, Fresnel lenses in America remained uninstalled experimental curiosities.

Competition among the transatlantic passenger lines and between shipyards in England and America striving to produce the fastest vessels started the practice of recording the precise timing of ocean passages. The great circle route between Bishop Rock in the Western Approaches and Sankaty Head on Nantucket, the two principal landfalls, was the most common track for calculating speed. Starting in 1838, the current record-holding vessel was accorded a symbolic "Blue Riband"—the award was more myth than reality. There was no material prize that could be passed from one ship to another, not even a blue ribbon—nothing but the honor of holding the ephemeral award and boasting of it to the world. It was a good time to boast. In 1838 American ships carried 90 percent of American trade, and the United States began to enjoy the greatest period in its maritime history.

Chapter 5

ROCKS AND SHOALS:
1838–1848

Even as New England shipbuilders gave up their self-imposed size limitations, they remained leery of steam propulsion. Considered unsuitable for long voyages, steam was put to work in tugboats and short-distance haulers; a few innovators developed small "donkey engines" for winches and anchor windlasses on larger sailing ships. Steamship service thrived on inland waters, but ocean traders were reluctant to rely on coal replenishment in ports distant from fuel supplies. With that short-sighted view they missed new opportunities to develop coaling ports and deliver fuel close to the places where it would be needed. Wind was God's gift to the trader and it was plentiful on the open ocean. The New Englanders saw speed as the proper response to the struggling steamers, to be achieved through evolving designs of hull and rigging. Long bows cleaving through the waves rather than pounding onto them gave rise to the term "clipper." The New England clipper ships were modeled on Baltimore's *Ann McKim.*

Shippers in the port of Boston, perennially troubled by lack of eastbound cargoes, were overjoyed when England's Samuel Cunard chose their city as the terminus for his Royal Mail Steam Packet Company. Boston's White Star packet line had found it necessary to collect southern cotton for the European market to support its transatlantic passenger service, a lengthy alternative to the direct, fast passages out of New York. Now, in an effort to gain on rivals in the passenger business, the port authorities refurbished the dock facilities in East Boston and in 1840 leased them rent-free to Cunard. One of Cunard's four steam side-wheelers arrived in Boston every two weeks, to the chagrin of New York, which at the time operated only one transatlantic steam packet. The *Britannia,* Cunard's prize ship, received a festive welcome at the East Boston wharf with every arrival. In the bitter winter of 1844, when deep ice might have kept the *Britannia* in harbor, the Boston merchants put out crews with axes and saws to cut a channel for it, sustaining Cunard's interest in the port. Cunard's line thrived from the very beginning. It became famous for its conservative development of safe passenger travel, and Boston long remained the Englishman's favorite American port. Yet for American shipowners the steamship business remained tenuous.

Congress took notice of what appeared to be a Cunard monopoly and in 1845 authorized subsidies for American shipping lines, in the form of mail contracts with those that would build ships capable of conversion to warships. Soon the Americans had routes to Havre and Bremen and established Central American connections with lines on the Pacific coast; but Cunard retained its hold on the prosperous Liverpool route. Months passed. Then, in a reversal of the New Englanders' historic disdain for steam, Edward Collins submitted a proposal to the Senate, a plan, in his words, to "drive the Cunarders out of business." Another year and a half elapsed before the postmaster general entered into a contract with Collins and the brothers James and Stewart Brown to carry mail between New York and Liverpool. The three agreed to build steamships fitting naval specifications, and with them to make twenty round trips per year on the North Atlantic run. For this they were to receive a ten-year annual subsidy of $385,000. In December 1847 the United States Mail Steamship Company was formed, better known as the Collins Line.

America's maritime affairs, while prospering, were at loose ends, in need of unified direction. Nowhere was the lack of capable administration more evident than in the lighthouse service. The reports returned by the naval officers after their 1838 inspection revealed what coastwise mariners already knew—that the nation's principal aids to navigation were poorly maintained and managed, as hazardous as they were helpful. Lighthouses were plentiful along well-populated shores, but absent or dim where they were most needed, in areas with heavy offshore traffic. Twin lighthouses stood on Thatcher's Island, northeast of the rocky entrances to Gloucester and Salem. At Nauset, the outermost edge of

Cape Cod, three lights were under construction, 150 feet apart. Navesink, New Jersey, displayed a pair. Elsewhere, reflectors were found to be misshapen, lenses cracked, revolving machinery rusted, lanterns leaking in stormy weather, towers ill-constructed and potentially unstable. The number of American lighthouses had grown rapidly, from 16 at the turn of the century to 204 in 1838, plus 28 lightboats. Stephen Pleasonton, the fifth auditor of the Treasury, who was responsible for lighthouse administration, was neither corrupt nor careless in his position; he simply misunderstood his role. Influenced by a parsimonious Congress, he strove solely for economy, tolerated political appointments of light keepers, and remained unaware of or uninterested in technical progress. By keeping his eye on the books, he weathered repeated criticism and held on to the post for thirty-two years—the archetypal federal bureaucrat. His severest critics were the brothers Edmund and George Blunt, publishers of the *American Coast Pilot,* who consistently delivered the complaints of seamen to congressmen and other federal officials. Governmental reactions were sporadic and failed for years to solve the problem.

A former sea captain, Winslow Lewis, was at the root of the technical shortcomings of American lighthouses, despite his maritime experience. He had improved a well-known European lamp and reflector, making the light brighter than any predecessor and energy-efficient too—it burned half the oil of older lamps. That appealed to the tight-fisted fifth auditor. Lewis obtained a patent for his system, then offered to sell it to the government and undertake refitting of the lighthouses to accommodate the new equipment. Pleasonton had Lewis draw up the specifications for the proposed work and allowed him to bid on his own proposal. In 1812 Lewis was awarded a seven-year contract to install and maintain his system in all forty-nine stations, a task he finished within three years. Lewis was a shrewd businessman and before long obtained a monopoly as supplier of the lighting system, closing out his only competitor by consistently underbidding. Pleasonton undoubtedly approved of that. Lewis had such a firm grasp on the business that any later consideration of the Fresnel lens, an expensive but enormous improvement on what he offered, was ignored.

The vendor and the fifth auditor got along famously. In 1835, when Lewis changed the characteristics of the Mobile Point Light from fixed to revolving, he did it without notifying the superintendent of lights. Unfortunately, the new characteristics matched those of nearby Pensacola Light. Mariners approaching or ranging the coast were faced with two lights, forty miles apart, with identical characteristics, one not conforming to published specifications. The Blunts and several shipmasters complained. Pleasonton defended Lewis, and the light remained as changed. There was no evidence of collusion or dishonesty in the Lewis-Pleasonton relationship, but the fifth auditor's favoritism toward the sharp entrepreneur is undeniable.

Edmund and George Blunt sent off a broadside against Pleasonton and the lighthouse service. They faulted the inferior workmanship and materials in several towers, pointed out the inadequate system of notification to mariners when lights were put out of service or their characteristics changed, and complained about the quality of the lights, especially as compared with those in England and France. In his stuffy, bureaucratic manner, Pleasonton wrote to Congress that he would be willing to experiment with the mentioned Fresnel lens, but that in his opinion its quality was only in the lamp behind it. Confronted with complaints from insurance inspectors and ship captains, Congress conceded the need for experimentation with the lens apparatus. In 1838, at the request of Congress, Commodore Matthew Perry sailed to Europe to study lighthouses on the continent and to purchase two Fresnel lenses. The lenses were installed in the twin towers of Navesink Station at the western entrance to New York harbor in 1840 and lighted the following year. Winslow Lewis did not get the installation contract. These were the first Fresnel lenses to be used in the United States, and before long they proved vastly superior to the older models. But progress in lighthouse service under Stephen Pleasonton remained slow. Over the next ten years, just two more Fresnel lenses were purchased. In 1847 Congress removed the responsibility for construction of six lighthouses from the fifth auditor and assigned the project to the Corps of Engineers. The move did little to solve the basic problem—a complete lack of understanding.

When the words "WHAT HATH GOD WROUGHT" clicked across a single copper wire strung from Washington, D.C., to Baltimore, Samuel F. B. Morse achieved the recognition he felt he deserved. Morse did not originate the telegraph or much of the code that bears his name, but he did get credit for his innovations. A Yale graduate, Morse was first a painter, trained in Europe and well known among the merchant princes of New England. It was he who painted the formal portrait of George Crowninshield Jr., that hung for years in the family manse. He was also a "natural philosopher," the term at the time for scientific tinkerer. (So, too, were Ben Franklin, Thomas Jefferson, and Robert Fulton; it was not a frivolous occupation.) In 1832, while abroad, Morse became fascinated by Ampère's idea for an electric telegraph. He saw a possible advantage in applying Faraday's and Henry's developments of the electromagnet to long distance transmission, and for the next twelve years he worked to produce a telegraph of his own. He modified a British code intended for semaphore and light signaling, recoding about a third of the alphabet, and used what he thereafter called Morse code in his telegraphic experiments. On January 6, 1838, Morse gave the first public demonstration of his electric telegraph. Six more years elapsed before he perfected the device, which later influenced the conduct of international trade and enhanced the safety of ships at sea. (Morse did no work on wireless telegraphy, but his code was used in that field by Guglielmo Marconi.) His 1844 demonstration for Congress followed twelve years of experimentation, during which he had not worked alone. Similar devices were already in use in Europe, but Morse's timing was opportune. With the coming of the railroad, the telegraph altered the nation's business methods, speeding the ordering and delivery of goods, shortening reporting times of arrivals, broadening the scope of commercial announcements. Morse's enthusiasm was not dampened by the need to defend his invention against other claimants. He foresaw the telegraph's potential in international trade and went on to experiment with a submarine cable. That idea was not realized in his lifetime, but before his death he gained worldwide acclaim for his telegraphic innovation and for the code known by his name.

A naval officer literally did the groundwork in specifying conditions for the laying of a transatlantic cable. Matthew Fontaine Maury, a native of Fredericksburg, Virginia, was permanently lamed at thirty-three in a stagecoach accident. At the time he was a navy lieutenant, and although unable to go to sea thereafter he applied to retain his commission. In 1842 he was put in charge of the navy's Department of Charts and Instruments, the predecessor of the U.S. Naval Observatory and Hydrographic Office. Maury originated and carried forward the idea of recording thousands of shipboard observations of wind, current, and ocean depth. He was the first to recognize what he called "the great plain of the Atlantic," a sea bottom free of deep crevasses and sharp crags, across which a cable between the continents might be laid. With new technology the message-transmission time between the two worlds would be reduced from weeks to seconds.

Maury's charts improved the Atlantic voyages of passenger liners, but not early enough for Charles Dickens's first visit to America. Dickens came to the United States in 1842 aboard the renowned *Britannia,* sailing during the worst month of the year before charts were available for alternative ocean routes. His satirical report gives a sense of the distraught state of passengers unaccustomed to the sea:

A head wind! . . . the wind howling, the sea roaring, the rain beating, . . . the sky both dark and wild, and the clouds, in fearful sympathy with the waves, making another ocean in the air. Add to all this the clattering on deck and down below; the tread of hurried feet; the loud hoarse shouts of seamen; the gurgling in and out of water through the scuppers; with every now and then the striking of a heavy sea upon the planks above, with the deep, dead heavy sound of thunder within a vault; and there is the head wind of that January morning.

I say nothing of what may be called the domestic noises of the ship: such as the breaking of glass and crockery, the tumbling down of stewards, the gambols, overhead, of loose casks and truant dozens of bottled porter, and the very remarkable and far from exhilarating sounds raised in their various state-rooms by the seventy passengers who were too ill to get up for breakfast.

Dickens boarded a Potomac River steamer after a night spent in a dormitory cabin sleeping on a shelf, with his clothes piled on the floor. He went to the fore-cabin and recorded what he found:

The washing and dressing apparatus, for the passengers generally, consists of two jack-towels, three small wooden basins, a keg of water and a ladle to serve it out with, six square inches of looking glass, two ditto ditto of yellow soap, a comb and a brush for the head, and nothing for the teeth. Everybody uses the comb and brush, except myself.

Dickens then booked passage on a western steamboat to Cincinnati, seeking a cabin in the stern. The reason for this, he wrote, was that "we had been a great many times very gravely recommended to keep as far aft as possible, 'because the steamboats generally blew up forward.'" More than one steamboat fatality had preceded his journey. In *American Notes,* he later described his exploration beneath the vessel's main deck, where he found

the furnace fires and machinery, open at the sides to every wind that blows, . . . the great body of fire, exposed as I have just described, that rages and roars beneath the frail pile of painted wood: the machinery not warded off or guarded in any way, doing its work in the midst of a crowd of idlers and emigrants and children who throng the lower deck: under the management, too, of reckless men whose acquaintance with its mysteries may have been of six months' standing: one feels directly that the wonder is, not that there should be so many fatal accidents, but that any journey should be safely made.

The author had a more pleasant trip aboard the American packet *Washington* on his return to England in June. By then a seasoned traveler, his lyrical report on the passage home was a travel agent's delight, all previously noted concerns about storms, explosions, fog, and outlying rocks forgotten.

As a youngster George Francis Train had had ample experience in clawing off life's lee shores. Born in Boston in 1829, the only son of Oliver and Maria Train, he moved with his family to New Orleans while still a toddler. There he saw his mother and three sisters die of yellow fever. The distraught father's last known act was to put his son, unaccompanied, on a ship leaving for Boston—this before the lad was much over eleven or twelve. From Boston young George found his way to his maternal grandmother's farm west of the city, where he briefly attended local schools. Threatened with being signed over as an apprentice, at fourteen he left home to take up work for a Cambridge grocer. He grew tall and dark as he came of age and once said of himself that he was an octoroon, but by then he was a man given to practical joking and sensational behavior. At the age of fifteen, when Enoch Train, a relative, inquired into his welfare, George countered with a bold demand for employment in the elder Train's shipping office. Objections notwithstanding, George soon began work as a clerk for the merchant shipowner.

Enoch Train was one of Boston's leading businessmen, a trader with activity in the Baltic and South America. His White Diamond ships were slow, and he often lacked outbound cargo. Boston's export fortunes were on the wane, and New York had developed a near monopoly in packet service. By 1844 the Cunard Line had a firm footing in Boston with its scheduled steamship service to Liverpool. It was in this adverse situation that Train established a new line of sailing packets for the Boston-Liverpool run, a venture that was viewed with skepticism. He had to elbow his way into a trade controlled by New York's Black Ball Line, the Cope Line of Philadelphia, and Boston's Cunard Line, which had the only steamships in the transatlantic trade. But Train's difficulties diminished when he took up with two people: his young kin George—the particular relationship is unknown—and a former Nova Scotia designer and shipbuilder, Donald McKay. Train commissioned McKay to build the *Joshua Bates* in Newburyport, a contract that marked the start of a long and profitable alliance. The Train Line, its house flag bearing a black *T* on a white diamond over a red background, grew under McKay's production. He built the *Washington Irving, Ocean Monarch, Anglo-Saxon, Anglo-American, Daniel Webster, Parliament, Staffordshire, Chariot of Fame, Star of Empire,* and many more—ultimately twenty-four packets running to Liverpool. Meanwhile the imaginative and adventurous George Train became the business's driving force. It was he who conceived what became the most famous of the clippers, an extreme clipper named *Flying Cloud,* which he contracted with McKay to build in 1848. George Train also became a columnist, published several books, was an active pamphleteer and speaker on behalf of the Union, undertook a number of sensational causes, and made a trip around the world in eighty days. (Several contributors to maritime advancement acquired more fame in other endeavors. Morse, a well-known miniaturist, participated in the early development of photography. Maury served the Confederacy as an agent in England and later became a professor of meteorology at the Virginia Military Institute.)

Donald McKay started his career as a ship-carpenter, became a shipwright, and then formed a partnership with master shipbuilder William Currier in Newburyport, Massachusetts. Impressed by the speed of the Baltimore clippers plying the Chesapeake, he thought he could produce a similar vessel and make it faster still by hollowing the convex bow. His first wife Albenia Boole, daughter of a shipbuilder, assisted him. Two New York packets reflected their ideas and gained the attention of Enoch Train, who chose McKay to design the *Joshua Bates* for his Liverpool run. McKay, by then primarily a marine architect, formed a new partnership in 1844 with shipbuilder William Pickett. Impressed with the results, Train convinced McKay to move and helped him establish his own shipyard in East Boston. For the next five years McKay produced plans for packet ships, while toying with new design concepts to turn out fast cargo ships along similar lines. Clippers, with their narrow forward sections, were inefficient cargo carriers. McKay thought he could retain the clipper lines, but build larger and rig taller and heavier in order to achieve both adequate space and speed. Before he reached his goal, however, his energies were diverted by the tumultuous events of 1847–48, which revealed his extraordinary talents, tested his courage, and won him fame.

Meanwhile, the practical application of steam propulsion made fitful gains, with mixed signals for investors. By the summer of 1847 a daily overnight steamer was operating between Baltimore and Norfolk. Cunard had so captured the ocean steamship trade that in that year no other company had regular steamship service across the Atlantic. Steamboats thrived on the inland waters, though with service that was far from genteel. Offering dormitory-style passenger accommodations, they were little more than floating flophouses for migrant river workers.

Sailing ships still commanded the seas through the 1840s. The *Washington*—the first sailing packet to include second-class accommodations, which provided an intermediate level of comfort between first class and steerage—took up transatlantic service. This was the ship on which Charles Dickens returned to England. Europe's failed potato crop generated a heavy demand for American grain, which was transported in sail-driven bulk carriers. Bryant & Sturgis had established a solid outbound trade by sending sailing ships around the Horn: in forty-eight years the firm had brought five million hides from California to be exchanged for dry goods, notions, clothing, wines, liquors, and shoes made from the hides. Boston traders Joseph B. Eaton and William Appleton joined them, and as long as no one shipped industrial equipment and people with the skills to use it, there was plenty of business for everybody.

Sail or steam—which could carry more and carry it faster? Which would dominate the latter half of the century? The still barely exploited territory of California beckoned. Sail was better suited than steam for the long haul around the two continents. The Pacific Mail Lines compromised by using the *California*, a sail-steamer, for passenger service from New York to San Francisco via Cape Horn. In 1848 the *California* sailed from New York and became the first steamer to pass through the Golden Gate. It failed to fulfill its projected schedule, however. Gold had been discovered north of San Francisco, and the crew deserted for the gold fields, leaving the ship to idle in a San Francisco cove.

Cunard's steamship *Persia* arrived in Boston from England in August 1848 bearing the sad news that McKay's *Ocean Monarch*, sailing out of Liverpool, had been destroyed by fire at sea. It burned to the water and nearly half of the four hundred souls on board were lost, mostly immigrants. In the same year, Donald McKay's helpmate, Albenia, died. The confidence McKay and Enoch Train had in each other helped sustain them through the year of tragedy. Still struggling to compete with Cunard's steamships, Train focused on the projected clipper ships. He and George were fascinated with the new designs and continued to order sailing ships from McKay's yard.

Chapter 6

CROSSING WAKES: 1848–1851

Spirited Irishman that he was, Edward Collins spent whatever it took to build four mail packets that outclassed any steamship afloat in grandeur and speed. Brigantine-rigged, each displaced about twenty-eight hundred tons, with sidewheels driven by a fifteen-hundred-horsepower, coal-fired engine. The Collins Line service began with the *Atlantic*'s departure from New York for Liverpool on April 27, 1850, to be followed before the year's end by the *Pacific*, the *Arctic*, and the *Baltic*. On average, their runs were one day faster than the Cunard Line's crossings. Within a year the elegant *Baltic* had won the Blue Rib- and for speed in crossing the Atlantic. Collins's ambitious challenge to Great Britain's domination of the steamship routes forced deep reductions in British ocean freight rates, and the Collins Line became recognized as the leader of a revived American merchant marine. Edward Collins may not have been the first to devise a technique for riding government subsidies to ultimate success, but he set a style that would be emulated for more than a century. Submit a courageous proposal, bid to win, spare no expense to exceed government requirements, outstrip all rivals, then plead for more money to maintain the newly raised standards. Two years after starting his service under the aforementioned $385,000 mail-contract subsidy, Collins convinced Congress that the service could be expanded from twenty to twenty-six round trips per year. For that his annual subsidy was increased to $858,000. Meanwhile he drew the best of the Atlantic passenger trade.

While East Coast sailing fleets were occupied with the Liverpool packet runs and trading elsewhere in the Atlantic, gold glinted in the West. It was the most sought-after prize in the ocean contest for speed and efficiency. Swift, big ships were needed to get people to the gold fields. Some headed around the Horn, others crossed the Isthmus of Panama. The ships were powered by steam or sail—whatever would put rivals behind. Matthew Fontaine Maury's charts defined the routes. Two men would decide the means of travel, Cornelius Vanderbilt, with ambition and money, Donald McKay with courage and talent.

Mariners had sensed for decades that the winds were not random, that there were patterns in the weather that swept over the seas. In 1820 a European, H. W. Brandes, became the first to chart weather reports over extended areas. By midcentury a Dutch physicist, Buys Ballot, had formulated an important principle concerning the relationship of wind to atmospheric pressure in the area of a storm. He observed that winds tend to flow counterclockwise around low-pressure areas in the Northern Hemisphere, clockwise in the Southern Hemisphere. Thus, in northern latitudes if a mariner puts his back to the wind an atmospheric low will be to his left, the approximate direction of the storm center. At about the same time, Maury was compiling his pilot charts. His "Abstract Log for the Use of American Navigators" was distributed among American ships for recording meteorological information. Paper, pen, and patience were the tools he applied in reviewing hundreds of voyages, millions of logbook entries, then collating and plotting them to form seasonal wind and current diagrams of the Atlantic. The resulting government-published Pilot Charts outlined the trade winds and the Gulf Stream, and confirmed with greater accuracy Ben Franklin's early work. Maury's charts also showed that of the various possible routes around South America, those that curved into the mid-Pacific as they followed currents and prevailing breezes could be faster than the shortest straight-line courses. Within five years after the publication of the first Pilot Charts, shipmasters reduced the usual 180-day passage from New York to San Francisco to 133 days and thereby saved their owners millions of dollars annually.

By 1849 the feisty Cornelius Vanderbilt had already made his mark on the New York waterfront. He had begun his entrepreneurial life before the age of twenty by running a ferry service between Staten Island and Manhattan. During the War of 1812 he provisioned the forts of New York harbor and acquired coasting schooners to set up a shipping business in the Hudson River for trade between New England and Charleston. Vanderbilt was a rustic individual, his language that of the dockside, and he loved nothing better than a good fight. But coarse as he was, he had vision and style. He came to the assistance of Captain Robert Gibbons, a shipper attempting to break Robert Fulton's monopoly of the New York waterway, and made Gibbons's struggling venture profitable. The Vanderbilt-sponsored Hudson River steamboats were fast, luxurious, and comfortable. Somehow Vanderbilt acquired the title "Commodore," probably self-assigned in response to rejection by New York society. The Commodore didn't care for arbitrary social acceptance; he could buy whatever acceptances he needed. When the California gold rush started, the tough-minded businessman looked to the Isthmus of Panama with a view to establishing a route from New York to San Francisco by way of Nicaragua. Vanderbilt proposed a grandiose scheme to improve the ocean-to-ocean muleback route but found no financial backing. Undaunted, he undertook the project on his own. With the cooperation of the Nicaraguan government, he built docks on both coasts and a twelve-mile macadam road connecting the West Coast terminal to Lake Nicaragua, which he hoped in turn to connect to the Caribbean by digging a sea-level canal from the east. (The canal was never built in the geographically and politically unstable country.) Eight new steamships of his new Accessory Transit Company offered departures from New York and New Orleans, connecting the Atlantic-based United States Mail Steamship Company with its counterpart, Pacific Mail Steamship. The combined "ocean-and-land" voyages to California took less time than the circuit of South America and cost less. Vanderbilt's ships developed a reputation among his competitors for being cheaply built and unsafe in the extreme, but nevertheless, the bulk of the two-ocean, trans-Isthmian mule-path business fell to his Nicaraguan venture. His major competitors were not other steamship companies but the fast, highly regarded "round-the-Horn" windjammers.

During the year 1849, eight hundred ships brought ninety thousand men from the East and Gulf Coasts to the port of San Francisco. New York cleared 240 ships for California, Boston was second with 151, and the little whaling port of New Bedford ranked third with 42. Upon anchoring in Yuerba Buena cove, ships were often abandoned by crew and skipper alike—such was the pull of gold. Within a decade the harbor yielded as much treasure for ship-breakers as did the gold fields for travelers with pan, pick, and shovel.

In the seagoing world of the 1850s the search was for speed, and uncertainty continued as to whether it was best delivered by steam or sail. Samuel Hall, a shipbuilder on the swamp-edged North River, south of Boston, advocated

6-1. *Surprise* of East Boston, 1850. PRINTS AND PHOTOGRAPHS DIVISION, LIBRARY OF CONGRESS

wooden sailing vessels. Hall and associates purchased forested land along the Niagara River, the lumber supply around Massachusetts Bay being near exhaustion. They built a sawmill on Grand Island and shipped its timber to Boston on Erie Canal barges and Hudson River packets. Hall was respected by the young marine architects who were then establishing offices in Massachusetts, and he had ample backing when he set up a shipyard in East Boston. Samuel H. Pook, at twenty-three, delivered plans to him for a 1,261-ton tall ship that became Boston's first clipper. When it was launched fully rigged in 1850, Hall named it *Surprise*. On its maiden voyage the *Surprise* reached San Francisco in ninety-six days, beating by one day the record set by the New York clipper *Sea Witch*. The race was on.

In December 1850, sixty days after laying out drafts of his first clipper, Donald McKay launched the *Stag Hound*. Like Hall's, it was small by subsequent standards, displacing only 1,534 tons, but had all the characteristics of later clippers—sharp lines, a mast two hundred feet in height, and eleven thousand yards of white cotton duck. McKay's designs called for a robust but narrow, deep draft hull, a prow leaping forward from the main deck like a porpoise, tall spars, and heavy canvas and cordage even in the uppermost rigging, to withstand any weather. Here were ships suited for doubling Cape Horn at the fastest pace, summer or winter. Each vessel was larger than the last, and the costs of construction soared. With the additional expenses of operation and maintenance, the ships required greater investments than traditional merchant traders could produce. The maritime world separated again into two factions: on one side were designers and builders setting the styles, on the other were shipowners and traders searching for financing.

McKay was an idealist with a designer's intuitive sense of beauty and proportion. With characteristic energy he attended to the finest details in the construction of his vessels, practical and unstinting in his concern for the outcome. He was a big man, handsome and clean-shaven, with curling dark hair, broad cheekbones, and dedicated, piercing eyes—a man esteemed by his competitors, admired by his employees, and respected as one of Boston's more prominent citizens. A year after his first wife's death, McKay married his secretary, Mary Cressy. Mary McKay did not have the shipbuilder's eye of her predecessor. More of a romantic, it was she who named her husband's most famous ships. McKay fathered fifteen children by his two wives, most of whom survived him when he died in 1880 at the age of seventy.

Even in his perfectionism Donald McKay would have had to admit that any ship is an assembly of compromises. A full-rigged ship carries at least three masts with six or seven sails on each, one above the other, each sail capturing its own share of the wind's force. The main mast with its upper spars stands tallest and carries the largest spread of cloth. The main mast alone may require a crew of more than a dozen on deck and aloft to handle its sails and rigging, and the same number again will be needed at each of the other masts if the sails are to be set together. A broad pine pole stepped on the keelson at the bottom of the hull passes upward through successive decks that shoulder it into an upright position. The raking masts of the first Chesapeake clippers gave them the appearance of speed more than the accomplishment; in comparison with later ships, they served to allow a longer rather than higher press of sail, while a modestly lower center of gravity kept the shallow hulls less crank in a crosswind. McKay sought height and speed, to be purchased with sturdy spars and heavy rigging.

The clippers carried the most complex rigging ever produced. Rising from the chains along the sides of the main deck, wire stays converged at the stubby masthead, stiffening it in place. There a platform, called the top, provided a base for the next level of shrouds and stays, which secured the overlapping topmast to the main mast's upper portion. To gain the top, sailors fearlessly climbed "ratlines"—ropework ladders fastened horizontally to the shrouds. After a few weeks at sea even a green landsman learned to roll with the ship and to climb with the wind at his back pushing against the abruptly angled shrouds. Most sailors felt work aloft to be safer than running across a sea-wet deck, with the ever-present threat of flailing blocks or a sailor's marlinespike falling from above.

The climb to the next higher level was standard duty for any sailor hoping to be rated as able-bodied. Topmast shrouds rose from the top's outer edge to converge at the topmast cap, where a second platform framed the base for the topgallant rigging. At this height the ratlines were narrower, the shrouds steeper. Rising above the platform at the head of the topgallant mast were further vertical extensions, the royal and skysail masts, stayed like all the lower sections from the main deck. Footage was narrow in the dizzying height of the upper platforms, limited to sets of short crosstrees at the base of the royal and skysail masts, the aeries of the agile and courageous. The crosstrees accommodated no inner shrouds, the next rise of stays being close to vertical. Above the uppermost mast a pole was rigged to fly a pennant or flag.

A horizontal spar or yard, suspended by a lift from the topmast, was positioned against the mast just below the top. The upper edge of the mainsail, pulled taut against the yard by rope earrings at the upper corners, stretched to the outboard ends. Above the main course the topsail was bent onto the topsail yard in the same way, and above that were the topgallant, royal, and sky sails, all fixed to appropriate yards, all yards held in place by braces and trimmed to the wind by sheets—lines leading aft of the mast. Between the braced sails there was room for more canvas to be added. Triangular sails, suspended from the fore-and-aft stays from bowsprit to mizzenmast, assisted when the wind was on or forward of the beam. And still others captured following breezes—studding sails, light cloths hung like bedsheets from booms that reached outboard beyond the ends of the squared yards, gull wings over the flowing waters.

There is very little that is square on a square-rigger. McKay's sails often reflected the golden section, beloved of painters and architects, taking the shape of an approximate rectangle in which the width exceeded by not quite two thirds the length of the vertical leeches when set to the wind. Many landscape paintings and picture postcards have similar dimensions. The form, while aesthetically pleasing to a distant observer, perhaps is not to a sailor engaged in reefing sail as he hovers over the yard above it. As McKay's sails reached higher, their width grew proportionally: one of his ships was equipped with a 120-foot yardarm. Given a five-foot reach, that would have called for two dozen men stretched out along the yard. As sailors pushed against footropes seized at intervals beneath the spars, they were troubled by the immense spread of canvas that formed the upper sails, having to fist stiff lengths to furl or fold them under reef-points.

A Boston shipmaster, Robert Bennett Forbes, eased the problem when he invented the double topsail in 1841 by adding an extra wooden spar aloft and splitting the spread of canvas into two parts. The upper topsail's yard could be lowered to the additional yard fixed between the two sails, so that the overlapping canvas was easier to bundle for furling. Frederic Howes, a Cape Codder and master of several clipper ships, took a similar approach higher in the rigging of the *Climax* to form a double topgallant, and patented the concept. Both arrangements enabled quicker reduction of sail and required fewer hands aloft. McKay experimented with both designs; his *Reindeer* was one of the first ships to incorporate Forbes's double topsail. McKay's clippers were towering cathedrals of canvas, spritsails and stunsails their flying buttresses—famous ships instantly recognizable as his work.

The *Flying Cloud,* displacing 1,783 tons, was launched in April 1851 for Enoch and George Train. They sold it at once to a New York firm for $90,000,

6-2. McKay's *Sovereign of the Seas.* Courtesy, Peabody Essex Museum

twice the amount they had paid to have it built. In June of that year the ship departed from New York under Josiah Perkins Creesy of Marblehead, and sailed around the Horn to San Francisco in eighty-nine days, twenty-one hours—a record passage matched only twice, once by the ship itself. The success of the *Flying Cloud* led McKay to design and build the 2,421-ton *Sovereign of the Seas,* so large that conservative American shipowners had no interest in it. Undisturbed, McKay built it on his own account and put his brother Lauchlan, shipbuilder and master mariner, in command. A giant of a man, standing well over six feet, Lauchlan McKay sailed the *Sovereign* on two voyages before it was sold to the British. The ship became famous under the British flag and brought the McKays international renown.

Captains often held a financial interest in the vessels they commanded. For most of the nineteenth century it was common for them to take their families to sea. The owners looked with favor on such domestic support, provided the voyages were profitable. Wives adapted readily, finding that in spite of the small quarters in the after-cabin, the housekeeper's role was pleasanter and simpler than that of a sea captain's wife left behind to worry about her mate. Provisions were supplied, trash went over the side, stewards and cabin boys took care of the cleaning, sweeping, and cooking. The captain's wife could attend to sewing, quilting, and the education of the children without having to attend to the care of horses, harrowing, and harvesting. Many took on the job of unpaid purser, keeping the ship's accounts, and some learned to assist in navigation. In the 1830s a school on Martha's Vineyard advertised a course on navigation as part of its female department. There was little communication between the captain's family and the forecastle hands. The fifty feet between them and the distinct separation of classes kept them worlds apart.

Music of a sort was not uncommon aboard windjammers, born from the union of intense work and a sense of accomplishment. Sea chanteys arose spontaneously when four to eight men were heaving and swaying up a halyard or pushing at the bars of a capstan and straining against the anchor rode. Locking pawls clanked into place with each few inches gained, their rising tempo joined by the rhythmic gasps of the sailors when the rode came up short. As the sailors strained harder to break the anchor's hold, they added grunts to the cadence. Someone put words and a simple tune to the beat. Somehow it lightened the load, brightened the prospects of a new voyage, or diverted minds to thoughts of home. The typical chantey had two beats to the measure. A short, rhythmic chorus followed a deep-voiced solo:

We're all bound for Liverpool, I heard the Captain say
Chorus   Heave away, my Johnnies, heave away
As I was walking out one day, down by the Clarence Dock
Chorus   Heave away, my Johnnies, heave away

And so it went, telling a tale, expressing a wish, sustaining a mood. Music was endemic to the life of nineteenth-century laborers, and it was a rare crew that didn't have a fiddler among them. In off-hours, when the barometer was high, men grouped on the fo'c'sle, and sang the simple, often ribald verses of the chanteys, or with a bit of grog under their belts, danced an impromptu jig. The seaman's lot, eased by the prohibition of flogging and other forms of physical punishment, demanded more courage and skill in manning the tall ships. Who could not be proud, exhilarated, given to merriment, while standing under a clipper ship's acre of canvas?

In those watershed mid-century years for mariners and ship operators, the unresolved destinies of sail and steam yielded to the forces of civilization and nature. The telegraph created a greater demand for swift ocean carriers and increased the risks inherent in the competition for new speed records. Shipwrecks became more common with the growing traffic in the absence of clear safety standards. Compounding the tragedy of the *Ocean Monarch,* the Trains lost the *Anglo-Saxon* off Cape Sable. In the North Atlantic, the sailing packets yielded their markets to the comfortable and efficient steamships of the Collins Line, but the long haul to California was still dominated by the fleet-winged clippers. Sailors emerged on deck from stifling engine rooms while others looked down from high in the rigging to see that, in the race for leadership, their ships were crossing each other's wakes.

Chapter 7

LEE SHORES AND CROSSCURRENTS: 1851–1860

It was a heady period for the merchant marine. Courageous entre-
preneurs braved high risks on the way to great accomplishments. But these
gamblers navigated near the lee shores of fragile economies in crosscurrents of
competition and government intervention. While Europe eyed the startling
growth of its maritime rival across the waters, contention emerged between the
American industrial north and agrarian south. At midcentury the captains of
the maritime industry must have wondered about their own destiny, shaped as
it was by forces beyond their horizon.

Donald McKay's work was in demand. In 1852, after completing *Sovereign
of the Seas,* he produced the clippers *Westward Ho!* and *Bald Eagle.* The following year, in his most ambitious project, McKay built the *Great Republic* for his
own account, intending to use it for a world-circling run by way of Australia.
The big ships commanded high fares, close to $1,000 for the 14,000-mile trip
from New York to the Golden Gate, usually paying for themselves in one or
two voyages. The *Great Republic* was the largest sailing vessel ever built. It measured a few inches over 334 feet in length, with a 53-foot beam and a draft of
25 feet. It had a cargo-carrying capacity of 6,000 net tons, although it was registered at only 4,555 deadweight tons thanks to a complex system of measurement dating from colonial times. More than four thousand oak trees were

needed for its timbers, more than a hundred acres of forestry stripped. The McKay shipyard became a city of wood, stacked for drying. The main truck of the four-masted ship soared 210 feet above the deck and was rigged with Forbes's double topsails. (This was the vessel mentioned in chapter 6 that carried a 120-foot main yardarm.) The fore skysail yard was forty feet long. It was said of the men sent aloft to the skysails that by the time they returned to the deck their hair would be gray and their youngsters married. A spanker mast abaft the mizzen supported three fore-and-aft sails. The complete sail plan called for more than one and a half acres of canvas, topsail bolt-ropes of eight-and-a-half-inch hemp (fiber rope is measured by its circumference) and fore and main standing rigging made of four-stranded, twelve-and-a-half-inch hemp—the best that could be brought from the Baltic.

The *Great Republic* was taken to New York under tow and tied up at the South Street docks. There, on Christmas Day, just before its maiden voyage under Lauchlan McKay, a dockside warehouse fire spread to the great ship's rigging and onto the deck, where it burned for two days, almost to the water. To save the hull it was scuttled in its berth. The ship was razeed and some time later rebuilt with reduced rig as a 3,357-ton bark. Nathaniel Palmer, the man who had discovered the Antarctic Peninsula, supervised the work. When the *Great Republic* returned to sea, it achieved speed records of its own and became one of the most famous sailing vessels in the American merchant fleet. In 1856, under the command of Captain Joseph Limeburner, it sailed from New York to the equator in fifteen days, nine hours, and from New York to San Francisco in ninety-two days. One can only guess what it might have accomplished under its original rig, as nothing was ever built that could compare with it.

Great ships continued to slide down the ways at East Boston (imagine the poetic Mary McKay, stars in her eyes, penning the names): in 1853, the *Empress of the Seas,* the packet *Star of Empire,* the clippers *Chariot of Fire* and *Romance of the Seas;* in 1854 and 1855, six clippers for the Liverpool-Australia trade, including two that would win world speed records, the *James Baines* (2,515 tons) and the *Lightning* (2,084 tons). In 1854, under the command of Charles McDonnell, the *James Baines* sailed from Boston to Liverpool in twelve days and six hours, and also achieved a round-the-world record of 134 days. In the same year the *Lightning,* under James Forbes, recorded a day's run of 436 miles, a new record in the history of sail.

McKay's ships became smaller as he saw that the days of the extreme clippers were ending. But never did they lack the exquisite beauty that it seemed only Donald McKay could design. Interviewed by a Boston news reporter for the October 29 *Boston Daily Advertiser* after he had launched thirty-two clipper ships from his East Boston yard, he stated modestly, "I never yet built a vessel that came up to my own ideal; I saw something in each ship which I desired to improve."

While the clipper ships enjoyed a heyday, so, too, did the steamboats of the Great Lakes and the Mississippi. The New York Central and Michigan Central railroads linked their routes with those of passenger steamers crossing Lake Erie, an early effort in intermodal transportation. Shipbuilders took a lesson from locomotive engineers: they replaced their leaky boxes with cylindrical boilers and installed compound engines to cycle steam at much higher pressure two and three times through the cylinders. These triple-expansion engines consumed less coal and were so economical that they soon killed the bulk sailing trade on the inland waterways.

Riverboats were often the testing sites for steam plant layouts that were later applied, with minor modifications, on oceangoing vessels. As solutions were found for the technical problems that had limited steamship travel on the ocean, supply stations for fueling and repairs appeared in more ports. Great Britain was building a worldwide coal-bunkering network. The California gold rush brought repair and refueling facilities to San Francisco and Central America. New York's East River and Virginia's Hampton Roads became centers for ironwork and steamship repair.

In 1852, concerned about the dangers inherent in the use of fire and steam at sea, Congress expanded on its earlier maritime legislation and established the Steamboat Inspection Service, merging it with the Bureau of Navigation under the Department of Commerce. Congress also passed forty-four laws to be enforced by the Treasury Department, which required, among other things, the licensing of every engineer and proof of competence for masters, mates, and pilots. Within three years, twenty-five hundred engineers and two thousand pilots were licensed. Specifications were established for the lights on barges and tugs, the original "rules of the road" for inland waters. Marine engineers, unhappy with these steamboat regulations, formed associations to intimidate the inspectors. After the enactment of the new rules, the National Marine Engineers Beneficial Association was formed as a fraternal organization for western river steam engineers. It soon became their principal union nationwide.

Also in 1852, in response to an investigation conducted the previous year, Congress formed a nine-member Lighthouse Board to oversee the troubled Lighthouse Service. The investigation had been extraordinary in its thoroughness. Shipmasters and seamen were interviewed, every coastal lighthouse visited and examined, comparisons made with England and France, supply lines analyzed, training of lightkeepers evaluated. The study's dreary conclusion was that the service suffered from inadequate management, careless administration, and wasteful spending; it needed a complete revamping. The Lighthouse Board, created on the recommendation of the investigators, faced an enormous task. To manage it the board established twelve lighthouse districts and appointed an inspector and later an engineer in each one. Under the board, the nation's navigational aids improved remarkably. Among the more important benefits were the annual publication of *Light Lists* and the frequent distribution of corrections known as "Notices to Mariners." One of the inspectors appointed during the Lighthouse Board's early years was a navy commander from Alabama, Raphael Semmes. So impressed was the board by his dedicated service that in time he was appointed secretary to the board. Dedicated he was—to the causes espoused by his home state in a nation drawing closer to civil war. Within a few years he destroyed more American ships than all the country's defective lighthouses had inadvertently drawn to their rocky shores.

The first immigrants to arrive at American ports by steamer traveled on the British Inman Line under ruthless, vile conditions. Passenger health was of little concern to companies. The poverty-stricken travelers were packed into fetid holds, offal and sewage sloshing in bilgewater inches below them. Because cholera was common in steerage, the hatches were battened down to keep contagion from the first-class passengers. In 1853 the American sailing packet *Washington* arrived in New York with sixty active cases of cholera, having lost one hundred passengers to the loathsome disease while on route from Liverpool. The statistics of port authorities measured cholera's results; no international regulations prevented its spread.

In 1853 Commodore Vanderbilt took his first vacation. A half century after George Crowninshield Jr. built *Cleopatra's Barge,* the Commodore built a steam yacht at the same level of ostentation. The *North Star,* as capacious as some sailing packets, took Vanderbilt, his twelve children, their spouses and children, guests, and a personal chaplain on a European cruise. It was the first passenger steamship owned outright by one person. When finished with his seagoing toy, Vanderbilt decided to sell it for $400,000 to the shipping combine that supported the Panamanian route to the West Coast. Competition was fierce among the various lines that shipped through Central America to California. Political instability compounded the problem. In a clever piece of fiscal legerdemain, Vanderbilt offered to give up his troublesome Accessory Transit Company and its Nicaraguan route in return for the purchase of his yacht and a $40,000 monthly "stipend" from his former competitors. He later got the stipend increased by 40 percent when he threatened to reopen his Nicaraguan connection.

California, Oregon, and Washington were annexed in the 1850s, bringing the combined length of the nation's coastlines to some three thousand miles. The territory of the United States now spread coast-to-coast across the midcontinent. Legal entry into the long-used ports of San Pedro and San Francisco became easier, and the path was open for a lucrative coastal lumber trade from the Columbia River and Puget Sound. The gold fever moderated, curbing the one-way traffic from the East Coast. Commodore Matthew Perry, the U.S. Navy's personal secretary of state, led a naval expedition to Japan to force the opening of its ports to American ships and to initiate trade relations between the two countries. The Pacific Ocean became the broad stage for a new West Coast maritime industry.

Transatlantic sail was not about to luff up to the steam packets. In 1853 in Newburyport, Massachusetts, the keel was laid for a modified clipper called the *Dreadnought*, to be operated by a group of New York merchants. This packet was built by and for one of the toughest sea captains ever to sail the high seas. It is difficult to imagine anyone with a livelier maritime background than Samuel Samuels. He ran away from home at the age of eleven to sign up as a cabin boy on a Philadelphia coastal schooner. According to his critically studied autobiography, in subsequent years he survived a shipwreck on a Florida beach, evaded a sentence of flogging on a revenue cutter, was shanghaied on a cotton ship bound for Liverpool, dodged pirates in the West Indies, and while sailing around the world encountered cannibals in the South Pacific. He became a mate at seventeen, and by twenty-one took command of a ship bound for the Mediterranean. In the meantime, he married a passenger he had met on a voyage out of New Orleans and, on a day when the sea was as smooth as glass, witnessed the birth of his daughter on the freighter *Manhattan*. ("The only squall we knew," he wrote, "was from the young mermaid.") It was in the Med that his adventures surpassed the wildest pulp fiction. He was offered an admiral's position in the Turkish navy, which he declined, rescued a Swedish lady who had been enslaved in Egypt from the Constantinople harem to which she had been dispatched, and was attacked by bandits near Pisa and by pirates off the coast of Leghorn. He survived cholera, which he had caught in Hamburg, and was washed overboard off the Cape of Good Hope. He had settled down to command the sailing packet *Angelique* between New York and Amsterdam when he was selected to supervise the building of the *Dreadnought.*

The new ship put to sea under Samuels's command in February 1854, flying the house flag of the Red Cross Line (which seems also to have been known as the Saint George's Cross Line). Given his background, Samuels could be nothing but a rugged disciplinarian and uncompromising driver. The *Dreadnought* was heavily sparred, and Samuels was inclined to keep it under full sail when others would be reefing topsails and rigging storm canvas. He preferred the northern great circle route between New York and Liverpool and followed it on the seventy-eight fast voyages that he commanded, ignoring the dangers of ice and gale.

On the first eight crossings of the *Dreadnought* the average passage time was twenty-four and a half days. In 1859 Samuels established a packet speed record of thirteen days, eight hours from New York to Liverpool. So fast and consistent were his passage times that the owners were able to set freight rates higher than those of the rival sailing packets, though still below steamship rates, and promise a full refund if deliveries were not made on schedule. In the quiet of the *Dreadnought's* passenger cabins, people who had signed up for their voyage months in advance knew little of Samuels's dealings on deck with his rowdy, Liverpool-recruited crews. One group threatened to throw him overboard. Writing of his famous ship, Samuels said, "She was never passed in anything over a four-knot breeze . . . and possessed the merit of being able to bear driving as long as her sails and spars would stand." Stand they did, and so did their sturdy skipper. He drove the *Dreadnought* for eight years and continued at sea in more subdued activities for another eight, before engaging in various business endeavors and dying peacefully at his Brooklyn home at the age of eighty-five.

Disaster struck the two most famous packet lines in 1854, the year that Samuels started racing out of New York. On September 27, in a fog off Cape Race on the southern coast of Newfoundland, the iron-hulled, propeller-driven French ship *Vesta* rammed the Collins Line's paddle-wheeler *Arctic.* Within five hours the famous liner, on its homeward voyage, went down stern first. Nearly all on board perished—three hundred persons, including the wife, son, and daughter of owner Edward Collins. The *Arctic's* loss marked the beginning of a long decline in America's maritime fortunes.

Fog again brought disaster, when, on December 30, the sailing packet *Staffordshire,* heading from Liverpool to Boston, struck a rock off Cape Sable

7-1. Wreck of the *Arctic*, 1854. Prints and Photographs Division, Library of Congress

on Nova Scotia's southeast coast. A McKay ship, one of the Trains' White Diamond fleet, the *Staffordshire* had once made San Francisco from New York in 101 days. The ship foundered, and of 214 aboard only 44 survived. In both disasters, speed was a contributing cause.

Undeterred by the loss of the *Arctic,* Collins replaced it with the 4,114-ton *Adriatic* in 1855. Then, in January of the following year, his *Pacific* sailed from Liverpool for Boston with forty-six passengers and was never heard from again. That put the Collins Line in serious trouble, and Cornelius Vanderbilt, no amateur when it came to financial manipulation, took advantage of it. In October 1856, seven months after the *Pacific* was lost without a trace, a motion was submitted to Congress to withdraw the Collins Line's generous additional subsidy of 1852 with six months' notice. The motion, which was passed, also specified that Cornelius Vanderbilt be given a contract to operate a competing line subsidized at the original $385,000 rate. Determined to capture his share of the Atlantic steamship trade, the cunning Vanderbilt offered to carry the mail to Havre without charge and, to that end, built three ships for what he called the Atlantic Line, including a superbly outfitted vessel he named for himself. Collins fought to stay in operation, but his company's three remaining ships began to miss their scheduled sailings. The Panic of 1857 did him in. The vaunted Collins Line went bankrupt, and to satisfy its creditors the famous ships were auctioned off for $50,000. The line never did return a profit to its owners. Nor did Vanderbilt find his new venture profitable over the ensuing years. Nevertheless, the economic downturn proved timely for him. With the clear insight of a hard-headed gambler, he knew when it was time to fold. He turned to the development of railroads between New York and Chicago, ulti-mately his most profitable set of investments.

High-speed passages around Cape Horn continued to make records, criti-cal to shipowners in drawing new business. A race between the clippers *Intrepid* and *Neptune's Car* from New York to San Francisco was proposed after the lat-ter ship set a new record. Captain Joshua Patten, the skipper of *Neptune's Car,* was impressed by the capabilities of his wife, Mary, a girl of sixteen when they married, and took her on a second voyage. On their first record-breaking voy-age she had done some of the cooking, dispensed medicine, and proved, in Captain Patten's words, "uncommon handy about the ship, even in weather." She was nineteen, pregnant, and reasonably skilled in navigation when they raced for Cape Horn in July 1856. Before departing they heard rumors that crew members had been paid by an opposing line to retard the progress of

7-2. *Adriatic,* largest ship in the world, *Harper's Weekly,* 1857. PRINTS AND PHOTOGRAPHS DIVISION, LIBRARY OF CONGRESS

Neptune's Car, and so it appeared. Chief Mate Keeler abused the crew, was insubordinate, shortened sail without orders, and then fell asleep while on watch—the last an unforgivable act for an officer. Patten relieved him of duty and put him in irons. The second mate was incompetent and illiterate, and knew nothing of navigation. Captain Patten took up Keeler's watch but, as the ship approached the Horn's westerly gales, he fell sick, became delirious, and lost much of his eyesight and hearing. The chief mate expected to be restored to duty, but Mary Patten disagreed. With the crew's support she took command and headed for the stormy cape. For fifty days at winter's height, hove-to much of the time, she inched the vessel through the southern passage. After a period of forty-eight hours on deck, the ship rounded the Horn and put the wind on its quarter, even before she could carry enough canvas for her to make an entry in the logbook, "A hard beat to windward under reefed topsails and foremast staysail." The captain, still confined to his bunk, released Keeler, who changed the ship's course, gave the crew orders to head for Valparaiso, and may then have attacked Mary. There was some sort of ruckus on deck and the mate was found prostrate with a lump on his head, Mary back in charge, and the ship on course for San Francisco. With Keeler in irons again, *Neptune's Car* logged three hundred miles on one day in its northbound trip. The winds failed and the ship was unable to match its earlier record, but it arrived ten days ahead of the *Intrepid* on November 15, 1856. When people heard who had commanded the ship Mary became world-famous, though less for the speed of the passage than for having achieved it as a female. The underwriter awarded her $1,000 with a commendation for her devotion, her watchfulness and care of her husband, her control of the seamen, and her confidence in handling a large and valuable vessel. Mary's baby was born four months after the ship's arrival, and three months later Captain Patten died. As a widow and mother of an infant, Mary could no longer take up seafaring. Sad to relate, she contracted typhus and died herself at twenty-three.

The opening of the Sault Ste. Marie (Soo) locks in 1855 gave Chicago, Detroit, Cleveland, and Buffalo access to the iron ore and wheat of Lake Superior. During the lock's first year of operation, 106,296 tons passed through; by the end of the century the annual figure was eight million tons. Ships built of iron would have increased the efficiency of bulk carriers and produced an almost immediate tonnage growth had there not been a countercurrent in the form of the economic downturn of 1857, which cooled all business activity. The failure of the Collins Line turned investors away from maritime business. Enoch Train's Boston packet ships furled sail for good. After fifty years,

Philadelphia's Cope Line went out of business, followed by the Ocean Line mail carrier. Most lamentable, perhaps, was the layup of the steamer *Western World* in 1858, the pride of the Great Lakes. Built in 1854 by the New York Central and Michigan Central railroads, its four-story-high paddle wheels had churned with pride across the waters for four years before the ship was done in by the Panic of '57.

Little-noticed events took place in Europe that further shaped America's maritime destiny. It was a time of peace among the nations of western Europe, an opportune occasion to modernize the international laws of the sea. The medieval Laws of Oléron, named for the island in the Bay of Biscay where they originated, are believed to have been brought from Rhodes by the Roman occupiers of Normandy and promulgated in the thirteenth century by Louis IX. (Rudimentary maritime law was known in Rhodes as early as 900 B.C.) Contemporary maritime law can be traced back to the Middle Ages, when it was drawn up in separate codes by the English, Spanish, and French. For six centuries these codes formed the basis of various maritime customs.

Ocean warfare in the eighteenth and nineteenth centuries created a need for new, international formulations. Privateers were ignoring the rules of battle at sea that made clear distinctions between the ships of neutral and belligerent nations. The difference between pirates and privateers was a piece of paper— the letter of marque or reprisal that indicated backing by a warring government. If a nation at war lacked an adequate navy to defend its maritime rights, as did the United States in both 1776 and 1812, the belligerent would commission privately owned vessels to capture its enemy's civilian ships, allowing the owners and crew to keep a share of the prize. When the booties were high, the privateers were apt to take the law into their own hands. Policing and enforcement were difficult to achieve, and violations were flagrant during the War of 1812.

Again the French took the lead as they attempted, with multinational cooperation, to codify the laws of the sea. Their efforts resulted in the 1856 Declaration of Paris. Because the American Constitution required all admiralty cases to be assigned to federal courts, the United States did not participate in the Paris conference. Nevertheless, the federal government recognized an obligation to observe the precepts as set out.

The Declaration of Paris outlawed privateering. Only commissioned warships were permitted to halt or attack a belligerent's civilian ships. An enemy's goods shipped under a neutral flag were protected from capture, except for those useful in the prosecution of war. Properly notarized manifests and vessel documentation would establish the nationality of a cargo or ship. Contraband was loosely defined and not always easy to identify—sulphur and saltpeter, for example, the constituents of gunpowder, were clearly materials of war, but lead and iron, unless cast into bullets and cannons, were difficult to categorize. A nation's waters were defined as those lying within a marine league (three nautical miles) of its coastline. No engagement for battle or boarding could take place in neutral waters. Loitering at harbor entrances, except to await a pilot, was forbidden. Blockades were binding only if they prevented access to an enemy's coast, thus requiring positioning of an extended offshore fleet rather than a single warship in the main channel. Belligerents were permitted to use neutral ports to make repairs and purchase noncontraband supplies. Laws regarding delivery of captured prizes to the harbors of neutral nations remained at the discretion of those nations. The most peculiar rule had to do with enemy confrontations in neutral harbors. A strike could not be launched from the neutral port against a departing enemy for twenty-four hours. Arrival in port was marked by putting down an anchor, picking up a mooring, or casting a line ashore. Could an armed ship cruise into a harbor and, upon sighting a more capable enemy ship within, turn about and leave without fear of pursuit for a full day? Who ran a clock against the anchor line of a vessel about to give chase?

Long-standing tradition tolerated the display of false colors by both pursued and pursuer until the engagement to board or fight, the latter indicated by the customary firing of a shot or blank across the other vessel's bow. False papers were easy to detect. Isolation and speed were the unarmed merchantman's best defense against enemy warships.

Until 1857, communication at sea between allies or enemies was haphazard, limited in the case of merchant ships to speaking trumpets and leather-lunged captains. Navies developed their own extended systems of coded communication, usually by flying combinations of foreign flags in proper or inverted positions. To address a broader need among merchant ships than could be filled by the handful of flag signals in general use, the British Board of Trade defined eighteen colored flags and compiled a list of seventy thousand signals proposed for international use. The system caught on and gradually expanded to include the forty flags and pennants that now make up the International Code of Signals.

Taking into account all of the nation's seagoing enterprises in 1860—fishing, whaling, ocean trading, and the meager naval force that defended them—the United States may well have been the world's greatest maritime nation, its number of vessels afloat close to and perhaps exceeding that of Great Britain. But America's mercantile arm had declined over twenty years. Undergoing an almost reluctant transition from sail to steam, suffering disastrous financial losses in the ruthless drive for speed, it now faced the inevitable conversion from wood to iron and steel. The Cunard Line's introduction of iron hulls helped it regain the dominance it had lost briefly to Collins. East Coast trade with California dwindled, even as new routes were opened in the Pacific.

Still the merchant marine had all the ingredients for success: the size of its fleet, the sheer tonnage it had afloat, the fame of its clippers and luxurious packets, its well-located shipyards and a ready supply of immigrant labor. It had access to skilled steel workers and steam engineers able to do for the shipyards what they had already done for the railroads. And it was backed by a nation largely supportive of its needs. The focus would soon be lost in the noise of momentous civil debates and internal dissent on slavery and states' rights, strong enough to cause secession and armed conflict.

Chapter 8

WRECKS, RAIDERS, AND REDUCTION: 1860–1875

Before the Civil War most American shipyards were located in the industrial northern states, and shipping companies based their operations almost exclusively in the North. The South's forty-ship navy offered scant defense of its half-dozen major seaports. The development of Southern shipbuilding was hindered by a lack of iron and heavy machinery for production facilities. The Tredegar Iron Works near Richmond and the naval shipyard facilities at Hampton Roads remained in Union hands until Virginia seceded.

On April 19, 1861, five days after the Confederate flag rose from the ramparts of Fort Sumter and war became a reality, President Abraham Lincoln announced plans to blockade the Chesapeake and all Confederate ports by deploying his own thin federal fleet of forty-two vessels. The U.S. Navy was quick to charter scores of merchant ships, arming them as warships to be dispatched to stations along the southern coasts.

By June 1861, four Union warships waited in deep water near the Mississippi delta, the smallest the twenty-one-gun *Brooklyn*, of 2,070 tons. The lowlands of the delta reach like tree roots into the Gulf of Mexico. South of Lake Ponchartrain the river runs through a long peninsula shaped like the claws of an osprey, the stream clutching at the Gulf in six narrow channels—the Passes of the Mississippi. The Pass à l'Outre, to the east, and the Southwest Pass, to the west, offered suitable egress to deep-keeled Confederate vessels that were bottled up near New Orleans. Once they reached the sea they could attempt to outrun the blockaders or sail by them unnoticed in low visibility. The challenge facing Southern skippers was to outguess the station-keepers, watch them turn from the channels, then, at the right moment, choose the route affording the best chance of evasion.

On the last day of the month a sweltering sun rose over the insect-infested grasses that sheltered a Confederate brig from the telescopes of the Union warships. A saturnine man, slender and of genteel bearing, stood near the brig's forward chains, his gray eyes intent on the southern horizon. Poised above tight lips, a long and heavily waxed mustache spread across his face like a semaphore signal. (The crew referred to him as "Old Beeswax" for the mustache, which his steward waxed for him daily.) He scanned the wind-swept skies in the east, and suddenly his eyes flashed with expectation. Commander Raphael Semmes, CN, called for his crew to get up steam and weigh anchor.

The CSS *Sumter* was a small ship, 184 feet long and bark-rigged. It had been built two years earlier in Philadelphia, then converted to a raider for the rebel navy. Armed with four thirty-two-pound, long-barreled howitzers in broadside, one eight-inch gun forward, and another on a pivot between the fore and main masts, it was no match for the USS *Brooklyn,* much less the larger Union ships lurking in the waters four or five miles distant. But Semmes thought the *Sumter* had a saucy air about her. Considering the ship's enlarged coal bunkers, able to carry fuel for a week of steaming, its funnel, hinged to aid in disguise, its new sails, and its ten-knot speed, he was satisfied that it would enable him to disrupt a large share of Northern commerce. Commanding a crew of ninety-two mercenaries, most of them green hands, led by hand-picked officers who were former members of the Old Navy, he now dared an attempt to slip by the four Union warships.

Semmes's career of more than thirty years as a naval officer was unblemished but not spectacular. At the age of fifty-one, married and the father of six children, he hardly seemed suited to take command of the Confederacy's only cruiser. His first duty as a passed midshipman was keeper of the naval chronometers in Norfolk, an assignment that led to a lifelong fascination with the precision instruments. (As there was no naval academy at the time, midshipmen were political appointees who learned their trade at sea and eventually were tested by a board of officers. If found satisfactory, they qualified for the rank of "passed midshipman.") As he rose to the rank of commander he took charge of four ships, two of which were lost from under him—one in an unavoidable grounding, the other in a squall at sea. Semmes was a humorless individual, bristly, his highest priority always the quick fulfillment of duty—a standard to which he held himself as well as his crew. He was known to be a stern disciplinarian, favoring rapid, harsh justice. Until flogging was outlawed in 1850, he was an overly frequent, albeit light, administrator of the lash. Semmes's last federal duties were with the refurbished Lighthouse Service, where he was appointed an inspector of stations, a job he combined with a private law practice. As a lawyer he often took part in naval courts-martial and, to his later advantage, became well acquainted with the emerging field of admiralty law. Mostly self-taught, he was indifferent toward slavery, considering it a necessary part of agricultural communities. He was an ardent secessionist and viewed the United States not as a single nation but as a set of incompatible societies under one government. Born in Maryland, he moved to Alabama, where he bought property and settled with his family. Semmes was well regarded in the Lighthouse Service and became secretary of the Lighthouse Board, responsible for a million-dollar annual maintenance budget. It was from that assignment that he resigned his federal commission at the outbreak of hostilities. He sought—and won—the same rank in the Confederate Navy.

In Semmes's view the major Confederate cause was not slavery but states' rights. He feared the North's economic domination of the South. Realizing that the South was ill-equipped to engage in ocean warfare, he proposed taking the battle to the enemy by destroying its commerce. This could be done with sea raiders purchased and equipped abroad. Someone would have to break the blockade and bring Confederate proposals, backed by money, to foreign shipbuilders. It was that for which Raphael Semmes volunteered, and on June 30 he got the brig *Sumter* under way, carrying $10,000 in gold.

The *Sumter* headed northeast, and Semmes sighted the *Brooklyn* not more than four miles astern, taking up the chase. His engineer raised the steam pressure from eighteen to twenty-five pounds, eking out a few more turns of the screw. The *Sumter* had the weather-gauge and Semmes called for full sail, hauling closer to the wind, aware that the brig with its great fore-and-aft mainsail could also handle well on a bowline. He started his fresh water, pumping fifteen hundred gallons over the side, and jettisoned one of the howitzers. Then, as if on command, a rain squall separated the two ships and they lost sight of each other. Semmes held his course. He was not yet free, for when the visibility improved the *Brooklyn* had closed the gap and was approaching with its guns run out.

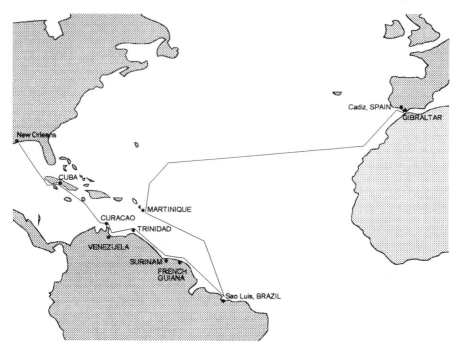

8-1. Cruise of the CSS *Sumter*

Just as Semmes prepared to deep-six the gold and strike his colors, the wind freshened. Now close-hauled, he found he could steer a tighter course than the square-rigger sailing in his lee. The chase continued for three and a half hours, the distance between the two ships widening as the *Brooklyn* was drawn farther and farther from its station. Finally, the Union warship gave up the pursuit and turned back to Pass à l'Outre. The *Sumter* was on the loose.

Three days later the Confederate raider encountered its first victim, the six-hundred-ton *Golden Rocket* of Brewster, Maine, traveling in ballast. Before setting it afire, Semmes confiscated the ship's cordage, sails, flag, and chronometer. (He made it a practice to remove the flag and chronometer from every ship he destroyed. The flag, no doubt, could be used as a relic of the capture, and the chronometer held a special attraction for Semmes.) The crew were taken aboard the raider, where they were granted limited freedom on deck. Excited by their first taste of potentially profitable adventure, the *Sumter*'s officers took up a collection among themselves for the *Golden Rocket*'s distraught skipper. They soon realized that they could not always be so gallant; this was the only time in three years of raiding that they were so generous. Nevertheless, Semmes and his crew treated their captives well. Later he wrote, "We were making war upon the enemy's commerce, not upon his unarmed seamen."

Raphael Semmes was not a swashbuckler who enjoyed gun battles at close quarters, bloody boardings, or swordplay. His quarries were unarmed merchantmen, and he approached them aware of the strictures of the Declaration of Paris. He conducted himself by the rules of war as a commissioned belligerent, not as a pirate or an outlawed privateer.

Semmes followed predictable procedures. Approaching his quarry, he flew the U.S. flag if he thought the ship was American; if in doubt, he chose either French or British. Once the target ship identified itself, the *Sumter* struck its false colors, raised the new flag of the Confederacy, and fired a warning shot, causing his victim to heave to. (Semmes was careful to stay within the letter of international law. The use of false colors prior to the establishment of belligerency was an age-old practice and was accepted as legal.) Then a *Sumter* lieutenant boarded the captured ship, or else the victim's captain was called over with his papers and cargo manifests to stand anxiously before the Confederate commander, who studied them without a word, alternately pursing and smacking his lips. A missing notarization on allegedly neutral cargo was enough to condemn it. Satisfied with his study, Semmes would make a decision: an American (Union) ship with an American cargo would be destroyed; an American ship with a neutral nation's cargo would be seized as a prize of war. Passengers and crews of the condemned ships were taken aboard the *Sumter* until they could be delivered to a neutral port. Southern chivalry prevailed: the prisoners had the run of the ship and were berthed and fed as comfortably as possible; the forlorn skippers were sometimes invited to eat with their taciturn captor.

The next day the *Sumter* stopped two more down-easters, the *Cuba* and the *Machias,* both carrying British sugar. Semmes put a prize crew led by a midshipman aboard each of the captive ships, and took the lead, heading for the Cuban port of Cienfuegos. Two more sugar transports fell to him on the way, both American, carrying Spanish cargoes, and both placed under prize crews. During the night, the captured *Cuba* broke away from the convoy, and two weeks later it arrived safely in New York after a harrowing voyage. Semmes captured six ships with Spanish cargoes during his first week at sea and sent all of them to the sanctuary of Cuban ports, after relieving them of their chronometers. He was dismayed to discover later that Spain, unwilling to vex the United States, arranged the return of the captured ships to their owners. The Spanish justified their decision by stretching the definition of territorial waters to claim that the ships had been captured within Spanish boundaries. By the time the Northern merchants learned of the raider's activities, their call for naval support was but a whisper in the cannon blasts of the bloody confrontations taking place in the Virginia hills.

After a damaging storm at sea, three weeks passed while the *Sumter* refueled and refitted in a Dutch port. Confident after his successes, Semmes made the fateful decision to send his next capture under the command of a midshipman to run the blockade into Pass à l'Outre. The unfortunate prize crew ran into the formidable USS *Powhatan,* commanded by David Porter, son of Commodore Porter, famed in the War of 1812. The younger Porter knew Semmes from the time when they had worked together in the Old Navy. He recaptured Semmes's ninth prize and discovered aboard a dispatch Semmes had written reporting his successes to the Confederate secretary of the navy. This led Porter to express interest in pursuing the now infamous raider, claiming he understood his strategies. Soon the North's leading naval figure was engaged in an oceanwide hunt, often close on the trail of the pursued but never successful. In his postwar writings, Porter spoke of Semmes with admiration, marveling at his luck and praising him for his skill.

Meanwhile Semmes was wearing out his welcome in the Caribbean. The U.S. consuls, aware of his ravages, had advised their hosts that the rebellious Southerners were pirates and not entitled to the rights of nations legally engaged in war. By the time Spain had freed the *Sumter*'s tenth capture, the little raider had the West Indies in tumult. Yet the harvest was thinning. During the three-month period from August through October, only two ships had been captured, both destroyed. Semmes, although unaware that he was dodging Porter's Federal fleet, sensed that it was time to move.

After five months at sea, the *Sumter* was worn out—its boilers and hull fittings leaked, and it was too slow to escape a warship's pursuit. Winter approached, and despite the risks of crossing the Atlantic in a tired ship not designed for long periods at sea, Semmes decided he could be more effective in European waters. The *Sumter*'s presence there would send the North's insurance rates soaring. More ships would have to be pulled from the blockade to find him. Before they did, he might succeed in exchanging the weary little ship for a larger and more seaworthy vessel. He headed east at the end of November, and at once his decision was rewarded with the capture of the *Montmorenci,* a New England square-rigger of 1,183 tons—the largest ship he would ever capture. It carried a neutral cargo, which led Semmes to resort to another legal ploy. He released the ship under a ransom bond of $20,000 due to the Confederate

States, and went on his way. The next day he torched a schooner carrying American barrel staves, for two centuries a staple Caribbean commodity.

Destruction by fire became the raider's favored option—after the quarry's crew was taken aboard and enemy cargo judiciously removed. The *Sumter* had little room for the latter, with a few exceptions: money of course, food and clothing for the Confederate crew and their captives, and coal if it could be transferred with ease. Semmes would add any captured chronometers to his collection. He permitted his crew no plundering at will and was careful to leave neutral cargo untouched. He did not enjoy charges that he was a pirate or privateer. His guns fired mostly blanks, and unlike the war being waged on the North American continent, his activities had caused no loss of life.

With the sixteenth capture, one third of the people aboard the *Sumter* were prisoners. The weather during the crossing was terrible, thanks to an unusually severe North Atlantic winter. The *Sumter*'s crew was getting rowdy. The men were tired of sharing their meager quarters with the Yankee captives and wondered how big their share of prize money could be when so many ships were burned. Fearing an uprising, Semmes ordered that the prisoners (excluding officers) be handcuffed, half of them at a time in alternate shifts. The captives, otherwise treated well, were understanding. But when word of the handcuffing got to the Northern press, Raphael Semmes was vilified as a scoundrel worthy of execution.

Communication across the waters was remarkably efficient, considering that it was conducted solely by ship movement. Mail packets traveled frequently, bringing news port to port. Sailing ships with common interests, meeting in midocean, would often lie to and, weather permitting, have a "gam"—send boats across to each other, or failing that, trade information by speaking trumpet. It was a sociable practice among people who spent months away from home. With that in mind, captains carried newspapers printed just before their departure. The papers were passed captain-to-captain, then circulated among the officers and crew. This was the only way, beyond rarely delivered private mail packets, for seamen to follow the doings of those they had left behind.

In January 1862 while gamming with an English bark off the west coast of Africa, Semmes learned that he was no longer the sole Confederate skipper in the eastern Atlantic. That news may have sustained him when he found himself unwelcome in Cádiz, denied permission to dock, discharge his prisoners, or make repairs. After a week-long delay, the *Sumter* was shunted to a nearby Spanish naval port, where the prisoners were sent ashore and thirteen crew members deserted. Knowing he would be better off in a British port where he could communicate with Confederate authorities in London, Semmes refueled the *Sumter* and headed for Gibraltar. But after three days of repair work in a Spanish drydock, he was low in funds, down to $51 by one reckoning. He had no time to lose as several Union ships were closing in on him. On his way to Gibraltar he disposed of two more ships at one stroke, the first with military cargo for Boston—sulphur, which burned spectacularly in the middle of the strait, visible from both coasts. The second, which carried neutral cargo, Semmes released in bond. Finally, safe within the confines of the great port at the base of the Rock, Semmes and his officers received a warm welcome and were able to relax. The neutral British, dependent on Southern cotton, were anxious to keep friendly relations with the Confederates.

Two Union warships entered the port but were restrained by the prohibition against fighting in neutral waters. Without anchoring, the USS *Tuscarora* moved out again to its Spanish station up the coast and was replaced by the new steam sloop USS *Kearsarge*. Under international law, should the *Sumter* elect to depart, the anchored *Kearsarge* had to give it a twenty-four-hour lead before pursuing it. But a battle could legally take place in international waters, a maritime league beyond neutral shores, where the *Tuscarora* presumably waited. The *Sumter* had run out of coal and could not even attempt evasion. It was trapped.

During its seven-month cruise, at an operational cost less than the value of one of its smaller prizes, the South's first raider had confronted eighteen Northern ships, destroyed seven, and collected bonds on two. It had tripled the rates for war insurance on American ships and forced the North to begin transferring its ships to British registry. Semmes sold the *Sumter* to a British agent of the Confederacy to get it out of Gibraltar, then went to London for further instructions. The havoc he had created was little more than an opening salvo to the destruction he would accomplish before meeting the *Kearsarge* again.

The Union merchant fleet won a few small victories. The story of the *Cuba*'s recapture by its crew was published half a century after the event, recounted in the words of the ship's captain. It was midmorning when the *Sumter* captured the *Cuba* and took it in tow. Semmes told the dour Captain Strout that he was a prisoner of war and sent him back to his ship under the prize-master Midshipman Thomas and a well-armed crew. That night the towing hawser broke in high seas and the *Cuba* was on its own. Thomas allowed the unarmed Yankees to stay on deck, and Strout quietly conspired with his first and second mates to regain control of his ship. Their chance came when Strout found Thomas asleep on a cabin top. With a tussle, Strout, his mates, and the cook got hold of the arms and distributed revolvers and a cutlass to their shipmates. The prize crew drew sheath knives, one found an axe, and they ran after the rebellious prisoners, climbing over the bundle of the doused mainsail toward the quarterdeck where the *Cuba*'s crew had mustered. Strout shouted, "If you stir, I will blow your heads off!" and ordered the prize crew to surrender. They yielded, and the Union crew put Thomas in irons, together with three of his men who were considered to be the most threatening. They bound the others with ropes. Later in the day, Strout turned over two of his prisoners to the brig *Costa Rica* and set course for New York.

The adventure wasn't over. A week later Midshipman Thomas begged that the troublesome irons be removed, Strout complied, and the wily Confederate managed to grab a pistol and climb to the maintop. Lighting up a cigar, he shouted down to the captain, "Do you intend to carry me to New York?" With a laugh he added, "Well, you'll never do it alive. . . . It's your turn to dodge." With that, he fired down at Strout, the bullet striking the deck at the skipper's feet as he ran below for his own pistol. Another shot cracked out minutes later as Strout emerged from below, hatch splinters flying through his hair. Bullets flew from deck and maintop as the two men dueled, missing one another until the rebel exhausted his ammunition. Then Strout fired off a well-aimed shot that struck his adversary above the right elbow. Arm broken, Thomas dropped his weapon, tossed his cigar away, and climbed down to surrender on deck. On Sunday, July 21, Strout took the *Cuba* into New York with its cargo intact and turned his prisoners over to the authorities. Thomas feared being hanged as a pirate, but after a period in a Northern jail he was sent back to the South.

In London Semmes and his first lieutenant, John Kell, met with Confederate agents. The agents had already worked out a plan with the British for the secret construction of steam-powered vessels for the Confederate Navy, worth a total of $1 million. The first of six ships had been delivered, unarmed, with a skeleton crew under the British flag, and sent on a trial run to Nassau. There it was armed in neutral waters and commissioned as the CSS *Florida*. All of this was accomplished within the confines of international law. After some delay, during which Semmes went to Nassau, he was told that he had been promoted to captain and that he should return to London and assume command of a ship with the curious name *290*. The name was nothing more than the British shipyard's tag to preserve secrecy. By the time Semmes arrived in Liverpool, the vessel had been launched as the *Enrica* and sent down the Mersey for its first trial, fully dressed, with a sportive group of men and women aboard. The partyers, it turned out, were maritime riffraff from Liverpool and their waterfront lady friends. The seamen among them were offered a month's advance pay for a voyage to Havana with the possibility of intermediate stops. Those who chose not to remain aboard were transferred to a tug and returned to dock along with the females, who left with a good part of the departing seamen's advance money tucked into their bosoms. Then the *Enrica* set sail for the Azores. There it joined the *Agrippina,* which was to be its tender on raiding voyages, and a second vessel, both carrying armaments and potential crew for the *Enrica.* Semmes went to the Azores to take command of the new ship.

The *Enrica* was twice the size of Semmes's former ship: 1,040 tons, 220 feet long and 32 feet wide, with a 15-foot draft. Bark-rigged like the *Sumter,* it had a retractable funnel for disguise. Two 300-horsepower engines drove a twin-bladed screw, retractable for better speed under sail. The ship carried an eighteen-day supply of coal and spare parts for a year at sea. The carefully planned arming and transfer of registry took place not in Havana but in an obscure seaport in the Azores. The ship mounted six 32-pound cannons broadside, a 110-pound chaser with rifled barrel on a pivot at the bow, and a 68-pound gun astern. Once armed, it was renamed and commissioned as the CSS *Alabama.* A round of grog was served to the scruffy workers, and Raphael

8-2. CSS *Alabama.* National Archives

Semmes climbed onto a gun carriage, read his commission as commanding officer of the man-of-war, then gave the last recruiting pitch the sailors would hear. He explained that the *Alabama* was a commerce raider, not a privateer, emphasized the lucrative possibility of prizes, warned that the men would be under naval discipline and might face battle with the U.S. Navy, and laid out the prospect of travel anywhere in the world. He mentioned again the probability of prize money and noted the risk of boarding a quarry in heavy weather, then asked those who wanted to join the Confederate Navy to sign up at once. Those who declined would be returned to the dreary life of the Liverpool waterfront. The Stars and Bars flew from the masthead, a band played "Dixie," and the recruits lined up at Mr. Kell's table to sign the articles of war. A few of the men shook their heads and climbed aboard the returning ship. After it departed a crew of eighty seamen, two thirds of the allotted number, manned the newest Confederate warship.

The rules changed at once. The Liverpool rats were sobered up, washed, dressed in uniform, put to work clearing and holystoning the decks, and exercising the guns, and sorted into watch and watch. They reported through hard-bitten petty officers to the side-armed officers of the Confederate Navy, several of whom were former *Sumter* shipmates. The *Alabama* set out to remove the U.S. flag from the waters of the world.

It was September and the American whaling season was at its peak. The *Alabama* headed for the feeding grounds northwest of the Azores. In two months Semmes destroyed ten ships, all but one from Massachusetts ports. The exception was the *Alert* from New London, the same ship that had brought Richard Dana back to Boston. It was now a supply ship for the Indian Ocean whaling fleet and marked for destruction. Semmes was no longer interested in sending captures to Spanish ports where they were likely to be freed, and he became more legalistic in examining the papers, accepting nothing as protective that carried any suspicion of inauthenticity. His efficiency grew with experience. Even as a quarry's captain stood nervously before him, the raider's boat drew up alongside the captive ship, ready at a signal to offload the crew, retrieve the flag and chronometers, and set the fire. The boarding crews did their job with dispatch, and the *Alabama* wasted no time waiting for a flaming ship to sink. Semmes burned one ship, the *Elisha Dunbar,* even before examining its papers, so certain was he of its American registry. (Testy sea-lawyer that he was, he knew his actions were ultimately defensible under the law.) Most of the burnings took place during the day because a whaler's fires could light up the night for miles,

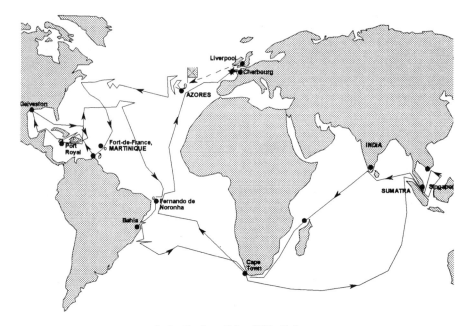

8-3. Cruise of the CSS *Alabama*

attracting unwanted attention. Once destruction was certain the raider got under way, towing the victims' whaleboats, which would later be used to put the prisoners ashore. At one point the *Alabama* had seventy captives aboard, nearly matching its own crew size; all were delivered via their whaleboats to the Portuguese island of Flores. Semmes used the Provincetown whaler *Courser* for target practice, exercising his crew at the guns before sending it to the bottom. Having raked the whalers' waters clean, he turned toward the Grand Banks to confront the transatlantic carriers of his enemy's fall grain harvest.

Cruising off Newfoundland, close to the New England shores, Semmes had even greater success. In the next phase of his mission, despite being trapped for several days in an October hurricane, he destroyed ten more ships and bonded three, two of which he sent back to the United States with his latest collection of prisoners. One of the bonded ships was the Philadelphia packet *Tonawanda*. It was a legitimate prize, but with sixty passengers, half of them women or children, it could only have encumbered him. The *Tonawanda's* arrival in England, even with its cargo and people intact, aroused concern in Liverpool. British consignees began withdrawing their shipments from American flagged vessels, in fear of loss to the raiders.

Semmes found that he could follow American news about the war and even discover details concerning the deployment of federal gunboats by reading the newspapers from ships just out of port. On October 15, he captured the *Lamplighter*, bound from New York with tobacco, and read news reports of his two captures twelve days earlier. On November 2, he destroyed the New Bedford whaler *Levi Starbuck* and confiscated its four-day-old newspapers. He read with mixed emotions of the terrible loss of lives in the raging land battles at home, aware that his own operations had not inflicted one injury or cost a single life. He turned vengeful upon reading in captured papers that the Northern general Nathaniel Banks was fitting out a combined land and sea force to invade Texas. Semmes had harbored a dislike for Banks since before the war and intended to cut short his expedition by raiding New York harbor. But he was short of fuel following his brush with the hurricane and abandoned the scheme. It distressed him to be referred to in print as a "privateer" and "pirate" without respect for his legitimate commission as a naval officer of a new republic. Reading between the lines, he saw that his activities were putting intense economic pressure on the hated Northern merchants.

The man had an uncanny sense of timing. He could estimate how long it would take, after the release of prisoners, for the news of a capture to travel back to the Northern merchants, and how long before their cries for vengeance would spur the navy to start a search of the area. A day or two before the arrival of the first Northern warship he would depart for new territory. If potential captives were plentiful in an area where he was working, he would delay the first breach of secrecy by holding the prisoners aboard until overcrowding became a problem. When he finally transferred them to a bonded ship or neutral shore, he knew that his time was limited and hastened to clear the field.

Semmes had scheduled a refueling rendezvous with the *Agrippina* in Martinique for late in November. Before sailing south he destroyed the *Thomas B. Wales*, on its way to Boston. The ship was carrying several passengers, male and female, and a cargo of saltpeter, an essential ingredient of gunpowder. Semmes picked up the trade winds, crossed the Gulf Stream, and headed for the Caribbean. The *Agrippina*'s bibulous skipper had been far from discreet about his reason for coming to the French island with a load of coal. Two Union warships picked up the news and closed in on the port. Under cover of night the *Alabama* and *Agrippina* slipped out behind them—another narrow escape for Semmes—and sailed for the coast of Venezuela, where they were able to sequester themselves north of Caracas in an obscure island cove.

Semmes got greedy and set out to find ships returning from Panama with California gold, a search that proved barren. Instead, he planned to raid a flotilla of a hundred or more Union ships that were hovering off the Galveston shoals, an exercise that would take him well beyond his commerce raider's charter.

Cruising near Jamaica in the meantime, he fanned his arrogance by capturing the California steam packet *Ariel*. There was little he could do with five hundred passengers, many of them women and children. After learning that some of the ladies were in hysterics at the presence of a Confederate warship, gallantly he sent one of his handsomest officers to inform them that they would not suffer at the hands of Southern gentlemen. Although their possessions qualified as legitimate prizes of war, he took nothing but a ransom bond and sent the passengers on their way. Semmes thought that the vessel was still owned by Cornelius Vanderbilt. (As it happened, the cunning steamship promoter had sold off all his vessels but the *Vanderbilt* during the early months of the war. He had received $3 million for his Atlantic Line, equipped the *Vanderbilt* as a warship, and turned it over to the federal government.) The *Alabama*'s short voyage across the Spanish Main netted one burned ship and two others released in bond.

The year ended and Semmes started 1863 by racing toward Galveston. He approached the Union flotilla in the dark of night. When hailed by the old side-wheeled warship USS *Hatteras*, Semmes vocally identified his own ship as "her Britannic Majesty's steamer *Petrel*." Suspicious, the captain of the *Hatteras* sent a boat over. The *Alabama* then properly identified itself, and the combat began. In thirteen minutes it was over, the slower and less maneuverable *Hatteras* outshelled by the *Alabama*. Semmes had drawn his first blood—two killed and five wounded on the sinking *Hatteras*, at the cost of one wounded on the slightly damaged *Alabama*. The Confederates rescued 118 Yankee captives before the Union ship went under. Once again Semmes was forced to flee his old nemesis, the *Brooklyn*, but now with a good lead and in a faster vessel. The ever gallant Southern skipper offered the hospitality of his cabin to the forlorn captain of the *Hatteras*. Within two weeks the prisoners were put ashore in Port Royal, Jamaica. Soon after, the *Alabama* moved out, on its way to the South Atlantic to resume plundering. Semmes and his crew were still tantalized by the prospect of California gold.

Trade routes cross the oceans like ruts in a road. Maury's pilot charts showed that rhumb lines and great circle tracks were not always the fastest paths, port to port. Seasonal prevailing winds and ocean currents often made the longer routes faster. Semmes knew that the merchant skippers would follow the swiftest courses, deviating from them only to avoid adverse weather or pirate encounters. The South Atlantic was not known for either of these threats, and the standard routes northward from Cape Horn and the Cape of Good Hope were well populated.

Semmes prospered in the third phase of his adventures, begun so dramatically with the sinking of the *Hatteras*. He headed into the mid-Atlantic, south from the island of Fernando de Noronha, along the Brazilian coast, then toward Capetown. In seven months he sank a Union warship, destroyed twenty-three American merchantmen, bonded seven with neutral cargoes, and commissioned and staffed the Philadelphia packet *Conrad* as the CSS *Tuscaloosa* to join him in pursuing the Yankee prey. On five separate occasions he found two ships traveling together, gave chase to one at a time as they separated, then captured and torched both. Hundreds of displaced Northern mariners and passengers, including women and children, had to find their way home from as far away as southern Africa at the expense of the U.S. government. Semmes remained meticulous in following the protocols of war, disdaining any unnotarized documents that identified cargoes as neutral. From his captures he collected food, clothing, a set of guns (with which he armed the *Tuscaloosa*), a splendid set of binoculars, replacement spars, cordage and lumber, the doomed ships' flags, and always his precious chronometers. Beyond that, he permitted no individual plundering. The boarding crew must have been severely tempted when they discovered the cargo of the *Olive Jane,* bound from France to New York with brandy, wines, tinned pâté, olives, and other delicacies. Pausing for rest and an overhaul of his vessel at Saldanha Bay near Capetown, he used the known longitude to take sights and rate his collection of chronometers.

The *Alabama* had been in commission for a year when it prepared to steam into the Indian Ocean. Its first conquest there was the *Sea Bride,* headed from Boston to East Africa. When a Capetown businessman offered to buy the *Sea Bride,* Semmes arranged to move it to an unpopulated part of the coast and there sold it for one third of its value. The final phase of his adventures starting in the waters east of Africa brought him over a period of nine months to the East Indies and into the China Sea, where he destroyed six more ships in protected waters and allowed his prisoners to row themselves ashore. Perhaps the greatest material loss at the hands of Semmes and his crew was the burning in the China Sea of the extreme clipper *Contest*. The demise of that graceful ship saddened Semmes himself. On his return voyage he destroyed one more ship in the Bay of Bengal and two in the South Atlantic.

When the *Alabama* anchored in the French naval port of Cherbourg in June 1864, it had traveled sixty-seven thousand miles and could count sixty-five vessels of presumed Union registry either sunk, sold, or converted to Confederate use, including nine released in bond and forty-two destroyed by fire. Then the rebel raider met the USS *Kearsarge*. Semmes was trapped in harbor but confidently went out to neutral waters to do battle. He must have had a sense of foreboding, however, for he sent his paymaster ashore with the warship's funds and payroll, and—although it isn't mentioned in his memoirs—his collection of seventy-five chronometers. (The eventual sale of the chronometers was the only source of prize money accrued to his officers.) The *Kearsarge* was commanded by Semmes's former shipmate from the Old Navy, Captain John Winslow, USN. Winslow had come five thousand miles to end the raider's destructive tour. The adversaries were evenly matched except in two respects: the *Alabama*'s ammunition had deteriorated in the long period at sea, and the *Kearsarge*'s wooden hull was for all practical purposes ironclad (lengths of iron anchor chain had been suspended over the sides and covered in wooden boxes, protecting the vulnerable machinery within the hull). Despite some testimony to the contrary, Semmes insisted to the end of his life that he had been unaware of the iron protection and would not have undertaken such an unequal combat had he known.

Crowds gathered along the cliffs to watch the contest taking place some four to five miles offshore, battle-watching as common along the coasts of the English Channel as it was on the hilltops of Virginia and Maryland. The French painter Édouard Manet sailed out with his sketchpad and later produced a painting of the battle, which now hangs in the Louvre. Seven times the two ships circled each other like snarling dogs while firing shot and shell at close range. A potentially deadly shell from the *Alabama* lodged in the *Kearsarge*'s stern post, but its cap failed to explode and tear off the ship's after-end as it could well have done. (The shell and the timber in which it lodged are on display in the museum of the United States Naval Academy.) Meanwhile, the *Alabama* was holed below the waterline and began to sink. Raphael Semmes struck his colors, nine of his men killed and twenty-one wounded. Within minutes the *Alabama* went to the bottom of the sea. Semmes was saved not by his enemy, under whom he would have become a prisoner of war, but by an English yachtsman out from Southampton to observe the confrontation. He returned to Virginia, where he was promoted to admiral in the Confederate Navy. He took command of the James River Fleet in defense of Richmond and there witnessed the Civil War's end.

More than two hundred Northern merchantmen had been destroyed in the war. Six Confederate raiders, two under Raphael Semmes and one commissioned by him, brought about the devastation. Semmes was directly responsible for seventy-one Union losses, more than a third of the total. The British had built the three most destructive vessels, and after months of negotiation, the United States collected $15.5 million from Great Britain for direct damage done by the *Alabama,* the *Florida,* and the *Shenandoah.* Of that, $6.75 million was attributed to Captain Semmes.

During 1862–63, nearly five hundred Northern ships changed flags, and in a self-destructive act of punishment, the government prohibited their repatriation after the war. Dozens of others rotted on their moorings, holed up in Chinese ports. Half of the U.S. merchant marine vanished, 110,000 tons destroyed and 800,000 tons sold, while foreign shippers closed in on the business. The nation never regained its supremacy in ocean commerce. American traders found they could achieve lower insurance rates and lower operating costs under foreign flags. What incentive did they have to return?

To his last days, long after the war, Semmes remained an unreconstructed Confederate. He much admired Yankee seamanship, speaking highly of it in his memoirs but always ending on a spiteful note. "Slanderous," "mendacious," "tyrannical," "oppressive," "miserly"—his inventory of descriptive words for his Northern counterparts seems inexhaustible. The reader of his narrative, exciting as it is, suspects that even a Southern victory would not have pleased the famous Confederate raider unless it placed him in the uppermost class of a nationwide aristocracy.

In 1865 the war over, ten years after the British adopted what was known as the Moorsom system for tonnage measurement, the federal government adopted it for American vessels. It encouraged the design of sleeker, longer vessels and closed the gap between cargo capacity and registered tonnage, although it did little to curb the practice of overloading.

Even before the war the prosperous shipping industry was plagued by wrecks, so numerous they exceeded the ability of local salvors to keep up. Thirty-five American ships were wrecked per month, hundreds of lives lost, millions of dollars wasted. Salvage work attracted opportunists who often did more harm than good, lacking seamanship and engineering skills. The Board of Marine Underwriters was determined to put salvage on a businesslike basis and in 1860 appointed Israel J. Merritt as general agent for the Coast Wrecking Company. Merritt had been doing salvage work in Long Island Sound since he was a lad of fifteen. At twenty he had taken command of a mackerel schooner to do similar work on his own. During the war he fitted out several expeditions to pull ships out of the surf, and in 1865 he patented a special pontoon-equipped device for raising submerged vessels. He served with Coast Wrecking for fifteen years before forming his own business, Merritt Wrecking, which later merged with Chapman Derrick & Wrecking to form the largest salvage fleet in the world. It continues today as Merritt, Chapman & Scott.

The American Shipmasters' Association was formed in 1862 under the leadership of John Divine Jones, president of Atlantic Mutual Insurance Company. The association, which changed its name in 1898 to the American Bureau of Shipping (ABS), stands as a beacon in American maritime history—a rare example of self-regulation in industry, successful from the beginning and highly regarded throughout the world to the present day. One of the association's first initiatives was the promotion of skill and character among the masters and mates of commercial vessels through testing and certification in nautical science and seamanship.

Overheated steam boilers contributed to as many losses as did overloading, poor charts, or coastal storms. In April 1865, the passenger steam vessel *Sultana*, carrying two thousand homeward-bound Union prisoners of war, exploded on the Mississippi, killing more than seventeen hundred people. The tragedy remains the worst marine disaster in the history of the nation. But shipwrecks were not just an American problem. In 1873 the British Board of Trade published a map displaying the enormous number of wrecks along the British coast and established the earliest rules to reduce vessel overloading. In the same year, licensing examinations for steamship captains and mates became mandatory in the United States.

Meanwhile, despite the *Sultana* tragedy and several other boiler explosions on the western rivers, the popularity of the Mississippi River steamboats grew. Their operators exploited them for entertainment as well as for passenger and cargo transportation. Before the war, Captain Thomas Leathers of Natchez had established a line of elegantly outfitted river packets. Colorful craft, they had wide, shallow-draft hulls, tall paired chimneys with smoke billowing from their scalloped tops, white, gingerbread-trimmed promenades circling the upper decks. Their steam whistles announced every curve in the river as the great paddle wheels churned the muddy water on each side. Cargo was loaded onto an open lower deck, quickly trundled across broad gangplanks. Inside, fifty or more staterooms surrounded a three-hundred-foot, carpeted saloon; the ladies had a separate section aft, "removed from the boilers." Overhead gaslights in frosted glass globes, plush-covered benches, and marble-topped tables added an air of elegance to the "floating palaces," a departure from the once rough-and-ready steamboats. The Leathers packet *Natchez* was the uncontested queen of the river, famous from St. Louis to the Gulf. After the war John W. Cannon, a friend of General Grant, launched the *Robt. E. Lee* and set new records for fast shipment of cotton. To compete, Leathers built a new *Natchez* with eight boilers driving giant pistons. The two boats were well matched, and a race was inevitable. On June 30, 1870, they got under way from New Orleans within minutes of each other, steaming toward St. Louis, 1,250 miles upriver. Captain Cannon of the *Robt. E. Lee* traveled light, with only a few passengers and no cargo. Captain Leathers of the *Natchez* assumed confidently he could do business as usual. He carried a full load, stopping first at Cairo and again upon encountering fog. The *Lee* ran nonstop with refueling barges following alongside. Three days, eighteen hours, and fourteen minutes after leaving New Orleans, the *Lee* steamed by crowds waiting on the levee at St. Louis and established a record that has never been broken. The *Natchez* tied up to the pier six hours later. The race marked the peak of self-propelled passenger transport on the Mississippi. It cannot be said to have proved that either vessel was faster.

The famous battle of the ironclads in Hampton Roads introduced the Monitors, a new class of warship that was adopted almost at once by navies worldwide. It also kindled interest in the construction of screw-driven iron and steel passenger liners, usually about four thousand tons register. Sailing packets lost their utility and were withdrawn from regular service. Only six American shipyards could produce good metal ships, however. The Clyde shipyards, producers of the Cunard steamers, maintained Great Britain's supremacy, and the new British White Star Line joined Cunard in the transatlantic trade. The head of White Star, Thomas Ismay, shrewdly recognized the benefit of connecting his steamers to rail lines. In 1869, with the driving of the golden spike that completed the American transcontinental railroad, Ismay offered through passage from London to San Francisco on White Star liners, outfitted luxuriously. The Pennsylvania Railroad tried to emulate Ismay but failed in its efforts to purchase a sound British shipping line that could meet its railheads. By 1870 the only American steamships on the transatlantic run were the Keystone Line's *Pennsylvania, Indiana, Illinois,* and *Ohio.* In 1873 the Penn invested in the construction of four iron screw-steamers by a Philadelphia shipyard. The steamers would be operated by the former Keystone Line, reorganized as the American Line, later to become a major part of the twentieth-century United States Lines.

In 1867 the United States made a fifth addition to its coastline with the purchase of Russia's Alaskan territory. The world was ready to be laced tighter in ocean routes. The sea-level Suez Canal opened in 1869, and in 1870 a proposal was put forward for the construction of the Panama Canal. Had the American merchant marine been better organized after the division and devastation of the Civil War, it might have risen once again to lead the world in ocean commerce. President Grant, aware that American bottoms carried less than one third of the nation's import-export trade, complained of "the tragedy of our drooping merchant marine." He repeatedly urged maritime industry leaders to investigate the question why the United States was no longer competitive in world shipping markets. Troubled by a scandal-ridden administration during his second term in office, he failed to attract attention to the issue. Congress, long uninterested in ocean trade, listened distractedly to shipowners' complaints about increased desertions. No one asked why the sailors were deserting. In 1872 Congress passed a bill attaching criminal penalties to the act. Two years later the law was repealed, replaced by a revised law containing a little-noted but important clause that eliminated the requirement that seamen sign articles on short coastwise voyages. Shipowners were happy to be relieved of the paperwork—until the legislation backfired.

In 1858, in a joint Anglo-American venture, the first telegraph cable was laid over Maury's "great plain of the Atlantic." It sputtered out a few Morse-coded messages and then failed. In 1865 the British put their behemoth *Great Eastern* to work as a cable ship. It had both screw and paddle-wheel propulsion, five funnels, and six masts. It finished laying the first two successful transatlantic cables in 1866, enhancing international politics and business relations. The time for the transfer of information between continents changed from weeks to minutes. Policies affecting relations between nations could be implemented faster, invoices for foreign-ordered goods delivered upon an ocean carrier's departure rather than transported with the cargoes, and orders could be submitted or canceled even while materials were in transit. The race was again to the swift. Struggling with its post-war reconstruction, the United States gave low priority to the recovery of commercial shipping. By 1875, so devastated was the American merchant marine that it carried only 28 percent of its own foreign trade.

Chapter 9

TRANSPORT IN TRANSITION: 1875–1894

S tiff competition for overseas trade, tension in the ranks, and fragmentation of the industry marked the continued decline of the merchant marine in the last quarter of the nineteenth century. In 1875 the marine engineers formalized their Cleveland-based fraternal lodge into a labor union, the Marine Engineers' Beneficial Association, and began carving out their rights in the developing steam plant discipline. In 1878 the Lake Seamen's Union was formed. By 1880 less than 9 percent of the nation's trade in foreign goods moved on American ships, much of that on the Great Lakes. Under the leadership of one man, the Great Lakes shipowners, unlike their West Coast counterparts, showed consideration in the seasonal employment of the hardworking Scandinavians manning their ships. Former Great Lakes captain George P. McKay was elected in 1883 as secretary-treasurer of the Cleveland Vessel Owners Association, later named the Lake Carriers' Association. McKay sponsored schools to train sailors to become ship's officers, set up savings plans for seamen, and introduced several widely effective safety reforms. He pioneered construction of the long steel freighters known as "lakers" to replace the Great Lakes' enduring wooden-hulled sailing steamers. One of the foremost contributors to the growth of the freshwater merchant marine, McKay held his position as officer of the Carriers for thirty-five years until his death in 1918.

Meanwhile, sail yielded its primacy to steam in ocean passenger service while it struggled to keep the long ocean routes of its bulk carriers. On the Atlantic coast, shipyards turned out towering arrays of sails, iron hulls, complex steam plants, and spacious coal bunkers. The diversity of demand drove up ship-building costs so high that the traders were forced to draw a line between "merchant" and "marine." Capital was divided between trade and transport: the merchants settled into countinghouses near their warehouses, and shipowners operated their fleets from dockside offices. Thereafter, the two functions were combined only in the conveyance of special commodities. Three classes of commercial shippers developed: small "tramp" operators, running their few ships between mostly foreign ports, wherever a paying cargo could be found; liner operators, their freighters and passenger ships sailing according to announced schedules, descendants of the packets; and proprietary shipping companies, owners of the bulk cargoes they transported—iron ore, coal, fertilizer, and later, oil and fruit.

Waterfronts were populated with taverns, boardinghouses, chandleries, and draymen's barns; warehouses moved to locations where goods could be processed or repackaged. A block or two closer to the city center stood the customs houses and dingy brown offices of shipping agents, underwriters, foreign traders, and commodity traders, removed from the musty smells of cordage, canvas, and the sea. Transport rather than trade became the domain of the merchant marine.

Succumbing to financial pressures brought on by the transition, shipowners strove to reduce crew size and shorten turnaround time, paying little attention to the skills, safety, or welfare of their workers. As steamships grew larger, the average number of crew members per unit of size grew smaller: two men per hundred deadweight tons on a sailing vessel where six men would have been hired a century earlier; no more than three men per hundred deadweight tons on a steamship. Merchant seamen were among the most neglected laborers in American industry. During the first half of the century seafaring had been an honored profession for the young and hardy. Many devoted their full working life to it despite its harshness. But as the nation spread westward, so too did its labor supply. By midcentury the rise of industry and the attractions of forests and plains drew once-dedicated sailors away from a hard life that had become even harder.

The thinning ranks of American seamen were filled by immigrants. Many of the newcomers brought seafaring skills from Europe, which made up for their limited knowledge of the language and of American ways. The newcomers would do any work aloft or below—loading cargo, reefing topsails, shoveling coal—all on a lower, European pay scale. Bred to indenture by the laws of the sea, mariners accepted brutality along with other routine rigors of life on the water. Officers, at one time trained in navigation and ship handling by mentors dedicated to the profession, now chiefly came from the forecastle to the quarterdeck. Their unmerciful treatment of foremast hands arose from a misguided view of discipline: they passed on and even magnified the rough handling they themselves had received. The 1835 law prohibiting physical punishment without justifiable cause proved ineffective because courts and juries consistently found assaults to be justifiable. In the absence of flogging, one of the cruelest punishments was "tricing up": the transgressor was manacled hand and foot and suspended from the overhead or rigging by wrist irons, feet barely touching the deck, for hours at a time. Slavery had been abolished ashore; it continued without subtlety at sea.

Shipowners held the line on wages, often by devious means. They encouraged drivers to batter crews into submission and to beat off malcontents. The port made the wage, and sailors were paid the going rate of the port where they signed on. Predictably, foreign ports supported lower rates. Some captains were not above forcing sailors with whom they were dissatisfied to resign or jump ship in ports where replacements could be had for lower wages. From 1865 through 1885, the average American sailor's wage grew not at all. It ranged from $18 to $20 a month, with $1 to $5 extra for working below at a blazing stokehole near the pounding engine. It was no wonder seamen became embittered as they saw the government routinely allied with the shipowners. Their grumbling in the forecastle was heard no farther than the gangway, for few ashore would lend an ear, much less take corrective action.

In 1886 Andrew Furuseth, a lanky thirty-two-year-old sailor with firmly set jaw, high cheekbones, and unruly hair, walked almost daily from San Francisco's Embarcadero to the local library before returning to his boardinghouse. An unmarried, unschooled immigrant who cared little for social life of any kind, Furuseth was intent upon educating himself in American law and customs. Soon after arriving from his native Norway, he became interested in the plight of the sailor in his adopted country. His interest was fired by an extraordinary intelligence, which in time would command the respect of government, management, and labor's rank and file. Furuseth's path to recognition as one of the nation's most sensitive and effective labor leaders, an honor he never sought, was strewn with obstruction and strife. But he never deviated from the course he had set.

Furuseth arrived in San Francisco by way of a British freighter, signing off to take up work on a coastal lumber schooner. Given the name Anders at birth, he anglicized it and became Andrew. For five years he grew increasingly troubled by the harsh treatment and injustice in the life of the merchant sailor. The International Workingmen's Association (IWA), a branch of Karl Marx's First International, had formed in San Francisco, and the Coast Seamen's Union (CSU) was affiliated with it. Furuseth joined the CSU in July 1885, with reservations. Part of Furuseth's problem with the union was that it was run by an Advisory Committee made up of IWA members, in accordance with the CSU's constitution. Thus the IWA, not the membership of the CSU, dictated its policies.

Shipowners systematically looked for nonunion sailors who would work for lower wages, the "open shop." They kept "crimps"—procurers, prone to duplicity or coercion—in their employ. The crimps toured taverns and boardinghouses in search of drunks and greenhands, flashing the articles before them. Once a signature was on paper, they hustled the unwary sailor aboard. (The practice became known as "shanghaiing," a reference to the Oriental ports to which many found themselves destined.) Because scab laborers were often inexperienced, the practice of using them lowered the quality for which the American merchant marine had been known in better days.

The CSU had two thousand members and its own boardinghouse. Although it had failed to curb the most blatantly unjust hiring practices, it grew by 50 percent during 1885–86. Meanwhile, a separate Firemen's Union struck John D. Spreckels's Oceanic Steamship Company. Aware of its own strength, the CSU joined in sympathy, its members forfeiting their wages under maritime law. The steamship operators reacted to the strike by forming the Shipowners' Association of the Pacific Coast, and stated that all hiring would be done through their own shipping office—their crimps, of course, hard at work. Earlier, the shipowners had begun issuing continuous discharge books for seamen to use as proof of employment. Seamen called them grade books since masters were free to include notes when signing the documents at the conclusion of a voyage, thus identifying those they found undesirable. Now the Shipowners' Association ruled that a grade book would be issued at the time of hiring only in exchange for the sailor's union book, his proof of paid-up dues. The effect was that he must renounce his union membership. In response, the unions threatened to fill West Coast ports with unemployed seamen by calling off all three thousand members from coastwise vessels. But the sailors were desperate for employment, and after some delay the unions' leadership was forced to give up the fight.

Furuseth saw a way out of the trap. At the end of August 1886, as a member of the union's Finance Committee, he spoke eloquently to the membership. His studies had convinced him that there was a loophole in the Desertion Act of 1874. Because a coastwise sailor signed no articles for short trips, he was a free agent and could not be charged with desertion if he left the ship. On the basis of that, Furuseth devised a job action that became known as "the oracle": union men would accept the new directive to exchange their union books for the grade books on coastal vessels, and go aboard without signing articles. Just before departure the crew would throw their dunnage on the dock and jump ship, leaving the captain with no alternative but to hire another crew. The next crew, of course, would do the same thing, delaying the ship at financial loss to its owners. Furuseth's speech encouraged the CSU to resume the fight. The oracle forced the owners to hire union men and to give up the grade book as a condition of employment. In addition, the CSU negotiated a raise to $35 a month for qualified seamen. These successes brought Andrew Furuseth into the limelight.

The following January Furuseth was elected to fill the vacant position of CSU secretary, making him in effect the head of the union. Paid $13 a week, he collected dues, kept the financial records, handled grievances, and maintained liaison with other unions. Without the demands of family and other work, Furuseth put in long days. The union absorbed his life.

He had never cared for the IWA's socialist views or the powerful role of its Advisory Committee in the CSU. As secretary he was in a position to do some politicking to change the bylaws. Ultimately, he would succeed in abolishing the Advisory Committee and send the CSU off on its own. But before that he had other work to do. First, he felt a need to return to sea. His resignation in 1889 from the secretary's office proved his worth. During his absence membership dropped by a third, and a new treasurer disappeared with $2,000 of union funds. That brought Furuseth back at an opportune time.

Enmity had developed between sail-trained seamen and the new breed of steamship sailors. Steam vessels became more efficient than sail and their crewmen earned marginally higher wages. In reaction to the disdain of the deck hands toward the "floating blacksmith's shops" of the steam crews, an IWA man formed a union of steamship seamen. The new union was short-lived, however; in July 1891 Furuseth persuaded the two unions to combine as the Sailors' Union of the Pacific (SUP). Again he went to sea, this time on a fishing boat, but was called back once more to serve as secretary of the SUP. He held that job for forty-four years, during which his salary never rose above $75 a month. Steamship cooks and stewards were making that wage in 1870.

Full employment might have strengthened the union, but the nature of the maritime trades put it at a disadvantage. Ordinarily, at any given time 80 percent of the members were at sea or in port under contract and would be considered deserters if they joined a strike. Only those on shore could wage the battle for better conditions, and the oracle could be used only for coastwise trade.

Maritime unions had also formed on the Great Lakes and the Atlantic and Gulf coasts. Furuseth met with Samuel Gompers, who had founded the American Federation of Labor (AFL) in 1886 in Columbus, Ohio, and was its first president. As a result of that meeting, in 1892 Furuseth instituted the National Seamen's Union of America and affiliated it with the AFL; he later changed the name to International Seamen's Union of America (ISU). The union had few members and very little money when Andrew Furuseth set his sights on the U.S. House of Representatives.

By 1893 a worldwide decline in shipping once again had produced a surplus of seamen. West Coast shipowners revived the grade book, and sailors reinstituted the oracle. Furuseth, fearing conflict, advised caution. The shipowners hired a new secretary for their association, a shady character who was dodging criminal charges in Michigan for bribery and perjury under the alias G. C. Williams. On arrival in California he stated his view that "a dose of cold lead has a wonderful effect in quieting disorders." Sailors reacted by cutting the cables of nonunion ships. There were beatings, riots, murders, and finally a bombing in which five people were killed, the last blamed on the SUP. The shipowners lobbied Congress to correct the loophole in the Act of 1874. When the law was revised, the union lost its strength. Comparing indentured seamen with the nation's former slaves, Furuseth said, "We hold up our manacled hands," and declared he would move the battle to the nation's capital and fight for proper legislation.

Shipowners routinely tolerated overloading of vessels even though many shipwrecks could be attributed to the practice. In Great Britain, Samuel Plimsoll pleaded for more than six years for regulation to prevent overloading. Finally, in 1876 a law was passed, conforming to the International Load Line Convention, requiring the use of Plimsoll's precautionary mark as part of Lloyd's classification of oceangoing vessels. Violators were subject to prohibitive penalties. The Plimsoll mark or load line symbol on each side of a hull indicated the maximum drafts under various conditions in fresh and salt water to assure a safe degree of reserve buoyancy. More than half a century elapsed before the U.S. Congress, at the behest of insurers, passed a similar law.

Coastal shipwrecks continued to occur with alarming frequency. In 1875 the SS *Central America,* returning from the West Coast, sank in a hurricane off

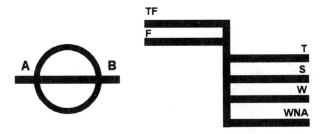

9-1. Plimsoll mark and load lines. AB identifies the classification society, American Bureau of Shipping; lines labeled for tropical fresh water, fresh (inland) water, tropical ocean water, summer ocean water, winter ocean water, and winter North Atlantic.

South Carolina with 578 passengers aboard. Only 153 survived, and $1.2 million in gold bullion was lost. Part of the problem was lack of reliable charts; in 1876 the Coast Survey expanded its mission to publish government-endorsed charts reflecting its geographic observations and became the Coast and Geodetic Survey. In 1877 when the steamer *Huron* was lost off Kitty Hawk, the nation's most popular periodical, *Harper's Weekly*, editorialized about the lack of lifesaving stations. A year and several losses later, Congress authorized the formation of the U.S. Life Saving Service. Stations were established at selected beachheads and equipped with volunteer crews, surfboats, and Lyle guns—devices for propelling lines from shore to the decks of foundering vessels. With proper rigging between deck and shore, passengers could be trundled to safety above the surf, one at a time in breeches buoys.

Travel was safer in midocean. By the 1880s regular transatlantic service had been maintained for forty years, dominated by British lines. Passage time was about a week, and several steamship captains had made more than five hundred Atlantic crossings. Shipping lines, each with their unique characteristics, drew distinct clientele. Immigrant carriers with ample bookings now had a central place to dock: on the last day of 1890, Ellis Island opened as an immigrant processing center and turnback point for unacceptable applicants. Without moderately good health and employability, the destitute foreigner would be sent back up the gangway to return to Europe.

With innovations, European lines took the lead in hauling specialized cargo. In February 1880, the British SS *Strathleven* arrived in London from Australia with the first successful shipment of refrigerated mutton. In 1886 the first steam-powered tanker was launched in England, in anticipation of the demand for worldwide oil shipments. Kerosene was already being sent from the United States in small lots aboard passenger ships, in five-gallon tins packed in wooden crates. When packed in this way the kerosene was referred to as "case oil." Concerns for safety in connection with the shipping of oil in any quantity, especially in proximity to engines, gave rise to specialized transport on oil sailers, wind-powered cargo ships dedicated to carrying case oil.

In 1884, motivated by cross-country railroads' needs for clearly defined time zones, the International Meridian Conference was held in Washington and approved the two-century-old Royal Greenwich Observatory as site of the prime meridian. Greenwich had long been recognized as the location from which longitudes east and west were plotted. It was already the basis for the charts used in 70 percent of the world's shipping when the United States approved it. In 1889 America took the lead for a change when it drew up regulations for the prevention of collisions at sea and initiated the first International Maritime Conference to discuss them. The conference built on earlier legislation, such as Great Britain's Steam Navigation Act of 1846 and subsequent rules that were approved by thirty-two countries in 1863–64. Statutes initiated by the British Admiralty had required the lighting of steamships since 1848 and the use of sidelights by sailing vessels since 1858. The 1889 conference consolidated lighting, steering, and signaling rules. Brought into force in 1897 and subject to continuing revision, they became known as the International Rules of the Road. The steamship *Columbia* became the first vessel to use electric lights, installed under the direction of Thomas Edison. The ship's three electrical generators supplied electricity to sixty incandescent lamps, each of 16 candlepower.

Ulysses S. Grant had been several years out of office when he convinced Congress to look into the problems of the flailing merchant marine. The House Merchant Marine and Fisheries Committee was formed, but years elapsed before it proposed any beneficial corrective action. In 1891 Congress passed the Ocean Mail Act, assuring payments for mail transport in the western Atlantic. The act required mail service vessels to be "of the highest rating known to maritime commerce" and authorized the American Shipmasters' Association to survey and rate candidates for the service. Postal aid provisions gave rise to the Ward Line, which operated between American East Coast ports and Mexico, and the Red D Line, traveling to Venezuela. On the West Coast, Captain Robert Dollar put his steam schooner *Newsboy* into coastal lumber service as the first ship in the Pacific Mail Steamship Company, later known as the Dollar Line.

In most of its maritime deliberations Congress looked no further than the pierhead. Shipowners and naval leaders were left to their own devices in matters of professional training and standards—an unhealthy circumstance for the mariner. A shrewd naval officer, Stephan B. Luce, focused his energy on improving the efficiency of officers in both services, and the merchant marine was the first to benefit from his efforts. Luce was a pleasant, witty individual and a technically competent seaman who became a prolific writer, a source of inspiration to those who knew him. As a Naval Academy instructor, in 1863 he published *Seamanship,* the classic text on the subject until Austin Knight's *Modern Seamanship* replaced it in 1901. (Felix Riesenberg's *Standard Seamanship for the Merchant Service* recognized the specialized interests of merchant mariners and by the late 1920s became their standard text.) Luce advocated the formation of locally supported schoolships for the training of merchant marine officers. He proposed that the navy donate older vessels to any seaports or state governments that would organize the schools. Grants were authorized by a congressional act in 1874, and in that year New York became the first to undertake cadet training. In 1875 the USS *St. Mary's* appeared on New York's East River to be converted to a sail-training school for merchant marine officers. San Francisco took over the USS *Jamestown* the following year but gave up the project after one cruise, possibly troubled by that port's growing labor unrest. In 1885 the federal commissioner of navigation, supporting a view held by most wind-sailors, declared that steamships were not good places to learn seamanship and that more sail-training ships were needed. In 1889 the USS *Saratoga* traveled up the Delaware River to become Philadelphia's sail-training schoolship. All three schoolships, retired from the Naval Register, were equipped only with sail power and thus were useful only for training deck cadets. Then, in 1891 the Massachusetts Nautical Training School was proposed, and the engine-powered brig USS *Enterprise* was donated to Boston, enabling the city to enroll candidates for both engineers' and mates' licenses.

In 1890 Captain Alfred T. Mahan, USN, published a book that influenced the thinking of maritime nations worldwide. When Mahan was a midshipman on a Union warship, disturbed by the ravages of the Confederate raider *Sumter,* he had the temerity to write directly to Assistant Secretary of the Navy Gustavus Fox with the suggestion that the navy put out a decoy ship with a hidden pivot gun to meet the *Sumter* and disable it. Nothing came of Mahan's proposal or his bold circumvention of official channels, but his action was indicative of the kind of naval officer he would become. In 1886, as a newly appointed captain in the meager U.S. Navy, he was called by then-Captain Stephan Luce, who had become the first president of the Naval War College, to lecture on tactics and

9-2. Schoolship cadets, furling topsail and mainsail. NATIONAL ARCHIVES

naval history. Upon Luce's promotion to admiral, Mahan followed him as War College president and in 1890 published his lectures in *The Influence of Sea Power upon History, 1660–1783.* The book was translated into all major modern languages and circled the globe to be studied in the admiralties and chancellories of every principal maritime power. Mahan's theories were influenced by his predecessor. Luce was the author of the first paper in the initial issue of the *United States Naval Institute Proceedings,* published in 1873 under the title "The Meaning of Our Navy and Merchant Marine." The paper argued for improved training of officers in both services, and was influential in the decision by Congress to establish the schoolship grants. Interest in Mahan's book and his subsequent writings carried into the middle of the twentieth century; his works are still studied as naval classics, having abruptly changed the policies of Great Britain, Germany, Japan, and the United States. Analyzing England's rise to dominance of the seas, Mahan demonstrated that maritime activity played a critical role in shaping the destiny of nations. National security, he claimed, depended on worldwide colonization, or failing that, on solid alliances. Both required open sea lanes, vigilantly protected by capital ships. In another text, *The Interest of*

American Sea Power, Present and Future, Mahan defended the view that a healthy merchant fleet and powerful navy were not independent but supported each other's purposes. A navy's principal aim was to keep the oceans free for the conduct of trade (that is, to keep enemies from interfering in the nation's commerce—or perhaps to destroy the enemy's commerce). Nations that traded together strengthened each other economically and were unlikely to become adversaries; thus commerce supported the navy's aim of preserving the peace. A robust merchant fleet could also supply ships to the navy in wartime. The days of the privateer had ended with the Declaration of Paris. Now it was time to assure an adequate supply of merchant ships, designed for conversion to warships if necessary, and able to supply the far-flung bases of a worldwide sea power.

American shipping companies continued losing business to British interests, and J. Pierpont Morgan proposed another approach to regain a substantial portion of the transatlantic trade: since America couldn't fight the foreigners, it should buy them out. In 1893 he assembled a consortium, the International Mercantile Marine Company (IMM), having found a means to operate ships under other countries' flags—the earliest organized use of flags of convenience. At the same time the federal government introduced the first preferential cargo rulings, which required that substantial portions of American goods in foreign trade be carried in American-owned ships. These rulings were expected to counter Europe's near monopoly in shipbuilding, but they didn't succeed. In 1889 two ships were built for American interests on the River Clyde, the *City of New York* and *City of Paris*—two more contracts lost to British builders. The ships sailed under the house flag of the British Inman and International Line. Their American owners were not bound by the demands of American labor, nor were they obliged to operate under the federal regulations governing American cargoes, as long as the ships were registered overseas. In 1892, awakening to the potential for further erosion of the merchant fleet, Congress approved a proposal that the two ships be transferred to American registry, with the stipulation that two similar ships be built by American shipbuilders. William Cramp & Sons of Philadelphia produced the *St. Louis* and *St. Paul* for what was called the American Line. These four ships, "City of" dropped from the names of the two whose registry was transferred, became the lineal ancestors of the United States Lines fleet. At the time, they were among the six largest ships in the world. In 1894 the *St. Paul,* 554 feet long with a 20,000-horsepower propulsion engine, was launched before twenty-five thousand onlookers. Later it became the first vessel to carry a ship-to-shore wireless and was renowned for having crossed from New York to Southampton in six days and thirty-one minutes.

Pleased with itself for starting the recovery of the merchant marine, Congress might well have echoed Morse's words and asked, "What have we wrought?" Conflict lay ahead. Stability in transport depended on a healthy relationship between shipowners and shipboard labor, but government, management, and Andrew Furuseth could not agree.

Chapter 10

RESTLESS LABOR:
1894–1914

A down-on-his-luck seaman, empty-pocketed and burdened with debt, saw relief in any offer of advance payment for a job. Desperate wives argued for wage allotments, an arrangement the shipowners readily handled for those they hired. Waterfront outfitters charged mariners high cash-on-the-barrelhead prices for cheaply made clothing, quick to need patching and replacement in the hard and wet work at sea. One of the not-so-subtle tools used by the nefarious crimps was the offer of advance pay in return for the signing of articles. Assured that his dependents had enough of his earnings to survive, a man could equip himself for the new job and take his place among the crew. As the unwary sailor hauled aboard the last line to shore, he was often more than half a voyage in debt to the shipowner, at wages agreed to under articles that rarely recognized his worth. Goods drawn from the shipboard slop chest were priced at generous profit to the owner and charged against the sailor's earned and debt-free income. After long weeks at sea, his funds plucked from his account as fast as posted to it, in every port cash dribbled from his purse to bumboat vendors, tavern keepers, bawdy houses, tattoo artists, and the ever present men with dice and cards. When the ship paid off even a parsimonious seaman had little to show for his effort. Then the cycle started over.

Coastwise vessels, engaged in interstate commerce, came within the purview of the federal government. Toward the end of the nineteenth century interstate transport by steamship made remarkable gains on both coasts. In 1894 the Fall River Line linked New England with Manhattan, sending the *Priscilla* on a regular passenger schedule along the length of Long Island Sound, the first of what would be known as the "New York boats." Passenger liners ran overnight voyages up and down the Chesapeake, making multiple stops between Baltimore and Norfolk. Cargo flowed from New York and Philadelphia to Hampton Roads and Charleston. A thriving lumber trade continued by sea between Washington, Oregon, and California. Because shipowners had a looser grip on coastal crews, it was on the coasts that modest strides were made to protect the impecunious seaman.

Imprisonment had been the standard reaction to desertion until 1895, when Grover Cleveland signed the Maguire Act, abolishing punishment for desertion from coastwise vessels. When a seaman jumped ship it had been customary for owners to attach his clothing and add it to the slop chest for resale; that practice was prohibited. So, too, was the advance payment of wages to procure new crew members. Shipowners saw these prohibitions as dangerous precedents and lobbied Congress to hold the line on legislation which might adversely affect them.

When Andrew Furuseth was appointed Washington representative for the ISU in 1895, the union had few members and little money to support him. Four years passed before he moved to Washington, where he lived alone near Capitol Hill. He had become a capable negotiator through his experience on the CSU's Finance Committee. On his own he studied the complexities of working with congressional committees and learned how to get hearings in support of new legislation. He knew well the deplorable conditions in which his fellow seamen worked, and he came armed with descriptions of the cramped, unhealthy quarters about which shipowners did nothing, the brutal beatings by bucko mates, the unconscionable supply of inedible food (complaints about the food were so common that all grievances came to be known as "beefs"), and diets that still led to scurvy a half century after most civilized nations had mastered the disease. Now it was time to make his case.

At first he listened as he sat in on the meetings of the House Merchant Marine Committee, and was stunned by the committee's ignorance of maritime affairs. Shipping company representatives gave testimony that committee members took to be authoritative. From time to time Furuseth interjected a well-worded challenge, backed with hard evidence. At adjournment he returned to his room to type carefully constructed and often lengthy responses for next-day delivery to the committee. The case he made for the seamen was impressive. Soon the congressmen ignored his rumpled clothing as his words captured their attention. (It was said that he hand-washed his suits and pressed them, sailor fashion, between mattress and bedboard.) His seaman's dedication and cogent words drew the congressmen's respect. The shipowners fought back, aware that Andrew Furuseth was the most intelligent seaman they had ever encountered.

The behavior of bucko mates was well known. Richard Dana made the public aware of it before 1850. Furuseth blamed not inherent cruelty but lack of training in proper discipline. His recommendation: give worthy sailors skilled, experienced shipmates. Crimps were the source of the ill-trained riffraff, and it was the shipowner-supported allotment system and advance payment of wages that kept the crimps in business—practices Furuseth also said should be discontinued. He argued for more crew living space: 120 cubic feet per man. When the commissioner of navigation, lobbied by the shipowners, proposed 72 cubic feet, Furuseth responded that this was "too large for a coffin, but surely not large enough for a living man."

Furuseth spent seven months in Washington describing the deficient working conditions at sea and the nearly conspiratorial rejection of any form of correction by the shipowners, and pleading for laws to improve the sailor's lot. His time was running out. The SUP was crumbling, its membership giving up all hope of improvement. The case of the barkentine *Arago* fed their despair. The vessel ran coastwise in the Pacific but included one foreign leg in its route, thus requiring the signing of articles. When the sailors found the conditions aboard to be intolerable, a number of them jumped ship before it went foreign and were arrested for desertion. Lacking the protection of the Maguire Act, which covered only coastwise voyages, they brought suit in 1897, invoking their rights under the Thirteenth Amendment (abolition of slavery). Their case threaded its way to the Supreme Court, which found that the constitutional provision against involuntary servitude did not apply to seamen. Referring in their opinion to the Laws of Oléron, the justices stated that the seaman's contract, based on ancient maritime law, was different from other contracts. They argued that the Thirteenth Amendment was intended to apply only to Negro slaves, not to seamen, and that the seaman's surrender of personal liberty remained unchanged. In direct response to that decision, Congress passed the White Act of 1897. The act formally abolished imprisonment of U.S. citizens for desertion in American and nearby waters and put an end to corporal punishment as dispensed by bucko bullies. At the time, about half the active seamen on

American ships were citizens, many foreigners having been hired in an immigration surge. A year after the *Arago* decision, when the Court was petitioned for a new hearing, it refused to reopen the case—a conclusion as blind as that in the infamous Dred Scott case.

By 1910 more than thirty million people had migrated from Europe to the North American continent, most to the United States. By 1914 one third of the population of the United States was foreign-born. There being no citizenship requirement for crew members, the effect for seamen was to keep wages depressed. In the first few years of the twentieth century, a seaman's wage of $25 per month was considered good because it was substantially higher than the European rate.

Furuseth would not give up. He met with SUP locals, working to install professional pride among the members. His efforts were strongest on the West Coast, where he had the largest constituency. If firemen, policemen, and navy sailors took pride in their uniforms, why shouldn't merchant seamen? Furuseth arranged to outfit SUP members in sailor's uniforms with blue flattops, trimmed white blouses, and bell-bottoms, and organized groups to march in parades. As the sailors' union became better known, it acquired improved office facilities in San Francisco's Ferry Building. In recognition came growth, pride, and strength.

"They that go down to the sea in ships, trading on deep waters, these see the works of the Lord" (Ps. 107, 23–24). At the turn of the century a group of licensed merchant officers who had come together for Bible readings extended their focus to include technical matters and safety on the bridge. The American Association of Masters and Pilots was formed when the masters joined the already established American Brotherhood of Steamship Pilots. Masters are unique among seamen in that they directly represent the shipowners and therefore are excluded from most collective bargaining. In their own self-interest they recognized a need for alliance; it did no harm to ally themselves also with the Lord. Pilots as licensed masters had similar labor interests. They worked as independent contractors and from colonial times were practically a law unto themselves. Their associations were similar to medieval guilds, in some respect owing their origin to those twelfth-century organizations. Since the Federal era, pilots were under state jurisdictions; customarily, an overseeing board was appointed by the governor. Like lodge brothers, the pilots worked together to protect and advance their interests, ever ready to advise the political appointees who set the rules for their conduct in state-controlled rivers and harbors. In time, the pilots' associations dominated the boards. Meanwhile, shipmasters and pilots kept a wary eye on each other, always suspicious but rarely opposed in their interests. Mates, pursuing the same accreditation path as masters and pilots, joined with them in 1900 to form the National Organization of Masters, Mates and Pilots. Maritime unions proliferated—firemen, sailors, cooks and stewards, longshoremen, teamsters, and many others formed groups—as many as twenty individual organizations.

Engineers and firemen had their own concerns. By the turn of the century triple expansion engines were being built that required hotter steam produced by multiple furnaces in enlarged stokeholds. Firerooms with forced draft systems enabled use of poorer-quality, lower-cost coal, measured with care. The standard for hourly fuel consumption was a half ounce of coal for every ton of ship and knot of speed. The second decade of the century brought in a twin-screw fast cargo ship of ten thousand tons that carried three thousand tons of coal in its bunkers. Twenty furnaces heated five boilers by burning ninety tons of coal per day. An assistant engineer stood watch in the engine room, overseeing nine stokehold workers. Four trimmers moved the coal in wheelbarrows from the bunkers to the furnace doors, the trundling distance increasing with fuel depletion. Five firemen shoveled and pitched coal from the trimmers' piles into roaring flames, reaching inside the furnaces to patch neglected areas and spread the blaze evenly. The hair on their arms burned to stubble. They took up heavy iron slice bars to break clinkers and assure complete fuel consumption, raked the embers for dead clinkers and ash, then shoveled the hot and dusty residue into a lift for dumping overboard before the cycle repeated. Steel platforms deep in the ship's poorly ventilated caverns framed an earthly hell. Men worked in searing heat, surrounded by swirling coal dust, struggling to keep their footing in rolling seas. The steamy climates of Panama, Suez, the Red Sea, and the East Indies added to the agony and gave little respite above decks. Stokehold workers collapsed on the metal flooring from heat exhaustion, choked in clouds of dust, and doubled over with cramping, desperately seeking relief with too much water, swallowed too fast. It was no surprise that firemen frequently deserted. There seemed to be no escape, and few to take up their cause.

Divide and be conquered. Andrew Furuseth saw potential trouble in the proliferation of unions. Shipowners could break smaller, specialized groups with ease. Indeed, strikebreakers were working to make San Francisco an open-shop city, a practice that favored the employment of scab labor. Furuseth formed the City Front Federation to consolidate all the waterfront trades and called for a response to the strikebreakers. On Labor Day of 1901, twenty thousand union members stopped work to march on the Embarcadero in dress uniform. The cease-work failed to change labor-management relations, but it attracted enough attention to defeat the attempt to make the city an open shop. Furuseth walked a narrow path after the City Front strike, keeping the unions from making unreasonable demands that were sure to fail, eliminating the riffraff, and encouraging training programs for members. His work preserved the peace and kept ships in operation, but any admiration on the part of the shipowners was buried in enmity.

The Pacific Navigation Company exemplified the kind of management that was Furuseth's goal, and its success demonstrated the benefits to owners of fair labor practices. In 1907 the New York boats *Yale* and *Harvard,* owned by Charles W. Morse's Metropolitan Steamship Company, were reputed to be the fastest ships in the merchant fleet, rivaling even rail travel between Boston and New York. The voyage around Cape Cod took only fifteen hours, a credit to the men in the stokehold. But the operation failed, and Morse chartered his two ships to the Pacific Navigation Company, where they ran successfully for years between San Francisco, Los Angeles, and San Diego. It was neither ship design nor quality of crew that made the difference between the failed and successful operations; it was responsible shipping company management, which balanced the needs of the business with those of the people it employed.

Back in Washington at the end of 1909, Furuseth met the man who was to become his strongest ally. The pair had little in common. Robert La Follette, a first-term Republican senator from the dairy-farm state of Wisconsin, was a flamboyant speaker who would later have his eye on the presidency. One wonders what drew him to the self-educated seaman with the heavy accent. Like a magnet's opposite poles, they were attracted to each other and worked well together. Furuseth went often to La Follette's home for Sunday breakfast. For two years, over strong coffee, Furuseth retold the same dismal tales he had reported to the Merchant Marine Committee. The senator submitted to Congress a list of twenty needed reforms, including improvements in working conditions, better food, an increase in forecastle space, improved safety equipment, and lifeboats. While Congress deliberated, the shipowners mounted a stiff opposition. Then, in 1912 the *Titanic* went down. There followed a public outcry, strong enough to push a weakly worded bill slowly through both houses. When the bill was at last submitted to the White House, President Taft let the deadline pass without signing it. Three years of discussion, politicking, and pressuring were left hanging in a vacuum. The senator made a second effort under a new administration with a stronger proposal, which came to be known as the La Follette Seamen's Bill. While it was in discussion on the floor, several maritime nations, including Great Britain and Germany, filed protests against the provisions having to do with the arrest, detention, and return of deserting seamen. Despite objections, the bill was passed and sent to the president. In the last hour before the deadline on March 4, 1915, Woodrow Wilson signed it into law.

While the inexcusable loss of the great *Titanic* with so many lives brought to light the need for improved safety regulations, the financial disaster suffered by its American owners went unnoticed. The liner was British-built and had a British flag and crew, but its operating company, the White Star Line, was wholly owned by IMM. Troubled financially and distracted by the war in Europe, IMM did little to enhance the comfort or safety of seamen in its American subsidiaries.

The ocean trading routes of the early twentieth century centered on the mid-Atlantic like winds on the vortex of a hurricane. A similar but lighter pattern, centered on Hawaii, fanned out in the vastness of the Pacific, stretching from Vancouver to Melbourne, edged by the old but still familiar routes to the East Indies and the Orient. It was in the North Atlantic and adjacent waters that the bulk of maritime business could be found. After a long, stormy period of decline amid growing labor unrest, American shippers strove to regain their hold on the potentially rewarding North Atlantic routes while expanding into others worldwide. The American merchant service trailed behind Europe in the transition from sail to steam. Lacking central leadership, its factions were blinded by intense and narrowly focused self-interest. Traders, shipbuilders and operating companies, windjammers and coal-burners, deck hands and stokers, federal regulators, owners and labor unions all had their own agendas.

During 1898, in two separate transactions, the islands of Hawaii and Puerto Rico were annexed, along with the distant island of Guam. They were the sixth and seventh additions to the American coastlines, bringing U.S. expansion in the Western Hemisphere near to completion. (The Panama Canal Zone and the Virgin Islands would follow.) Hawaii's agricultural bounty and potential for ocean trading had been recognized for decades. Development efforts literally bore fruit in November 1895 when the first cases of canned pineapple were shipped from the lush islands, augmenting the well-known cargoes of sugar and oranges. As a U.S. territory, the islands were destined to grow commercially.

An interesting study in the evolution of trading routes can be found in the first twenty years of the American-Hawaiian Steamship Company. After the annexation of Hawaii, the firm sold its clipper ships that had been engaged in round-the-Horn trading out of New York, and allied with the islands' major exporter, Sugar Factors, Inc. The new shipping company was in the fortunate position of having ample East Coast cargoes for the westbound voyage and, through Sugar Factors, a major share of Hawaii's eastbound cargoes, enabling it to control the lengthy New York–Honolulu route. When the company switched to steam, the traditional ocean route became shorter. For the clippers the only safe passage around South America had been around Cape Horn; the currents and rocky shores of the Strait of Magellan were considered too dangerous for sailing vessels. The company's new steamships conserved fuel by cruising through the strait, and once the underwriters accepted that route as safer than the storm-swept path around the Horn, equivalent insurance rates were negotiated. Another problem was the lack of coaling ports between the West Indies and Chile. American-Hawaiian installed oil burners in its modern steel ship *Nevadan,* an innovation well beyond the imaginations of shippers still skeptical about the use of coal steamers on that route. The *Nevadan's* test runs were striking in their success: with oil the ship had more cargo space than with coal and took less time en route than the windjammers on their Cape Horn routes. The company soon added the *Nebraskan* and then two more oil-burning vessels to its long-haul fleet. The navy was impressed and began at once to convert its warships to oil. Then within four years a British-owned trans-Isthmian railroad at Tehuantepec, Mexico, challenged American-Hawaiian's lock on the intercoastal route. The land crossing was projected to reduce transit time by more than two weeks. American-Hawaiian had little choice but to capitulate to the British proposal that it service the Tehuantepec Railroad, splitting its cargo shipments into two parts and discontinuing its route through the Strait of Magellan. American-Hawaiian acquired more ships and instituted separate Atlantic and Pacific fleets, routed from New York to Puerto Mexico and from Salina Cruz to the American West Coast and Hawaii. The Pacific fleet soon added a second route between Salina Cruz and Puget Sound.

At Tehuantepec, the stevedores, never known for their honesty, gave the shippers difficulties in the double transfers of cargo. Mexican laborers at the Atlantic terminal were aided on the Pacific side by Chinese coolies unfamiliar with the mechanical cargo gear. Workers looted cargoes and wrecked trains to get at their contents. Twenty percent of the general cargo was lost to improper handling, bringing some shippers to specify the all-water route rather than pass their goods through Mexico. Discouraged by its difficulties in Tehuantepec, American-Hawaiian returned briefly to the strait, and when the Panama Canal opened after some delay, the first three commercial ships waiting to use the new waterway were American-Hawaiian's. The company was highly profitable and eventually operated the largest merchant fleet under the U.S. flag, thanks to its flexibility in routing and its tactical adjustment to oil-burning steamers. Then the new market created by the war in Europe enticed the company to put its fleet up for Atlantic time charters. In an ill-chosen, opportunistic move, in 1915 American-Hawaiian withdrew its island service to shift its vessels for greater near-term profits. The decision did not improve the company's long-term future. Except for some government-requisitioned wartime service between Hawaii and San Francisco, the company never returned commercial intercoastal service to the mid-Pacific islands, the focal point of its best years of operation.

The Hawaiian merchants were justifiably upset and set out to find a more accommodating partner. That gave a San Francisco shipper, William Matson, the opportunity to expand his fleet. A Swedish immigrant and sea captain, Matson had begun his business in the late nineteenth century with a few sailing vessels operating out of the islands. He started the San Francisco–based Matson Navigation Company in 1908 to offer regular service between there and Honolulu. The company competed in a small way with American-Hawaiian but more with Robert Dollar's well-established Pacific Mail Steamship Line. A canny Scotsman, Dollar was an eighteenth-century-style merchant. He had immigrated to Canada, first attracted to the lumber trade, then moved to California, where he leased timberland and set up sawmills; he also built mills in Oregon and in Washington. That led him to establish a one-ship coastal lumber transport business, which he expanded to form the Pacific Mail Line. He then looked to the Orient for new commodities never before shipped directly to the West Coast. The vast Pacific became Dollar's territory. Hawaii was more than a stopover, but with American-Hawaiian out of the picture, he graciously shared the locale with Matson. Their two companies dominated the Hawaiian market for the remainder of the century.

In 1908 the Moore-McCormack Line opened regular routes to Scandinavia. Trade between western Europe and the United States had grown tenfold since 1840, when Edward Knight Collins and American shipping ruled the Atlantic. Yet the British Cunard Line, which in 1907 introduced the thirty-three-thousand-ton ocean liners *Lusitania* and *Mauretania* into passenger service, had regained its dominance of the routes to the British Isles. The largest shipping company in the world, Germany's Hamburg-America Line, was transporting more than half a million tons between Europe and New York annually in its ninety-five oceangoing freighters. Meanwhile, America's International

Mercantile Marine Company (IMM), the federation of several companies assembled by J. P. Morgan to operate mostly under foreign flags, got off to a discouraging financial start in its attempt to command the Atlantic. At the end of 1902, with transatlantic freight rates forced down by European shippers, IMM acknowledged Germany's and England's leadership.

The first decade of the twentieth century brought several advancements in technology that were adopted internationally. One of the greatest enhancements to ocean shipping was improved communications, beginning with a 1901 amendment of the International Code of Signals, which brought the 1857 proposal up to its present standard. The International Radio Telegraphic Conventions were instituted in 1906.

There were occasional flashes of American genius in maritime technology. In 1908 a prolific inventor, Elmer Sperry, demonstrated a compass influenced not by the earth's magnetism but by its rotation. With little formal education beyond vocational school, Sperry applied his unusual combination of inventive talent, entrepreneurial spirit, and hardheaded business sense to a wide variety of

10-1. SS *Princess Anne,* carried the first gyrocompass. COURTESY OF THE MARINERS' MUSEUM, NEWPORT NEWS, VIRGINIA

creations. Starting with arc lamps and electrical generating equipment, at the age of twenty he founded Sperry Electric to produce lighting and dynamos. From there he moved to mining machinery, street railways, electric automobiles, batteries, and chemical processes, adding every year to his lists of patents. In his lifetime he started eight companies for the production of his inventions, but his crowning achievement was the development of the gyrocompass. Based on Léon Foucault's gyroscope, long known as an amusing toy, Sperry's device overcame the obstacles that had interfered with the gyroscope's continuous operation. Sperry powered the gyrocompass with an electric motor, which positioned the axis perpendicular to gravity's pull, aligning it with the earth's axis. By avoiding the errors introduced by nearby iron objects or the earth's eccentric magnetic field, the gyrocompass pointed consistently true north. In 1911 Sperry installed the first operational gyrocompass on the Old Dominion Line's *Princess Anne* for a trial run from New York down the coast to Hampton Roads. The experiment was successful, and the gyrocompass was installed on the USS *Delaware*. Sperry established the Sperry Gyroscope Company in Brooklyn and installed the devices on four other naval ships. The allied navies put the compass to immediate use, and not long after the Great War it was adopted by more than sixty steamship lines. Meanwhile, hardly noted by the mariners, their major nemesis was born. On a cold, breezy day in November 1903, on the shores of North Carolina's Outer Banks, the Wright brothers proved that man could fly. By 1914 Elmer Sperry had designed a stabilizer for their winged devices.

Circumstance and misfortune obscured the extent to which the United States lagged behind its European counterparts in the controlled use of the radio spectrum. An American subsidiary of the British Marconi Company introduced commercial wireless telegraphy to American shipping in 1904. The Marconi Company controlled the use of its invention by leasing out the equipment and putting wireless operators aboard ship as its own contracted employees. The invention's worth had been proven in England in 1899, when the Goodwin Sands lightship issued the first-ever radio distress call. On Friday, January 22, 1909, the fifteen-thousand-ton White Star liner *Republic* sailed from New York, bound for Gibraltar with 431 passengers. (White Star was a British subsidiary of IMM.) The next day found it some 175 miles east of Ambrose lightship, wrapped in a thick fog that had rolled down the coast from the Grand Banks. At five-thirty that morning the *Republic's* Marconi operator, Jack Binns, was at work in his radio shack, engaged in relaying commercial traffic to the Siasconset Shore Station on the southeastern tip of Nantucket. Suddenly he heard a series of blasts on the fog siren. He looked up from his papers, felt a heavy thud, and to starboard heard the sickening screech of metal against metal, the shattering of wood and steel. The ship rolled sharply to port, upsetting the loose gear in his already cluttered cabin. The *Republic* had been struck amidships by the eighty-two-hundred-ton steamer *Florida,* a new ship of the Lloyd-Italiano Line, half the size of the *Republic.* Headed for New York in near-zero visibility, the vertically stemmed vessel cleaved the starboard side of the *Republic* like an ax put to a tin can, slicing deep into the engine room. Engines full astern, the *Florida* backed its damaged prow out of the gash, while its stern swung and smashed hard into the lean-to wireless office aft of the *Republic*'s main housing. Then it lurched off into the fog. Tons of seawater poured into the *Republic*'s machinery space, surging up on the heels of the black gang clambering to safety on the main deck. The ship went dark, and Binns groped through his demolished radio shack for an oil lantern to illuminate the transmitting equipment. He checked the antenna cable leading down from the aftermast across the great porcelain insulators to the oscillation transformers and the ten-inch spark coil, tested the motion of the long-handled copper transmitting key, sat on a wooden box with his codebooks before him, and closed the knife-switch on the emergency circuit. The accident had occurred at five-forty, and by six o'clock Jack Binns was back in operation, his battery-powered transmitter broadcasting over a range of a little more than fifty miles. With that he sent out the Atlantic Ocean's first "CQD" message and became famous.

The Marconi operator at the Siasconset Station, sleepily relaying commercial traffic, was suddenly startled to hear a faint CQD. His headphones carrying the customary background chatter of distant signals went quiet as stations hearing the distress signal stopped transmitting. "CQD-CQD-CQD." CQ warns all stations hearing it to yield the circuit because an important message follows; D is the cry for help in a dangerous situation. CQD—some translated the arbitrarily assigned code as "come quick, danger." By international agreement in the previous year the SOS signal had been adopted in lieu of CQD, but the latter was so deeply ingrained in the minds of British and American operators that its use was still widely accepted. Who, after all, would ignore it on a technicality?

A Morse inker slowly recorded Binn's messages, preceded by the *Republic*'s call letters:

6:15 A.M.—Rammed by unknown ship 26 miles south of Nantucket. Latitude 40.17, longitude 70.

One hundred and ten miles from its sister ship, the White Star's *Baltic* was inbound, well east of Sandy Hook, when at seven o'clock it first heard the relayed message. It sent its acknowledgment with its own call letters as it changed course for the site of the collision. The *Pennsylvania* of the Hamburg-America Line, the Cunarder *Lucania,* the Anchor Line's *Furnesia,* the French liner *Lorraine,* and the *Minneapolis* of the Atlantic Transport Line all were operating along the coast and heard the relayed messages. From New Bedford the revenue-cutter *Mohawk* hastened toward the site, then ran aground in the fog at midmorning on a falling tide, where it remained stranded for nearly twelve hours. It managed to send a message to the cutter *Acushnet,* which got under way from Woods Hole, forty miles from the scene of the accident. Marconi had equipped 180 vessels with the new transmitting equipment, supplying them with operators and their codebooks and call-letter listings.

The *Florida* was without wireless. Its captain, concerned about his own caved-in bow, was ignorant of the state of affairs until the stricken *Republic* loomed again out of the fog. The pair, still alone, communicated by semaphore and voice to arrange the transfer of the *Republic*'s passengers to the *Florida.* The Italian liner was carrying 880 immigrants, many the recent victims of a massive earthquake at Messina.

Meanwhile, Jack Binns remained at his station, his messages recorded and relayed at the Siasconset Station:

Steamer *Florida* is alongside *Republic* taking off passengers.

12:30 P.M.— *Republic* can remain afloat but two hours longer. All the passengers and three quarters of the crew have been transferred to the *Florida.* Others preparing to leave the ship.

His batteries were low and his signals getting weaker as the responding ships closed in. Radio direction finding did not exist; the ships exchanged dead-reckoned plots throughout the day, their signals alternately fading and strengthening while persistent fog prevented accurate positioning. The *Baltic* continued to probe through the fading light for the crippled vessels. Before Binns's batteries failed, the *Acushnet* arrived on the scene, the first rescuer. Siasconset picked up more messages:

6:58 P.M.—*Florida* in bad shape, leaving for New York in need of assistance. *Lorraine* and *Lucania* searching for her. *Florida* not being fitted with wireless, it is difficult to obtain her exact position. *Baltic* is nearing *Republic,* which, still afloat, is directing the *Baltic's* steering.

7:30 P.M.—*Baltic* found *Florida* and *Republic,* and is now standing by them to render assistance.

10:30 P.M.—All hands off. *Republic* sinking fast. Capt. Sealby, in boat along-side, refused to leave her till out of sight. *Baltic* will convoy *Florida* to New York. Latter able to steam slowly.

With the arrival of the *Baltic* on the scene, Jack Binns brought fresh batter-ies aboard and continued at his wireless key, sending status messages until he escaped with the remaining crew members and the captain, minutes before his ship sank in forty-five fathoms.

Two sleeping passengers and four crewmen on the *Republic* were killed in the collision. Two others were injured—a remarkably small casualty count con-sidering the extent of damage to the ships. Five years after its American intro-duction, the Marconi wireless had dramatically fulfilled its most important purpose. Yet the startling sound of "SOS" crackling on the airwaves could not guarantee rescue, even for the most valued vessels. Three years later the HMS *Titanic* sank on its maiden voyage, its hull sliced by an iceberg. That tragedy reaffirmed the value of the wireless while spotlighting the widespread neglect of safety precautions aboard ship.

Sometimes when nature unleashed its power unabetted, no amount of caution could prevent destruction. In November 1913, the most disastrous midwestern storm on record swept across the Great Lakes. Ten modern steel steamships sank with all hands on Lakes Huron and Superior. Lake Erie's Buf-falo Lightship was lost with its full crew. A half-dozen steel-hulled ships on Erie, Huron, and Superior broke up or were stranded. Barges and old, wooden sailing vessels on the Michigan and Erie waters foundered or were forsaken in sinking condition. More than 250 sailors died as twenty-three lakers suffered unrecoverable damage or went to the bottom. At the south end of Lake Huron, thirty-two-foot waves were measured officially; estimates by many who sur-vived the storm were much higher. Shipping itself, on fresh or salt water, what-ever the vessel type, put life at high risk.

A decade or more after the turn of the century, Maine still had die-hard builders of oceangoing sailers and a handful of hardy men to command them. The

A. & E. Sewell Shipyard in Bath produced five steel, three-masted ships, starting with the *Edward Sewell* in 1899. Richard Quick of Bath, one of the last sail masters, captained the *Sewell* for twenty-one years. A native of Newfoundland, Quick first went to sea on a fishing boat at the age of twelve, got his mate's license at seventeen, and, the following year, became an American citizen and shipped as master for the Sewells. During his years under sail he had to amputate a sailor's arm, lost one man overboard, and suffered increasing difficulties with inexperienced crews. Eventually, the dwindling supply of men familiar with canvas led Quick to sell out to steam and take command of a series of oil tankers.

The last gasp of the windjammers came in 1902 with the launching of the *Thomas W. Lawson,* the world's first and only seven-masted schooner. The Coastwise Transportation Company paid $240,000 for the steel-hulled, fore-and-aft-rigged ship, which had been built by the Quincy yard of the Fore River Ship & Engine Company. Unrigged in the dockyard, the *Lawson* looked like a section of an oversize picket fence. It had eight steam engines aboard for handling cargo, pumping, steering and raising sail, but none to propel the hull. It carried a crew of fifteen to nineteen sail-trained seamen. Much controversy has surrounded the names of its masts. Jests circulated that they were named for the days of the week. There is general agreement that the first three were named fore, main, and mizzen. The son of the man for whom the ship was named claimed the remaining four were called spanker, rider, driver, and jigger, in that order. One of its skippers said that because of confusion over the sequence of names, the four after masts were finally called no. 4, no. 5, no. 6, and spanker. The ship turned out to be impractical and cranky to handle. In 1907 it was cut down and converted to an oil barge, and on Friday, December 13, on its first transatlantic voyage, it was wrecked on the Scilly Islands with the loss of all but two of its crew.

The sea-level Cape Cod Canal, envisioned for 287 years, opened in 1914 to provide a safer and more direct steamship route between Boston and New York. By cutting seventy-five miles and five to eight hours from the difficult passage around Provincetown, the canal ended sail-powered trade between New York and New England. The construction was privately funded and took four years. No tolls were charged. The property was sold to the federal government in 1927.

If any single event made hauling on halyards for commercial purposes obsolete, it was the 1914 opening of the Panama Canal. No more rigorous doubling of Cape Horn or hooking up with trains across Central America. George Washington Goethals's masterpiece of engineering tied the two great oceans together, knotted by a mountain lake amid three levels of locks, it completed the tropical circuit of the globe. The Panama Canal became the only place in the world where a commanding officer must yield operational control of his ship to a pilot; he is legally relieved of all responsibility for the eight-hour transit. Masters of sail, unlicensed for steam, soon found that they, too, were relieved of responsibility. The days of commercial sail were over, except for the pilot boats that continued operating at many ports for a half century or more—sturdy reminders of sail's glorious past.

Chapter 11

THE TIDE TURNS:
1914–1917

As the Great War spread across Europe, embargoes and blockades disrupted transatlantic commerce. Great Britain looked to America to supply grain, cotton, munitions, and other war material. Shipping activity revived, and both marine insurance and freight rates soared. Profiteers quadrupled the charges for transporting wheat in little more than a year; by 1915 the charge for shipping a hundredweight of cotton went from 20 cents to $1.30. Congress thought it could stem the surge in prices through competition, to be generated by encouraging expansion in the shipping industry; it reversed an earlier restriction on the transfer of foreign ships to American registry intended to encourage local construction. That did little to help the nearly defunct American shipyards. At any rate, foreign flags were no longer protective for the shippers. American operators stood ready to make their flag convenient for British shipping.

The United States remained neutral, although its many immigrants were inclined to sympathize with the factions they had left behind. The government exercised caution as it edged closer to war. On January 28, 1915, it merged the Lifesaving and Revenue Services into the U.S. Coast Guard and then prepared armed Coast Guard vessels to accompany merchant ships across the Atlantic. In February, the secretary of state informed the Germans that they would be held strictly accountable if they caused an American vessel or the lives of American citizens to be lost on the high seas. The Bureau of Standards had been experimenting with radio waves and in the process came up with a secret device for the detection of submarines, which it quietly began installing in American ships.

The 1915 La Follette Act was a sort of Thirteenth Amendment for sailors. It put an end to the crimping of indebted seamen as a means of recruiting. It eliminated the continuous discharge documents known as "fink books," which had been used to blacklist strikers. Seamen were given the right to collect half their unencumbered wages in any port where cargo was worked. The law established a three-watch system for those on duty in the engine room, retaining watch-and-watch for those on deck. Sixty-five percent of the deck crews were required to be "able-bodied," that is, to meet reasonable physical and professional standards. Seventy-five percent of the crew in any department had to be able to take orders in English. The law improved shipboard safety and working conditions, and it ended the imprisonment of seamen for desertion in American or foreign ports. There was a subtle ISU strategy in Furuseth's lobbying for the desertion clause. The union leadership expected that low-paid foreign seamen would jump ship in American ports, creating more jobs for union members and forcing international wage levels up to American standards. Were it not for the wartime shipping boom, the shipowners probably would have taken strong countermeasures and caused the strategy to backfire.

The owners were furious about the government's interference in their affairs and turned to the Department of Commerce for interpretations of the new law's poorly defined specifications. In most cases Commerce favored the owners. It attempted to prove that the requirement that 65 percent of deck crews be able-bodied seamen was impractical given the shortage of qualified A-Bs. Commerce also criticized the new physical exam standards for A-B certification, which disqualified sailors with as much as twenty years' seagoing experience on the basis of color blindness or a missing finger.

Before the passage of the La Follette Act, Robert Dollar's Pacific Mail Steamship Line had been operating with all-Chinese crews under white American officers. The Chinese were capable seamen and available at lower wages than Americans. Responding to the law that three quarters of the crews on American-registered vessels must understand English, the Commerce Department said that pidgin English would suffice. From that decision a shockingly cruel phrase arose among seamen—"Chinese fire-and-boat drill" meaning a confused reaction to an emergency. Pacific Mail Steamship gave up its low-paid Chinese crews, would not consider white English-speaking replacements, discontinued its transpacific service, and sold off the ships to Atlantic operators.

The Great Northern Steamship Company followed Dollar's example and terminated its plans for West Coast service between San Francisco and Portland, Oregon.

Frustrated by the recalcitrance of the shipowners, Andrew Furuseth offered to debate them publicly. Congress had followed the advice of the owners for 150 years, he said, and as a consequence the United States was almost without a merchant marine. He asked only that the La Follette Act (it came to be known as the Seamen's Act) be given a fair trial. He went to the Legal Aid Society for support and got an adviser for the union. The lawyer identified more than thirty possible violations of the Seamen's Act which Furuseth intended to present to Congress as evidence of the need for monitoring. With the government turning its attention to the wartime demand for an increase in shipping, the act was not enforced.

President Wilson reacted to the shipowners by facing them down. He offered them low-cost ships to be operated on government terms. If they wanted to adhere to their contrary practices, they had no alternative but to build their own more expensive vessels. Under the Shipping Act of September 1916, designed to overcome foreign domination of the shipping business, he created the U.S. Shipping Board, gave it a working fund of $50 million, and authorized it to subsidize a merchant fleet. He had ample reason to move aggressively to satisfy the increased demand. There were flaws in the Shipping Act, which would become evident after the war, but in the meantime Alfred Mahan's recommendation was being zealously fulfilled. The federal government entered into partnership with commercial shipowners. With the additional impetus of the war, 129 new ships were launched in 1915, and 200 more were scheduled for delivery the following year. Shipbuilding became big business on both coasts, on the Great Lakes, at both ends of the Chesapeake, and on the Gulf of Mexico.

Great Britain's losses to the newest weapon of war, German submarines, could not be ignored. The two belligerent nations tested the limits of international law, setting up reciprocal blockades, the Germans around the British Isles, the British on the North Sea. On May 1, 1915, a German U-boat torpedoed the neutral, American-flagged tanker *Gulflight* off the Scilly Islands, with the loss of three American lives. The neutral ship was in the company of two armed British patrol boats, which technically made it a combatant. However, the German ship had failed to send a warning before attack. The situation illustrated the futility of the 1914 International Law on the Conduct of War. Under the law, no merchant ship could be sunk without first being warned and inspected, unless it was convoyed, armed, or attempting to escape or resist intervention. False colors, widely used, were acceptable under the rules until a warning was given. Thus the Germans may have mistaken the ship's American flag for a *ruse de guerre*. If the U-boat had exposed itself by giving a warning, it would have been vulnerable to attack by ramming or firing. That left the German skipper with two alternatives—get away fast, or fire at the tanker as a carrier of contraband to the enemy. The *Gulflight* did not sink, and Woodrow Wilson, wary of increasing the tension, delayed his response. Then the event occurred that rewrote the laws of ocean warfare and threw merchant shipping into chaos.

It was common practice for seaport newspapers to report ships' daily arrivals and departures in shipping news columns. Since the early days of the scheduled packets, passenger lines had posted these departure notices for the convenience of travelers arriving in the port prior to embarkation. In New York, on May 1, 1915, the same day the *Gulflight* was hit, Europe-bound passengers who opened their morning papers to verify the RMS *Lusitania*'s departure time faced a troubling decision. Adjacent to Cunard's customary sailing notice was a warning posted by the Imperial German Embassy.

NOTICE

Travellers intending to embark on the Atlantic voyage are reminded that a state of war exists between Germany and her allies and Great Britain and her allies; that the zone of war includes the waters adjacent to the British Isles; that, in accordance with formal notice given by the Imperial German Government, vessels flying the flag of Great Britain, or of any of her allies, are liable to destruction on those waters and that travellers sailing in the war zone on ships of Great Britain and her allies do so at their own risk.

The *Lusitania,* the fastest steamer in transatlantic service, was scheduled to leave at ten o'clock in the morning on the return leg of its 121st round trip from Liverpool. There was little time between breakfast and boarding for the 1,257 passengers, including 197 Americans, to make other travel arrangements. The Kaiser had announced two months earlier that he intended to take the war to England's surrounding waters. U-boat activity had increased frighteningly since then, and two hundred ships had been attacked in the defined area. Newsreel cameramen and reporters flocked to the North River pier to record the embarkment of what some were calling "the last voyage of the *Lusitania*." Anxiety coursed through the crowd, and the departure was delayed for two hours.

At last the gangway was hauled away. Those with unweakened resolve stood at the rails of the passenger decks waving flags. A long, ear-shattering blast issued from the whistle, followed by three shorter ones, and the famous liner backed out of its slip.

The Germans lived up to their threat. Seven days later in midafternoon, when the liner turned into the Irish Sea, its lifeboats already hung out for lowering, it was struck by a torpedo. There were munitions in the cargo, but under the restrictions of wartime secrecy their extent had not been made public. The first detonation was followed by a second, more harmful explosion, and perhaps a third as the boilers blew up. Coal dust in the bunkers could have contributed to the effects of the first, and perhaps only, torpedo. Within eighteen minutes the *Lusitania* went down. Eleven hundred and ninety-eight passengers lost their lives, among them 128 U. S. citizens. Whatever sympathy the American people had for the Germans turned at once to outrage—but the United States took no action for nearly two years. (Fifty years later Cunard released the *Lusitania*'s cargo manifest from the last voyage. It revealed that there had been several thousand cases of small-arms ammunition aboard, though not highly explosive as packaged; there were also "bulk furs," which some charged could actually have been a cottonlike element of munitions, explosive when exposed to salt water.)

During 1916 Great Britain was restrained by the loss of more than a million tons of shipping. Germany had pledged unrestricted submarine warfare but fell subject to worldwide criticism over the *Lusitania* incident. Eventually it promised not to attack passenger ships without warning. However, it did not adhere faithfully to its promise and its U-boats continued to wage war against cargo carriers—so successfully that by the spring of 1917 England was close to starvation.

Tensions between the United States and Germany increased. On April 6, 1917, after breaking off relations with Germany, Woodrow Wilson led his country into the "war to make the world safe for democracy." The Great War became the World War. The ocean liner *Great Northern,* intended for the Pacific coastal trade until idled after the enactment of the Seamen's Act, was converted to a troopship to carry part of the American Expeditionary Force to France. Other ships followed into the Atlantic.

Before Pacific Mail shut down its transpacific operations, the *Mongolia* carried cargo and passengers in the Oriental trade for eleven years. In 1916 Pacific Mail sold it to the Atlantic Transport Line, an American-flag subsidiary of International Mercantile Marine. At 13,630 tons, the *Mongolia* was one of

11-1. SS *Mongolia*. SSHSA Collection, University of Baltimore Library

the largest vessels in the American merchant service. Its captain, Emery Rice, brought it around Cape Horn to be armed for the transport of munitions and other wartime cargo to Europe. On April 19, 1917, the *Mongolia* was taking soundings near shallow water off the English coast. A lowering sun gleamed through a late afternoon haze as the ship's gunnery officer joined the skipper and chief mate on the bridge. Suddenly the mate sighted a periscope on the port bow, too close for the U-boat to carry out its intentions. The scope went under while the sub maneuvered into firing position. Rice gave a helm order to circle to where the sub had left its descending swirl. Two minutes later the forbidding black hull emerged abaft the freighter; by this time, the *Mongolia's* armed guard had manned its stern gun. The gunner gave a single command to fire, the big gun flashed, and its shell exploded against the German's conning tower. Rice put on full speed to leave the scene, fearing that the damaged sub had a partner in the area. His attacker disappeared beneath the waves.

A curious chain of circumstances had brought about the incident. Shoddy treatment of maritime labor led to the Seamen's Act; shipowners' distress at the act's restrictive laws caused West Coast companies to sell out and send their ships into the Atlantic; the president reacted to the American labor conflict and the European war by intervening further in both, and arming freighters for Allied support; one of the largest cargo carriers that might otherwise have stayed in transpacific service became a prime target for the Germans. And in less than three minutes after sighting the U-boat, Emery Rice and his crew fired the first American shot in the World War. They damaged the sub and joined the ranks of the few merchant mariners who have taken the conflict to the enemy. Rice made eighty-two Atlantic crossings through the U-boat-patrolled waters before his death at the age of forty-one in 1919. A posthumously awarded Navy Cross was added to the distinguished service medal he had received while commanding the *Mongolia*.

Chapter 12

UNCONVENTIONAL SHIPMATES: 1917–1929

After the sinking of the *Lusitania* the German merchant fleet, fearing reprisal at sea, spent most of its time bottled up in neutral ports. Upon the United States' entry into the war, the new head of the Shipping Board, Edward N. Hurley, took fast action. He seized 600,000 tons of enemy shipping tied up at American docks—ninety German and Austrian vessels, including the largest ship in the world, Hamburg-America's liner *Vaterland*. He also established a Shipping Board subsidiary, the Emergency Fleet Corporation (EFC), and empowered it to build and operate three yards for the rapid assembly of subcontracted ship sections. In 1917 the EFC started building what would total 2,382 ships, nine million tons, most ordered for delivery within eighteen months.

President Wilson appointed the genial and energetic Charles Schwab as director general of EFC. Schwab, the founder, owner, and board chairman of Bethlehem Steel, had already proven his production capability by completing an order for twenty submarines, assembled in Canada to avoid any violation of neutrality. The Germans were so disturbed by his production rate that they offered him $100 million to have Bethlehem stop supplying their enemies with war materials. By the end of the war Bethlehem's orders exceeded a half billion dollars.

Within two years the Shipping Board was operating 178 yards, building standardized ships from prefabricated parts. The parts were produced inland by manufacturers who knew little about specialized shipbuilding requirements. In a remarkable act of showmanship on July 4, 1918, Schwab arranged the same-day launching of one hundred ships around the continent.

The largest shipyard in the nation's history was constructed at Hog Island, Pennsylvania, with fifty ways on the Delaware River south of Philadelphia. The major contractor was a Stone & Webster subsidiary, the American International Shipbuilding Corporation, whose production records were unsurpassed and would remain so for a quarter of a century. One hundred and twenty-two steel ships were built at Hog Island, assembled literally by the mile. During one sustained period a ship was launched into the river every five and a half days. Another dramatic event took place on May 30, 1919, when five Hog Islanders were launched within forty-eight minutes and ten seconds. The ships looked like giant bathtub toys sliced from an assembly line, flush-decked, slab-sided, with wooden booms and ungainly, tall stacks above coal-burning engine rooms. But seaworthy they were. The Hog Islanders formed the needed "bridge of ships" to England, and many of them continued to give reliable if slow service through World War II.

Stripped of its luxuries and converted to a troopship, the *Vaterland* was renamed *Leviathan*. Earlier British sailing vessels had also carried the sea mon-

12-1. SS *Leviathan*. SSHSA COLLECTION, UNIVERSITY OF BALTIMORE LIBRARY

ster's name. Woodrow Wilson is said to have chosen it partly because his wife liked its biblical origin and partly because of the enormous difficulty with the ship's disposition. The *Leviathan* was to be operated by the U.S. Navy under the Shipping Board's direction. Government agencies were not well suited to the management of monstrous ocean liners. The ship had been terribly neglected and even willfully damaged by its last German crew. All the diagrams of piping and wiring had been removed, obstructing the engineers' work, and seven months elapsed before the ship was ready to return to sea. Finally in operation, the *Leviathan* completed nineteen round trips as a transport, once carrying 14,416 soldiers—more passengers than had ever before embarked on a single ship. On its last voyage it carried some seven thousand returning troops. The Knights of Columbus, in an act of postwar exuberance, promised to pay for every soldier to send home a radiogram during the crossing. Lines formed at the ship's radio room, operators working around the clock to deliver the troops' messages. Many of the jubilant doughboys were disappointed; before they reached the booking desk the fast liner had docked in New Jersey.

After the November 1918 Armistice, the Shipping Board had to dispose of its captured commercial fleet. The American Merchant Line, a subsidiary of J. P. Morgan's IMM, took over a number of single-class German cargo-passenger ships, gave all of them names with the prefix *American,* and put them into service between New York, London, and Hamburg. Their red-painted stacks bore single white and blue stripes and the company logo, a blue eagle on a white oval background—a design that became well known later in the century. The Board had several German luxury liners on its hands as well. After trying without success to sell the *Leviathan* to both England and France, it decided to give the ship a new life in America.

William Francis Gibbs, the little-known marine architect chosen to head up the *Leviathan*'s second renovation, was a Harvard graduate with a law degree from Columbia, self-taught in naval architecture, unlicensed but learned, an austere individual with aristocratic taste. With his brother he had toyed at ship design since boyhood. During the war he was attracted by the immensity of the converted passenger liner, and when the *Vaterland*'s German builders demanded payment of a million dollars for the blueprints, Gibbs found his opportunity. Having nothing but the ship itself to work with, he assembled a team of draftsmen, who measured it from stem to stern and within a year delivered to the Shipping Board twenty blueprints, more than a thousand pages of specifications, and Gibbs's own recommendations for a $10 million restoration. His proposals ranged from conversion of the coal-burning plant for oil to improvements in the finest details of nautical decoration. Two years elapsed before the board gave full approval to the costly Gibbs plans and the ship was towed to Newport News for rebuilding. Gibbs's new employers soon learned that they had a perfectionist in charge, attentive to every aspect of the passenger liner.

At the turn of the century less than 1 percent of ocean shipping used oil for fuel. That portion rose to 15 percent by the end of the war. At that point Germany and Denmark were already introducing diesel machinery into their ships; the U-boats had used diesels exclusively. American engine manufacturers found that high-pressure steam fired by an acrid, black oil known as "bunker-C" offered surface ships the optimum combination of power and economy. The *Leviathan* burned more than ninety-five hundred tons of bunker-C per crossing, drawn from forty-six tanks built into its double bottom.

J. P. Morgan was never happy with his maritime endeavors, restricted as they were by multiple governments. The International Mercantile Marine Company had already gone into receivership in 1915 and never succeeded in monopolizing the Atlantic, in spite of England's wartime difficulties. It was the wartime shipping boom that kept the IMM afloat. In 1919 Morgan made one more effort to enhance his gamble. He assembled more than a million tons of shipping under both American and foreign flags, 106 steamships making up six different lines: American (also known as American Merchant or American Ship and Commerce), Atlantic Transport, Leyland, Red Star, White Star, and the White Star–Dominion Lines. The ocean proved too big even for this conglomerate. The IMM suffered from inept management; Morgan lost interest in shipping and turned back to his railroads. In 1921 the IMM divested itself of its foreign holdings, and the United States Lines, identified in its posters as "managing operators for United States Shipping Board," was formed from the IMM's American Line. When the nine-year-old *Leviathan* was ready to sail on its third maiden voyage on July 4, 1923, United States Lines took it over as its flagship. The *Leviathan* made a profit only sporadically during its twelve years of civilian service, but it carried the blue eagle house flag of United States Lines into the age of the illustrious passenger liners. For the company, the greatest benefit that emerged from that cumbersome beginning was a thirty-year relationship with architect William Francis Gibbs, which brought worldwide fame to the man, the shipping company, and the American merchant marine.

The terms and conditions established by the 1916 Shipping Act for the sale of government-owned vessels to private interests were long known to be too loosely defined. The need to tighten up the law resulted in the Merchant Marine Act of 1920, also called the Jones Act after its sponsor, Senator Wesley L. Jones of Washington state. The tireless senator spent the better part of a year promoting the bill, which then was rushed into passage with little debate and no recorded vote. One wonders whether the spirit of the departed Alfred Mahan hovered over the legislators as they wrote the new law. (Mahan had died in 1914.) The Merchant Marine Act directed the Shipping Board to do "whatever may be necessary to develop and encourage the maintenance of a merchant marine . . . sufficient to carry the greater portion of its commerce and serve as a naval military auxiliary in time of war or national emergency ultimately to be owned and operated privately by citizens of the United States." The act stated that the Shipping Board should operate government-owned vessels until sold to American companies; that there should be no foreign sales; and that the board should determine what lines should be established for both coastal and overseas trade, and should sell or charter its vessels to those lines. In short, the act socialized shipping. In theory, through the chartering provision new private operators would be enticed to gain experience before purchasing their fleets. The most enduring part of the Jones Act was its reaffirmation of cabotage, the policy that confined trade between any American ports, intra- and intercoastal, to vessels of American registry.

In retrospect, wartime ship production had been a case of too many ships too late in the game. The war ended sooner than anticipated, and shipyards had more than a thousand keels laid, ready for fulfillment of building contracts. The Shipping Board's great challenge was to put the nation's growing fleet of idle ships—augmented by the seized German ships—to productive work.

Commercial and government maritime interests made unconventional shipmates. For more than a century shipowners had tried to keep their distance from federal regulators, and the government had shown only a marginal interest in maritime affairs. Later, the Department of Commerce and then the Shipping Board became management's allies in labor matters. By 1921 the board owned or leased 70 percent of the merchant fleet. It had become the nation's principal shipowner and its policies reflected that situation. Shipping companies now were operators and not always owners, and they saw as their primary aim the near-monopolistic control (or at least American control) of private routes. The glut of ships available for charter gave them a free ride at government expense. From this new relationship stemmed most of the difficulties that beset the American merchant marine for the rest of the century.

During the war the high demand for seamen helped them gain concessions from the shippers. Deck hands were able to override the watch-and-watch provision of the 1916 act and work an eight-hour day on a three-watch plan for $90 a month, plus a dollar an hour for overtime. These were the highest seamen's wages in history. However, the rosy, federally ordained future anticipated by the Jones Act did not come to pass. Peacetime foreign trade failed to regain its prewar tonnage until after the next world war; in 1923 the volume was 20 percent lower than it had been ten years earlier. By 1928 freight charges had dropped below their 1913 rates. The IMM continued to flounder through the twenties, its White Star Line competing unsuccessfully with Cunard and the revived Hamburg-America Line for the bulk of transatlantic passenger traffic. Done in by the depressed worldwide economy of the 1930s, one by one the IMM's companies came to an unprofitable end, leaving only a remnant in shaky operation, United States Lines. Steerage passengers on the *Leviathan* made up for the empty cabins in its three classes of costly service; even then, on some crossings the ship carried more crewmen than passengers. Henry Ford bought a half-million gross tons of idle ships for scrap iron to feed his booming automobile factories. The shipbuilding surge ended as suddenly as it had begun. "Ghost fleets" of wood and steel formed in little-used upstream waters, one of the more visible being a group of four captured German luxury liners that ended up rusting at anchor, side by side, in Maryland's Patuxent River.

The industry was in deep decline in 1921 when the operators, in collusion with the Shipping Board, attempted to break the unions. The operators proposed a return to the eighty-four-hour week, elimination of overtime, a 15 percent wage cut, and reversion to the watch-and-watch system for above-deck sailors. Admiral W. S. Benson, the newly appointed chairman of the board, agreed and announced that the new rules would go into effect on all government-owned vessels on May 1. This amounted to a lockout because the government owned 70 percent of all commercial ocean carriers. Senator La Follette called for an investigation, Furuseth requested arbitration, and the ISU demanded a strike and reinstituted a job action, the oracle. The Masters, Mates and Pilots joined the seamen in sympathy, but the Pacific Coast Longshoremen's Union wouldn't join. Violence on the waterfront followed, and the shippers called for federal troops. When the job action failed, the strike withered of its own accord before the army arrived. The owners backed away from some of their draconian expectations, but the ISU's membership dropped to 16,000 from a postwar peak of 115,000.

Once more, Andrew Furuseth was on the defensive, losing to his own constituency, and not without cause. Under his leadership the Sailors' Union of the Pacific held to its policy that a member must prove himself a "real sailor." Candidates were examined by a committee of two elder A-Bs and asked questions about the ropes and gear of square-riggers. "Checkerboarding," or the integration of black workers into white crews, was not permitted, and for decades blacks were excluded from the West Coast unions. Asians and East Indians were admitted to the unions but segregated on the job, often working as stewards; they made up the entire nonlicensed crew on Dollar's Pacific Mail line.

Many seamen challenged the SUP as an obsolete craft union. It was autonomous at a time when the "Wobblies"—the Industrial Workers of the World (IWW)—were forming broader-based industrial unions. Attracted to the idea of a single, powerful maritime union, many members of the Sailors' Union joined the IWW's Marine Transport Workers Industrial Union, and the SUP and ISU grew weaker. A running conflict over jurisdiction continued between the sailors and the longshoremen, who disagreed on what constituted shipboard work and what was the proper domain of stevedores. They bickered over the topping of booms, the opening of hatches, and the tending of dock lines, and little was resolved to mutual satisfaction.

Furuseth's own ideas were harsh. He tolerated the racist status quo, having nothing to say on matters of integration. He protested against workmen's compensation because it relieved shippers of responsibility and made negligence profitable. Recognizing that marine insurance could make the loss of a vessel profitable to its owners, he opposed liability insurance as detrimental to shipboard safety. He fought against union hiring halls, saying they violated the seaman's right to seek employment without a middleman and the captain's right to select the best men for a safe operation. Sound as some of his arguments may have been, it was hard for the seamen to tell where he was coming from, and they often disagreed with him. But he remained as resilient as ever, continuing to lobby for enforcement of the Seamen's Act. Soon he would face the threat of Communist infiltration.

When Robert Dollar was unable to keep his Pacific Mail Steamship's coastal business profitable after the war, he discontinued it to pioneer a new opportunity. He became managing operator of the new government-owned Dollar Line and in 1924 initiated the first regular round-the-world passenger service with the passenger liner *President Harrison,* originally built at Hog Island as a troop transport. The company's name was changed to American President Lines (APL) to free it from the seamy reputation Pacific Mail had acquired under Dollar's management. The APL was one of several government-subsidized ventures in this period. A former longshoreman-turned-warehouse-operator, Henry Herberman, moved into shipping to become president of Export Steamship Corporation in

1919. In 1924 his company bought the Shipping Board's Mediterranean fleet for something like 30 percent of the original cost and changed its name to American Export Lines (AEL). The line transported major cargoes of Egyptian cotton but, even with the low start-up costs, was unable to make a profit until Herberman landed a subsidy in the form of a government mail contract in 1928. Also under Shipping Board directives, the New Orleans–based coffee shipper Delta Line gained routes to the Baltic and Scandinavia. Similarly, Moore-McCormack supplemented its Scandinavian routes with East Coast service to Brazil. In the Gulf, Lykes gained routes through the new Panama Canal to South America's Pacific coast, Farrell Line won routes to Africa, and Grace Line started carrying fertilizer from the west coast of South America. In its generosity the Shipping Board allocated routes to nearly two hundred managing operators.

The wartime shipbuilding explosion, hurried as it was, brought about extensive engineering improvements. New compact steam turbines replaced the plodding reciprocating engines and then, in turn, were replaced by even newer turboelectric and diesel engines. Oil tankers took up worldwide routes that hastened the discontinuance of coal burners. The growth of shipyards on the Delaware River and in Baltimore, Newport News, and Norfolk required improvements in the C & D Canal. In 1927 the canal became a sea-level waterway for barges, and a proposal to widen it for steamship passage was under consideration.

Occasional acts of bravery by officers and men at sea maintained public interest in the merchant marine. The Atlantic Ocean in the winter of 1929 provided a venue. "WNA"—Winter North Atlantic—is the label of the full-loading mark with greatest freeboard. Just the initials evoke chilling memories for those who have sailed during winter, loaded or light, on the storm-swept, mountainous seas between Cape Race and Bishop Rock, or through the frigid, turbulent weather that spreads deep into the lower latitudes of the North Atlantic. Even the sturdiest ships are at risk; small ones have no business being there. Nowhere on that wild ocean can a vessel take refuge, even for a moment—not in the trough, where waves cascade over the stern in curling white foam, not on the crest, where the ship is tossed about like an empty bottle until, twisting and momentarily free of gravity, the hull spirals down into a deluge of green water. The propeller churns violently in empty air, bites down, recovers, pushes up from the deep, then lifts again on the swell at some crazy angle, shaking its fastenings with unrestrained energy. Waves burst against the bridge, and tons of water course along the open decks to shatter lifeboats, carry away deck gear, and tear at hatch coverings. Icy sleet sheaths the rigging, straining masts which roll far over under the added weight. There is the ever present fear that cargo will shift in an unforgiving sea and introduce a deadly list. For weeks on end the sun hides under leaden clouds. Positions become uncertain as the compass swings wildly, four or more points on either side of the course. In the machinery space, stokeholds choked with smoke lose their draft, and water sluices down the ventilators, flooding the floorings and shaft alley. Within the housing everything is doubly secured, athwart ships, fore and aft; chairs are turnbuckled to deck padeyes. On good days the crew eats at a table covered with cloths dampened to restrain sliding dinner plates, edge-fiddles raised into place. On bad days it is better to eat sandwiches hand to mouth, braced in a corner and standing up. Sailors pull their mattresses onto the floor to sleep, propped against a bulkhead, a life jacket pushed under an edge to make a V shape. Gravity duels with the sea's lift and fall, motion never ceases, and there is always the clacking, creaking, shuddering, groaning of the working ship.

The third week of 1929 was among the worst on record for sailors on the North Atlantic. On Sunday, January 20, the British freighter *Teesbridge,* bound from Fowey for Philadelphia, sent an SOS with the message that it was foundering in westerly winds of gale force, three hundred miles east of Cape Race and facing gigantic seas. It then disappeared without a trace. On Monday the *Terne* was surrounded by ice near rocks at Friar's Head, Nova Scotia, and the diesel trawler *Mariner* was disabled off Nantucket. The westbound *American Shipper* and *Columbus* both signaled that their scheduled New York arrivals would be delayed for a day. The *Homeric,* due from Cherbourg, and the *Providence,* from the Mediterranean, encountered heavy weather in midocean and predicted late arrivals.

On Tuesday, stormy seas persisted and a two-day search for the *Teesbridge* was abandoned. The *Paris,* from Le Havre and Plymouth, reported that unusually severe weather would delay its New York arrival by a day or more. Just before noon the *Florida* issued an SOS, stating that it was seven hundred miles east of the Virginia Capes with its rudder broken and a lifeboat stove in by mountainous seas breaking over the decks. Another SOS followed from the tanker *Dannedaike,* steaming from Beaumont, Texas, to Ghent, Belgium, also with a damaged rudder, on nearly the same latitude one hundred miles east of the *Florida.* The *Florida,* a twenty-two-hundred-ton Italian Line freighter with a crew of thirty-two, had been headed from Pensacola to Italy. Three vessels responded to the calls—the German steamship *Yorck,* itself struggling through enormous seas, Dollar's *President Harrison,* and the liner *America,* next in line after the *Leviathan* as flagship of United States Lines—three hundred and fifty miles north of the two disabled vessels. The *President Harrison* interrupted its round-the-world passage and set out for the *Dannedaike,* and *America* turned south toward the *Florida.* After steaming for five hours, the *President Harrison* reported that it was hove-to, barely making steerageway with very slow progress toward its target. *America,* commanded by George Fried, continued its race through the whole gale.

Captain Fried, a Teutonic individual with a firm jaw, high cheekbones, and close-set eyes under his short-billed, cylindrical cap, was a taciturn skipper. Earlier, while captain of the *President Roosevelt,* the rescue of a freighter in wintry seas had earned him fame that he hardly acknowledged. Now, after the *Dannedaike* reported that it was proceeding toward Bermuda with a jury-rigged rudder and under its own power, all attention focused on *America*'s meeting with the *Florida.* During the thirty-six hours following Captain Fried's commitment of *America* to the rescue of the disabled ship, he dispatched few messages, just two for public consumption. He spent an anxious period of more than a day searching for the ship and then, on Wednesday at nine o'clock in the evening, issued the simple statement, "*America* now standing by the SS *Florida.*" At ten o'clock came the laconic report: "Rescue full crew of *Florida.* Total thirty-two. Chief Officer Manning charge. Whole westerly gale. Lifeboat lost. Proceeding. Full details later." It would be difficult to find a more heroic event than what had occurred in the single hour that passed between the two messages.

Had the weather been less severe, it would have taken Captain Fried about twenty-one hours to reach the *Florida. America* was sheathed in ice as it plowed through squalls of hail and heavy snow. It was impossible under the circumstances to maintain a normal, sixteen-knot cruising speed. The gale continued through the night, abating somewhat after daybreak. In midmorning the seas remained violent under clearing skies, and the winds had dropped below gale force. Fried sent his company a brief message that he was now running toward the site at full speed. *America* was the lone rescuer, the *Yorck* and *President Harrison* having dropped out of the race after a futile eight-hour search and loss of radio contact. The *President Harrison,* between *America* and the mainland and short of fuel, continued to relay messages ashore from *America,* which reported it too had lost contact with the *Florida.* Some time later, contact was regained after the troubled ship enabled its emergency equipment.

Fried asked for a position report, and the *Florida* replied that its navigation books had been destroyed when waves carried the bridge away. The master had a sextant and reported his observations by radio to *America,* where they were worked out, revealing that the *Florida* was 150 miles north of its last assumed position. The two ships had passed during the night. *America* turned at once and retraced its route, using its radio compass. Invented in 1915 by F. A. Kolster, a research scientist at the Bureau of Standards who had observed the directional characteristics of radio waves, the radio compass could indicate the direction of a transmitter by rotating a receiver's loop antenna on a vertical axis and relating its position to the compass as the intensity of the signal increased or decreased. The Kolster receiver and radio compass (later called a radio direction finder, or RDF) was kept secret during the war while used to spot German submarines, providing additional protection for transatlantic convoys carrying troops and supplies through the U-boat barriers. After the war, ships were equipped with the easily recognized diamond- or ring-shaped metallic antennas above the radio shacks. By this time radio equipment had found its way to the uppermost portion of the house, abaft or above the bridge.

It developed that the *Florida*'s skipper, fearful of capsizing, had kept the screw turning over, the better to keep the bow into the seas. The ship moved northerly at about three knots. Now, the signals received by *America* became feeble, sometimes fading entirely. Nightfall approached, clouds closed in, and the winds increased. Both ships had been close to the eye of the storm and now were groping for each other in its southeast quadrant. *America* turned on a searchlight and told the *Florida* to keep a lookout for it. At six-thirty, *America* sighted the *Florida* dead ahead and took a position on the stricken ship's weather-beam about five hundred yards away. Snow squalls reduced the visibility as the liner attempted to close in on the freighter. The *Florida* listed heavily to starboard, lee rail awash, every roll of its hull sending a heavy surge toward the rescuing ship.

The crew of the *Florida,* now almost entirely without radio communication, was prepared to abandon ship. Given the state of the sea, Fried would not have been negligent had he done no more than stand by to pick survivors out of the water. What little practice sailors get in lifeboat seamanship takes place in placid water as they prepare for annual inspection. A rescue craft attempting to cross between the two vessels could easily capsize with subsequent loss of life.

Chief Mate Harry Manning and eight selected seamen stepped forward. Lifeboat number 1 was lowered away with nine life-jacketed men aboard, the chief mate at the tiller. They rowed at a quick pace, hastening to close the gap while *America* afforded a lee. Halfway across, the boat was temporarily lost to observers on *America*'s bridge, eclipsed as it shot down the further side of a swell, then sighted as it rose a long minute later, a boat's length farther away.

The spotlight tracking the rowers caught them on every rise, eight grim faces, shoulders hunched over as they bent to their efforts in unison, the distance to the rescue shortened foot by foot. Manning maneuvered the lifeboat as close to the lee of the foundering ship as he dared, near enough to heave a line up to the slanted deck. The *Florida*'s crewmen were near despair as he shouted to them to ease singly down the line, then pull themselves through the icy water to the lifeboat, where they would be hoisted aboard. *America*'s Italian bowman acted as translator for the foreigners. One by one, they eased over the railing, lowered themselves into the water, and worked hand-over-hand toward the lifeboat. Half of the crew had been rescued when a wave surged the length of the slanted deck and carried the line away. A man nearing the safety of the lifeboat had to be hauled back aboard the sinking freighter. There was not a moment to lose as another line was sent over, while Manning maneuvered the lifeboat to close the distance without getting under the rolling hull. Finally the *Florida*'s captain climbed over the gunwale and informed Manning that there were no more men behind.

America's crewmen bent again to their rowing, thirty-two survivors shuddering beneath them, exhausted from their long ordeal, soaked, their clothing torn, some nearly naked. *America* had worked to leeward of the sinking *Florida*. Wind tore the ocean into long sheets, wave tops tumbling in watery chaos. The gale intensified, accompanied by blinding, wet snow and heavy swells. The gravely burdened lifeboat swung wildly, now much lower in the sea and taking water aboard, combers gripping its rudder and breaking across the stern. The passenger ship was well lit, easy for the rowers to spot as they ran in the darkness, chased by biting, horizontal sheets of spray. Approaching the liner they found its starboard side strung with cargo nets, rope ladders, and knotted lines. None of the *Florida*'s crew could climb up unaided. A makeshift breeches buoy was fashioned from life rings, and one by one the thirty-two dazed survivors were eased into the apparatus and lifted aboard. One man fell overboard and had to be fished from the water. Another tumbled on top of Manning. His back injured, Manning was able to steer up under the swinging falls as his sailors reached to grasp the loose, heavy steel blocks and hooked them to the lifeboat. But it proved impossible to hoist the boat to the deck with its crew aboard. Swaying just above the waves it crashed against the side, and at the last minute the shattered boat had to be released as the seamen grabbed knotted monkey-ropes and climbed upward, foot by foot, Manning the last to leave. He collapsed as the first assistant engineer pulled him onto the deck. The darkened

12-2. Hardy survivor of a hurricane in the Gulf of Mexico, the SS *Rochester* was mercilessly torpedoed and shelled, and finally sank on January 30, 1942. It was the fourteenth American ship lost to submarines on the East Coast in World War II. MOBIL CORPORATION

Florida was lost, as was *America*'s lifeboat, but within the hour Harry Manning had rescued all thirty-two crewmen and his eight exhausted sailors.

Three thousand people met *America* at Hoboken when it docked at the end of the week. Fried and Manning were lionized the following week with a ticker-tape parade and a reception hosted by the mayor of New York. They received medals from Benito Mussolini on behalf of the Italian government and letters of commendation from the U.S. Congress. Captain Fried insisted on giving full credit to his chief officer, and when later sent on a speaking tour to tell of their adventure, he turned over the command of *America* to Manning. Troubled as United States Lines was financially, it gained new respect with mariners like Fried and Manning commanding its ships. Coincidentally, Captain Manning and designer Gibbs would meet as shipmates, a world war and nearly a quarter of a century later.

Chapter 13

IRISH PENNANTS:
1929–1940

Frayed sails, unsecured small stuff, loose ends flapping in the wind—sailors call them "Irish pennants." They are untidy, unproductive, and beg for attention. The merchant marine of the 1930s had its own Irish pennants in need of trimming or tying down. From an oversupply of qualified manpower in 1929, fewer than sixty-four thousand men found work on American oceangoing vessels. Ships were plentiful, but there was no well-defined plan to use them in competition with the Europeans. There were unresolved labor issues and shipboard safety requirements forgotten or ignored in the face of trade reductions. Maritime development in the Pacific had been neglected since the 1916 Shipping Act. Shipyards lost the incentive to innovate, held back by an idle reserve fleet moored in inland waters.

Troubled by the monster-of-the-deep *Leviathan,* United States Lines lurched from one deficit to another. In 1929 the Shipping Board sold its fleet to the Paul W. Chapman Company, which promptly reorganized it, determined to operate it in a businesslike manner. The trade decline that followed the World War continued into the worldwide depression of the 1930s, and Chapman was soon in arrears. He refused a bid by the IMM to purchase the line, and the Shipping Board prepared to resume control. But Chapman, unwilling to step aside, joined with Kenneth Dawson and Stanley Dollar, son of the West Coast shipping magnate, in a deal that set the course of liner trade in both the Atlantic and the Pacific for the next three decades. They faced two IMM representatives across the bargaining table: Kermit Roosevelt, son of Theodore Roosevelt and owner of the Roosevelt Steamship Company (American Pioneer Line), and John Franklin, the son of P. A. S. Franklin, one of the IMM's founders. The IMM, looked upon in the United States as a marginal, largely British, holding company, was fighting for survival. The Dollars, more interested in the Pacific than the Atlantic, haggled to gain supremacy in Pacific coast shipping and exclusive rights to the use of the name "President" for their liners. United States Lines won preeminence in the Atlantic. When Robert Dollar, the white-whiskered patriarch of the Pacific, died in 1932, American President Lines had acquired two new sister ships for the Oriental trade—the *President Hoover* and the *President Coolidge*—and had become the largest commercial fleet to fly the American flag.

Some bright spots broke through the dark financial clouds. The *Seatrain* was launched in 1929, an empty hull with built-in railroad tracks for transporting loaded freight cars. The original containership, it was the ancestor of roll-on, roll-off vessels. The same year, the state of California, seeing a potential need for licensed officers in the commercial shipping industry, established the California Maritime Academy. Thus it revived the short-lived educational initiative of 1875, when the schoolship *Jamestown* was delivered. In 1931 the Matson Line—perhaps inspired by the success of its four-year-old, Gibbs-designed *Malolo*—announced the first completely air-conditioned passenger liner, the *Mariposa,* for West Coast service to Hawaii. Undiscouraged by the Depression, the company also contracted for the construction of its new flagship, the *Lurline,* named for Matson's daughter. The ship was built in Quincy, Massachusetts, and brought to the Pacific the following year. The Los Angeles Steamship Company (Lassco) purchased the *Yale* and *Harvard*—once reputed to be the fastest ships in commercial service—from the Atlantic-based Metropolitan Steamship Company, which had chartered them to Pacific Navigation since 1908. Lassco kept the two ships in coastwise trade and in 1935 reported that the venerable *Yale* had completed 1,330 voyages, covering more than 1,270,000 miles in thirty years of seagoing.

In 1932 the Bureau of Marine Inspection was formed, combining the ninety-four-year-old Bureau of Navigation with the Steamboat Inspection Service. The nation's new president, Franklin Roosevelt, continued housecleaning in the government bureaucracy, at least for a while. On June 10, 1933, he abolished the Emergency Fleet Corporation by executive order and assigned responsibility for ship acquisition and allocation to the Shipping Board's successor, the Shipping Board Bureau of the Department of Commerce.

Labor unrest persisted while labor leaders fought among themselves for power. By 1934, seamen's wages in San Francisco had dropped below $67 a month, sometimes as low as $30 or $40. Longshoremen earned 85 cents an hour if they could get work at all. Jobs were few, and a shady method of hiring called the "shape-up" emerged. Hungry men gathered outside piers on the Embarcadero where ships prepared to work cargo. Milling on the street with leather pads on their shoulders and cargo hooks at their belts—the hooks were hand tools, also suitable as weapons—they waited to be called by a straw boss holding a tally list of gangs needed for the day. A man had to present a blue book showing that he was a paid-up member of the Longshoremen's Association of San Francisco (LAS), a company union. Only if his "fink book" satisfied the straw boss could he be selected for work. The practice led to kickbacks. Uncalled men could do little but walk away in wild-eyed frustration. The waterfront was ripe for riot and Communist infiltration. Helped by the National Recovery Act, the American Federation of Labor formed an affiliate, the International Longshoremen's Association (ILA). Communists were quick to join, along with disgruntled members of the corrupt LAS.

The ILA's numbers grew, and it started making tough demands. Then on May 9, 1934, it called a strike. Ignoring the advice of Andrew Furuseth, disparaged as he was by the Communist contingent, the SUP stopped work in sympathy with the longshoremen. Two hundred and fifty ships at eighty-two docks along the Embarcadero stood idle. The shipowners brought in strikebreakers, and predictably, there were violent incidents, some of them fatal.

Labor had too many factions, and too many people within them striving to take control. Some of the divisions reflected differing needs—cooks and stewards, for example, shared little with stevedores. Some divisions were purely emotional, like that between the sail and steam crews. Many of the groups, such as the deckhands and longshoremen, had overlapping interests. Labor needed unified leadership. Yet if its leaders had one trait in common it was a contentious spirit, which they applied with the same vigor to their own constituents as to their adversaries in management. It was difficult to know where any labor leader stood on issues other than the advancement of his chosen causes. Communism further clouded the situation. Did the leaders tolerate it or not? Were they encouraging overthrow of a patrician government? Were they influenced by foreign interests? And was improvement in workers' lives synonymous with a rise of the masses?

The ILA strike shut down the entire city for days. The chief agitator was a native-born Australian, Harry Bridges of the International Longshoremen's and Warehousemen's Union (ILWU), head of the Joint Marine Strike Committee, and a Communist sympathizer. Joe Ryan, the ILA president, was concerned about Communist manipulation and came to San Francisco to meet with the shipowners. He tried to settle the strike through a secret agreement, but was rejected by his own membership, worked up as they were by Harry Bridges. The walkout spread up and down the West Coast.

Two days into the longshoremen's strike, the Seattle sailors sent Harry Lundeberg, the head of their local SUP strike committee, to meet with Bridges and the San Francisco local of the ILA. Harry Lundeberg was similar in some ways to Andrew Fureseth: Norwegian born, a seaman from age fourteen, at thirty-three ready for full-time union work. But there the two diverged. Lundeberg favored economic action over legislative reform and saw strikes as critical to improving the seamen's working conditions. His background had a pink cast; he had belonged to Norwegian, British, and Spanish unions. He transferred from the Australian Seamen's Union to the SUP and was reported to have joined the anarchy-favoring Industrial Workers of the World (IWW)— the "Wobblies."

The ILA strike gained little, except that it ended use of the company union "fink books." One wonders how the union rank and file in their tavern discussions used the acronyms—LAS, ILWU, ILA, SUP, ISU, IWW. Did they have their own terms for the scrapping organizations? Favorable or demeaning? Were the men hopeful of achieving fair treatment, or resigned to a dismal future at the hands of their political warriors?

The shipping companies remained headstrong. Lundeberg returned to Seattle, but not before he had impressed Harry Bridges with his militancy. Bridges saw Lundeberg as the means to stir up the SUP now that the elderly Furuseth was on the way out. Lundeberg became port agent in Seattle and Bridges nominated him for head of the new Maritime Federation of the Pacific. He won that election and used his position to shake up the SUP leadership. In 1935 the SUP rank and file elected him to its highest post, secretary-treasurer.

The SUP was still an affiliate of the crusty International Seamen's Union, which grew alarmed at the militancy of Lundeberg and others like him. The two groups split apart in 1936 and Lundeberg's SUP drifted without allies. He was reluctant to hook up with Bridges's ILWU. Harry Bridges was unaware that behind Lundeberg's truculent attitude toward the ILWU was dislike of Communists, of their methods, and of their cause. As leader of the independent SUP, Lundeberg began to advocate what he called "bread and butter unionism"— quick and incisive job actions to confront employers. This was a turnabout from the rabble-rousing approach of the Communists. The SUP membership liked Lundeberg as they had liked no one before him—not even Andrew Furuseth, the man who freed them from their bonds. Lundeberg was a strongman among common men, an abstemious but colorful individual who gambled heartily and swore like a dockhand. He always wore open-collared shirts, black dungarees, and, indoors or out, a flat gray cap that became his trademark. After his rise to leadership, the flat cap—gray for longshoremen, white for seamen—became part of the uniform of West Coast maritime workers.

In July 1935, Roosevelt signed the Wagner Act, establishing the National Labor Relations Board (NLRB) to oversee collective bargaining and ensure that it was properly administered. The following spring a wildcat strike on the East Coast led to the formation of the National Maritime Union (NMU). Atlantic and Gulf coast sailors were disillusioned by the racist ISU and through the new NMU compelled and won elections on those coasts to replace the ISU as their bargaining agent. The NMU was organized with CIO support in May 1937. The clouds of Communism swirled eastward. In September the NLRB ordered elections to determine representatives for collective bargaining with eighty-seven steamship companies on 756 vessels on the Atlantic and Gulf coasts. The NMU won by a large margin, and in November it signed its first contract with the Black Diamond Steamship Corporation.

Throughout the period of labor unrest ashore, lax shipboard operations remained unpoliced by many operating companies. It took the worst American peacetime tragedy of the century to instigate change, and then dreadfully slowly. On Thursday, September 6, 1934, the Ward Line's cruise ship *Morro Castle* departed from Havana, returning to New York to complete its 174th round trip. (The Ward Line, founded before the Civil War, was part of the Atlantic, Gulf & West Indies Steamship Lines [AGWI], and at the time was in financial difficulty.) Sixty-two years later the mystery of that voyage continues to unfold. On Friday night after dinner, complaining of indigestion, the portly captain, Robert Wilmott, retired to his stateroom and died, apparently of a heart attack. He was found dead by Chief Mate William F. Warms around nine o'clock, and Warms took command as acting captain.

During the subsequent mid-watch, a fire broke out in the *Morro Castle*'s writing room on the port side, forward of the midships passenger lounge. It was reported to the bridge by a night watchman at a quarter of three, and the second mate, Clarence Hackney, went to examine the situation. As flames spread to the walls and ceiling, the mate tried to fight them with a fire extinguisher. Ten minutes later he returned to the bridge to ask for water in the fire mains and a sounding of the general alarm. Believing that the fire could be contained, the acting captain waited another ten minutes before arousing the passengers with the alarm. While flames spread rapidly through the superstructure, doors and windows to the promenade deck were opened to clear the air. Smoke from the boat deck was sucked through the ventilating system into the engine room. Fearing they would choke to death, men on duty below shut down and abandoned the machinery spaces, while Chief Engineer Eban Abbott headed for the bridge and then for the lifeboats. Light and power were lost below decks, the water mains lost pressure, and the steering engine failed. The captain ordered an SOS to be sent at 3:15 A.M., and at 3:23 A.M., standard time, it went on the air. The ship was steaming through strong wind and heavy rain off the coast of New Jersey, headed for its scheduled docking the next day in Manhattan. Many of the 318 passengers were seasick or inebriated from what was meant to be their last night of revelry before landing. The wind had been on the starboard quarter and as the ship, without steerage, turned into it, the fire raged aft on the port side. Throughout the midships section, wooden stairwells and draperies burst into flames.

Several ships in the area heard the SOS and altered course to steam at full speed toward the disaster site. The cruise ships *Monarch of Bermuda* and *City of Savannah* headed south from Ambrose Light; the freighter *Andrea S. Luckenbach,* seven miles to the east, was attracted by the sight of the blaze; the liner *President Cleveland* hastened north. The scene was one of confusion and horror as dawn broke on Saturday morning and the rescue ships converged. They found the *Morro Castle* anchored off Shark River Inlet with smoke billowing from its housing fore and aft, surrounded by lifeboats, Coast Guard picketboats, desperate swimmers, and dead floating bodies. Four of the *Morro Castle*'s lifeboats had been launched successfully, six others were inaccessible. Dozens of passengers, trapped by the flames, jumped through the darkness into the water. Some were able to slide down ropes, others were pushed into the boats or into the sea. Many were injured, some left to die. Ninety-four passengers and 43 crewmen were lost. Of those saved—224 passengers and 189 crew—many spent hours in the water before rescue. At least five couples jumped together

13-1. *Morro Castle* survivors approaching *Monarch of Bermuda*. SSHSA COLLECTION, UNIVERSITY OF BALTIMORE LIBRARY

from the rails; two couples arrived exhausted on the Jersey shore; rescue boats picked up another pair; and two wives, before being saved, watched their husbands drown.

On Saturday night a Coast Guard cutter and two tugs attempted to tow the burning hulk toward Sandy Hook, but it broke away in heavy seas and stranded broadside, near the Asbury Beach convention hall. Thousands gathered on the boardwalk to stare at the abandoned vessel, fire still visible within, smoke streaming from the portholes even three days after the tragedy.

Accusations, recriminations, and denials clouded the testimony given during the subsequent investigation. Andrew Furuseth, called as an expert witness, said the fire was inexcusable. Both the Ward Line and the Steamboat Inspection Service were blamed. The federal government was found to have a larger financial interest than the Ward Line in the vessel. The crew was both commended and castigated. The acting captain and the chief engineer were convicted of negligence, but their convictions later were set aside by a federal appeals court.

Communists were blamed for plotting to stop the flow of arms listed on the manifest as "sporting goods," thought to be part of cargo kept for Cuba in a floating arsenal. Evidence withheld until 1996 suggests the fire was started by

13-2. *Morro Castle* off Asbury Beach, the day after the fire. SSHSA COLLECTION, UNIVER-
SITY OF BALTIMORE LIBRARY

a mentally unstable radio operator who had been planted aboard in an arson-for-insurance plot that went awry. The FBI suspected the man within a week of the tragedy, but then claimed that nothing had been found to justify an investigation. Two years later the radioman, George Rogers, was working for the Bayonne Police Department when he confided to one of the lieutenants that he had started the fire with an exploding fountain pen placed in a writing room locker. Regretting his disclosure, he sent a package to the police lieutenant that exploded and almost killed him. For that, Rogers was found guilty of attempted murder and sent to prison. Then, appallingly, his sentence was commuted so that he could serve as radioman on a supply ship during World War II. Discharged for cause from that assignment, he got a job in a defense plant. He was later convicted of murder in the bludgeoning death of two neighbors. Given life imprisonment, he died in 1958 while in Trenton State Prison, allegedly of a brain hemorrhage. High-level government officials, aware of the shunting-about of this pathological killer, remained aloof from the continuing cover-up of Rogers's records. Questions remain, particularly about who may have conspired with Rogers before and after the tragedy of the *Morro Castle*. If there were others involved, what did they intend to accomplish? Why the sustained government cover-up, which lasted more than sixty years? The *Morro Castle* story is not yet at its end.

After the *Titanic* tragedy Congress had called for a meeting to set international standards of safety, winning the immediate support of the British government. Regulations for lifesaving equipment and regular drills for passengers and crews were drawn up in the first Safety of Life at Sea (SOLAS) Convention of 1914, but never were ratified because of World War I. American ratification of the agreement was almost blocked by the ISU and the ultraconservative Andrew Furuseth. It took seven years for Congress to overcome labor's resistance; in 1936, convinced by the *Morro Castle* disaster, it finally ratified the 1929 regulations. Out of the disaster came long overdue laws on fire safety devices and a lasting memory of an avoidable tragedy. The new laws called for nothing not already known when the *Morro Castle* sailed. The Fall River Line, the originator of the seagoing steam whistle, had installed similar equipment on its ships for decades and regularly drilled crews in its use.

The glamour of the great ocean liners remained in European hands. In 1935 Harold K. Hales, a member of Parliament, offered a silver cup as the trophy for record-breaking Atlantic crossings—the first material "Blue Riband." The first recipient that year was the Italian liner *Rex.* Then in June the elegant French liner *Normandie,* on its maiden voyage, broke all records by crossing from Bishop Rock to Ambrose Light in four days, three hours, and two minutes. It wasn't long before Cunard's *Queen Mary* became the fastest liner, but holding common sense and safety regulations above speed, Cunard refused the award.

The Great Depression continued. Roosevelt's Works Progress Administration sought ways to put the unemployed into productive, government-sponsored work. Hundreds of jobless schoolteachers, accountants, and bookkeepers were given pencils, forms, hand-operated mechanical calculators, and a set of formulas. Their task was to work out the complex trigonometry involved with sextant observations of celestial bodies for every minute of latitude, every minute of longitude, and every minute of altitude—thousands upon thousands of calculations to be recorded, verified, and tabulated. The result was Hydrographic Office Publication No. 214: nine books of tables of precomputed altitudes and azimuths. Each book covered 10 degrees of latitude. No longer would navigators need to undertake the tedious work of finding a line of position by computing bearing and distance from an estimated position. An hour's work, fraught with possibilities for error, was reduced to the few minutes needed to find the solution in a table.

Again Congress studied the lagging state of commerce and defense. This time it came up with the most enduring legislation of the century. On June 29, Roosevelt signed the Merchant Marine Act of 1936, abolishing the Shipping Board Bureau and creating an independent agency, the U.S. Maritime Commission (MarComm). MarComm was authorized to regulate American ocean commerce, supervise freight and terminal facilities, and administer government funds for the construction and operation of commercial vessels. Any American company that was three-quarters owned by American citizens could apply for financial assistance in having new ships built in American yards. If a ship was put in what MarComm defined as service essential to foreign trade, a "construction differential subsidy" would be paid, based on the difference between the potential costs of foreign and home construction. Operating companies were offered twenty-year loans amounting to 75 percent of a vessel's purchase price. Aboard ship, tighter licensing requirements were specified, the three-watch system established for all departments, and specifications set for more comfortable crew quarters. Subsidized freighters were required to have fully American crews, passenger ships 90 percent American—(Filipino and European stewards held greater appeal for paying passengers). To modernize and keep the merchant marine efficient for national defense, ships constructed and operated under the American flag were to be ready for conversion to naval auxiliaries. Further, the 1936 act provided funds to support the training of officers for manning such vessels.

The shipyard labor force was down to twenty thousand workers. There were no more than ten yards that could build ships longer than four hundred feet, and half of the forty-six slipways were tied up in naval contracts. During the fifteen years from 1922 to 1937, only two dry cargo ships, a few tankers, and twenty-nine subsidized passenger ships were built. Roosevelt appointed Joseph P. Kennedy as first head of the Maritime Commission in 1937. Kennedy was quick to recognize the end of a failed era, stating that in twenty years the U.S. government had spent $3.8 billion on *not* getting a healthy merchant marine. He proposed a ten-year program to construct five hundred ships, and soon after, his eyes on loftier political assignments, he departed from the agency. His replacement was a commission member, Rear Admiral Emory S. Land, who moved to get congressional authority to build 150 vessels as soon as contracts could be written.

In March 1938 MarComm established the Cadet Corps and assumed the responsibility of selecting and training men through assignments aboard subsidized merchant ships. Richard R. McNulty, a captain (later rear admiral) in the Naval Reserve, was named as first supervisor of the corps, a post he held for twelve years. A graduate of the Massachusetts Nautical School, McNulty was charged with establishing a competitive selection process for formal schools to be located on the three coasts. Within a year, and with little more base of operations than was afforded by the ships they traveled on, more than two hundred cadet-trainees were working toward licensed positions on federally funded merchant ships.

In 1938 Emory Land started an ambitious shipbuilding program based on MarComm standardized designs. Classifications were developed by length and deadweight tonnage categories, identified as P- for passenger carriers, T- for tankers, and C- for cargo ships; C-1, C-2, and C-3 for ships of seventy-two hundred, nine thousand, and twelve thousand tons. Equipped with steam turbines, the new ships would be sleek, fast, and economical in fuel consumption. Contracts were put out at once for the first hundred ships, and a fresh breeze blew through the rusty and faltering merchant fleet. *America* was commissioned in 1940 as the new flagship of United States Lines. After a series of money-losing crossings, the oversized *Leviathan* had been given a four-year rest at a pier in Hoboken, then aroused for a final trip to the scrapyard, to be replaced by the elegant, new *America*. The passenger liner operators ignored the threat of competition from the new passenger airlines, which began trans-atlantic flights in 1937. High-speed ocean liners had captured the day with telephones in every cabin, service in superb continental style, shuffleboard and badminton courts, and a dazzling passenger list assured on every voyage.

Also little noticed but of major importance was a device that the navy was experimenting with, first developed in England. In 1938 the English were using bedspring-shaped antennas on masts placed along the coast to broadcast microwaves, radio beams reflected by large objects in the Channel, the return signals captured for display on cathode ray tubes. Both the British and American navies saw shipboard applications for radar, but kept the idea to themselves during its early years of development.

In 1939 the C & D Canal became a fully usable two-way passage for steamships, completing the inland connection from Philadelphia and Camden to Baltimore, Norfolk, and Newport News—a long, safe route protected from the rigors of the Atlantic. The significance of that protection was appreciated when the new war, which began in September, spread to the American coasts. Before then, to the American people the war was just another European affair; a roman numeral had not yet been appended to its name.

In a horrifying replay of history, England suffered heavily from German U-boat attacks, losing 150 ships, totaling one million tons, in the first year. Unable to replace its ships as fast as they were sunk, the British Admiralty looked to the United States. American shipyards had doubled their capacity. The United States was able to produce two hundred ships per year for its own purposes. The Admiralty asked the Maritime Commission to build twenty ships modeled on England's economical coastwise coal-burners. Emory Land was not interested in the production of plodding ships based on World War I designs for a country facing destruction, preferring to advance his own agenda. He called in the respected William Francis Gibbs to consult.

"You don't need them," Gibbs told the Admiralty representatives with a touch of sarcasm after studying their plans. "If you are that near winning the war you have no need for them." Instead, he proposed the design of a new freighter of ten thousand tons, with 2,500-horsepower reciprocating engines to achieve a standard eleven-knot speed, the hull built along classical, blunt-bowed lines. The English liked the idea and requested that thirty-two be built for them in American yards. But rather than start with fresh blueprints, Admiral Land wanted to implement the MarComm-designed C-ships which were better suited to proven American mass-production techniques.

Negotiations continued and a compromise was achieved on a simplified design. The ships would displace only 7,157 tons and would be welded rather than riveted for faster construction. The United States agreed to mass-produce sixty newly designed Ocean-class ships for Great Britain's account. The negotiators unknowingly had sown the seeds of renewal for the American merchant marine. The United States would blossom once more into a world maritime power.

Chapter 14

SAILING ON FRIDAY: 1940–1945

When the United States agreed to supply the British Admiralty with the requested sixty Ocean-class cargo carriers, there existed no organization better qualified to accomplish the work than that of Henry J. Kaiser. Kaiser's innovation and relentless drive spurred MarComm's slow-growing shipbuilding program to overcome daunting obstacles and ultimately to set new records. He shied from nothing to get a job done and done well.

The son of German immigrants, Kaiser had a humble beginning that was soon transcended in a series of increasingly successful ventures. While still in his twenties, after a period as a photographic supplies salesman, he opened a photography shop in Lake Placid, New York. Soon he added branches in Daytona Beach, Miami, and Nassau—the resorts of the wealthy. The Pacific Northwest attracted him as a land of greater opportunity, and at age thirty he sold his business to join a construction company in the state of Washington as manager of paving contracts. Two years later, in 1914, he founded Henry J. Kaiser, Ltd., the first of several construction companies. In 1921 he moved his headquarters to Oakland, California, where he would base his wide-ranging operations for the rest of his life. The year 1927 was a turning point for Kaiser. The nation was in a period of prosperity when he landed a contract to build two hundred miles of highways in Cuba. He could well have spurned the challenge, which involved delivering materials across the water to a country whose language he couldn't speak, then directing untrained labor in cutting paths through mountainous tropical jungle. Instead he took it on, and while businesses at home began to collapse with the advent of the Great Depression, Kaiser learned how to build teams of people capable of managing immense projects. As the depression worsened Kaiser was building levees on the Mississippi. In 1931 he founded Six Companies, Inc., to take part in the construction of the Boulder (Hoover) Dam. In 1933 he formed a new affiliate, Bridge Builders, Inc., poised to build the piers for the newly planned San Francisco–Oakland Bay bridge; that company later built the Grand Coulee Dam. Nothing stopped Kaiser. If he couldn't get suppliers to deliver what he needed, he would form a company to do it. Thus was born the Permanente Cement Corporation, the Permanente Metals Corporation, and the Kaiser-Permanente holding company.

The British request for sixty ships was on the desk of the Maritime Commission, and Kaiser joined with John David Reilly of Todd Shipyards in Oregon to win the bid. They built two yards in Portland, Maine, and completed the work in record time. Kaiser knew nothing about shipbuilding—never did he learn to refer to the bow and stern of a ship as anything but the front and back ends—but he was a master at assembling and organizing the people who did. He was a genial man, heavy-set, jowly. Looking as much like a baker or bartender as a business executive, he was approachable and easy to talk to. Yet when irritated he could spiel off a stream of epithets to make a stevedore's head turn. It is worth noting that this was the man who after the war would pave Waikiki Beach with hotels, develop and sell a compact car before its time, and introduce his workers to the new concept of managed health care.

In January 1941 Roosevelt felt the pulse of a worried American public and advocated a new shipbuilding program to support war-ravaged England. In February he announced plans to mass-produce an emergency fleet of two hundred vessels of the new E-C class, ugly ducklings he described as "dreadful-looking objects." The construction of the long-planned MarComm C-ships was deferred. Rapid delivery of the Ocean-class vessels took higher priority, followed by the E-Cs, modeled closely on the Oceans. The first ship, *Ocean Vanguard,* was launched in one of Kaiser's New England shipbuilding yards nine months later, seven months after keel-laying. The company's construction pace quickened with experience as it turned out more ships from more yards. As Kaiser completed delivery of the Ocean-class vessels that had been contracted to him, he turned his attention to the emergency fleet. By now he had seven West Coast shipyards, located in California, Oregon, and Washington.

14-1. First Liberty, SS *Patrick Henry* at launching. NATIONAL ARCHIVES

Admiral Land had a change of heart on his C-ship agenda. The first of the new all-American-class freighters was launched in Baltimore on September 27, 1941. To overcome the stigma created by FDR's reference to "dreadful-looking objects," Land took a cue from the ship's name, *Patrick Henry,* and announced the E-C as the first of a new Liberty Fleet. Thirteen sister ships were launched across the nation on the same day, which was named Liberty Fleet Day. Coincidentally, the event highlighted the rebirth of the United States as a maritime power. It took place on the eighty-seventh anniversary of the loss of the *Arctic,* the day that marked the downturn of America's maritime fortunes. Speaking of the "ugly duckling" freighters, President Roosevelt in an increasingly bellicose statement proposed that "these ships shall sail the seas as intended, and to the best of our ability [we] shall protect them from torpedoes, bombs, or shells." He had already moved the Atlantic sea frontier to the longitude of Iceland, where a contingent of U.S. Marines were debarked. On November 13 he amended the Neutrality Law to permit a return to the World War I practice of arming merchant ships. Because the nation remained leery of involvement in another European conflict, the change was undertaken slowly and without publicity. Two months later the desperate need for rearmament became clear.

The 1936 Merchant Marine Act improved the quality of the seaman's life, but jobs were hard to find during the worldwide depression. Joe Curran's CIO-affiliated National Maritime Union became dominated by Communists. On the West Coast the Seafarers' International Union (SIU) had formed, a confederation of small unions of mixed interests: fishermen, cannery and warehouse workers, and the sailors of the SUP. In 1938 Harry Lundeberg, needing an alliance for the SUP but wary of joining with Curran or his former advocate, the radical Harry Bridges, convinced the AFL to replace the disgraced International Seamen's Union with the SIU. It was a good move, as the SUP, headed by Lundeberg, dominated the group. Maritime labor coalesced into two major groups: the CIO's NMU on the East and Gulf Coasts, and the AFL's white-capped SIU on the West Coast. However, the mergers didn't bring appeasement. The union leaders continued brawling among themselves and threatening walkouts. Only a shipping boom could cause them to settle down with any degree of satisfaction.

Mariners took whatever jobs they could find. Once acquired, a billet could be retained for as long as the ship continued in operation if the seaman signed on for the next voyage immediately after being paid off for the completed one. (Fink books had not been abolished, but companies used them less than in the past.) Older seamen, though not always in the best physical shape, relinquished their positions only for urgent reasons of health or if a rare opportunity for something better beckoned. In the absence of suitable jobs, men with able-bodied seamen's papers were forced to work as ordinaries; third and second mates served as bosuns. Deck officers sailed two or three grades below their licenses. The situation was no different in the engine room. The men accepted reduced status in return for steady work, reasonable pay, and a chance to put money aside. A seaman's base wage in 1941 was somewhat lower than that for equivalent labor ashore, but with overtime pay, housing, and meals provided, the seaman was better off financially. Life aboard, except for the routine rigors of the sea, was comfortable, thanks to union efforts and the provisions of the Merchant Marine Act. Accommodations were clean and tight. Shipboard fare was bland and plentiful. A man could walk proudly down the gangway, fully employed with money in his pocket, and that was a blessing in those depressed times.

Under the three-watch system the four-to-eight bridge watch fell to the second mate who, by custom, was also the navigator. Star sights were taken at dawn and dusk. The morning and evening watches fitted well into the navigator's daily routine, which consisted of a quiet pre-sunrise period before the day workers roused out, free time during daylight hours, brief relief by a junior officer during the dog watches for the dinner meal, and an eight-hour rest as the ship settled down for the night. Such was the case until the U-boats converged.

Soon after the United States entered the war, Germany replayed its reaction to the American entry into World War I by sending U-boat patrols to the American East Coast. Tragically, the U.S. merchant fleet, Navy, Coast Guard, and shore facilities all were unprepared for the offensive. Lightships continued to mark the seaboard with their signals. In the first weeks of the war, vessels steamed nightly on coastal routes with navigation lights showing. For months, no blackout obscured the shore. The glow of street lights, hotels, and beach traffic provided an ideal background for prowling submarines to sight passing ships in silhouette. The submarines rarely engaged in twilight action. They lurked on the surface under cover of darkness, then submerged at daybreak to track their targets by periscope. A ship was most likely to be attacked while the navigator was off duty. Prudent navigators slept in their clothes with a life jacket nearby and made frequent updates to notes on the ship's position for passing to the skipper and radio operator. Most U-boat attacks came in darkness. The third mate stood the deadly twelve-to-four watch, with little to do but stare at the sea for signs of imminent attack—black waters sliced by a spine-chilling streak of green phosphorescence. With luck, he would make the sighting in time for evasive action. A daylight surface attack was likely to come from the sun's direction. Afternoons were spent in weary scanning for a periscope piercing the glare. Once a sub was in firing range, it could surface and man its guns in three to five minutes, and an unarmed freighter was helpless in the event. Two or three well-placed shells at the waterline were enough to send the impotent victim to the bottom.

The uneasy quiet of the mid-watch would be blasted apart by a bone-shaking explosion. Wreckage flew into the air, steam pipes burst, fires broke out, heavy smoke billowed across the decks, and lifeboats in their chocks were damaged by the upward blast. With luck the radio operator might get off a signal: SSS ("attacked by submarine"), followed by SOS and the ship's position. Hanging on the key until his messages were acknowledged, he had little time to save his own life. The skipper had to assess the situation quickly, sometimes within three or four minutes while staggering on a steeply sloping deck. He had to stuff codebooks and wartime manifests into a weighted bag to be deep-sixed, impose order on the men at the boat stations, and see to the rescue of those injured in the wreckage before issuing the final order to abandon. Men in their bunks grabbed clothing and life jackets, forsook their personal effects, and rushed to stations to start launching. In theory, the boats on either side could accommodate the entire crew unless they had been demolished or their falls jammed. But a steep list of the ship would prohibit the release of boats on the higher side. The men had to launch and depart swiftly from the low side before the ship rolled over in its last minutes afloat.

After a hit, the submarine typically maneuvered on the surface, circling the doomed ship to send off a second strike against its undamaged side. Not until a U-boat captain had noted the identity of his victim and felt confident of a sinking would he leave the scene. If the stern went under before its identity was known, the sub's skipper, casting a searchlight across the water, would approach survivors in their boats or clinging to flotsam and ask for the sinking ship's name and tonnage. No one would be taken aboard the sub's cramped quarters. A few merciful submariners handed down food, water, and navigational directions before heading off in search of their next prey. Survivors were left in the water with their dead companions to await rescue or perish.

Not always did the wrecked ships sink. People died in nearly every attack, but rarely were there no survivors to bring tales of horror ashore. The fates of the *City of Atlanta* and the *Francis E. Powell* were typical of these sinkings in the early days of the war.

In the darkness of the mid-watch on January 19, 1942, the old freighter *City of Atlanta,* 5,269 gross tons, was steaming south inside Wimble Shoals buoy near Cape Hatteras, the gleam of North Carolina's Outer Banks visible to the west. At two in the morning the ship was struck without warning on its port quarter. Thirty-three of the forty-seven-man crew were in their bunks. The detonation demolished the radio shack and darkened the bridge. Three men were killed instantly. The engines stopped and the ship developed a steep port list, preventing the lowering of the starboard lifeboats. Men lined the rails while the skipper came on deck and gave the order to abandon. He was last seen hanging on a rail, trying to overcome the failed launching of the lifeboats. Through the blackness the harsh glare of the U-boat's searchlight raked the sloping deck and hull as the keel lifted from the water, the crew now leaping over the sides into the wintry sea. The second mate was caught between two jammed boats, saved from broken bones by his padded life jacket. Afloat in the choppy water he managed to grab a broken door frame, push away from the sinking ship, and count eighteen men swimming amid the flotsam. An off-duty oiler, weighed down by a sheepskin coat, climbed onto a skylight near the grimy hull as it slipped below the surface. Several sailors hung on to a bench from the crew's quarters, gasping in the icy spray. The sub churned away and left the survivors adrift in the watery darkness. Hours passed as most of them succumbed to the cold, eventually losing their grasp on whatever had kept them afloat. At dawn, twelve miles south of Wimble Shoals, the *Seatrain Texas* came upon three survivors among the wreckage, the second mate and two oilers. No one else lived through the ordeal of more than six hours in the wind-whipped seas.

A week later, off Chincoteague, Virginia, twelve miles southeast of Winter Quarters Lightship, the northbound tanker *Francis E. Powell,* carrying eighty thousand barrels of gasoline and heating oil, was struck on the port side, aft of the midships deckhouse. The time was a quarter to three in the morning, again the deadly mid-watch. A biting rain swept down the coast. The explosion took away the radio antenna, part of the catwalk aft of the housing, and most of the port railing. Almost at once the captain gave the order to abandon ship, and within five minutes three lifeboats were put over. The crew got off into two of them—the third was lost in the melee—but the master reboarded the sinking ship, probably to dispose of the codebooks. Minutes later, the main deck awash, he climbed from an upper deck down a rope to board one of the boats and was crushed between the hull and the surging boat. The men in the boat hauled his broken body aboard as they rowed away, almost colliding with the partially submerged sub. The two boats spent the next seventeen hours in driving rain until a Coast Guard cutter found them near dusk. The skipper and three others were dead, an astonishingly low casualty list for a crew of thirty-one.

In the first three weeks of the American Battle of the Atlantic at least twenty-five ships were sunk off the U.S. coast. Five hundred seamen and civilians died, the toll equal to one sixth of the casualties at Pearl Harbor. There would be many more. On January19, one of the worst nights in that brutal period, three ships went down off Cape Hatteras, almost in sight of each other. The submarines found they had freedom to range the whole coast undisturbed. Five days earlier, a German sub had entered the main channel of New York harbor undetected, its crew aghast at the lights of Manhattan.

Entire seaside communities were devastated by the offshore attacks. In Mathews County, Virginia, many young men were raised to become merchant mariners and Chesapeake Bay pilots. There, tiny Gwynn Island, with a population under seven hundred, counted nineteen sea captains among its fifty-seven men who served the nation in 1942. Of the first sixty-one ships torpedoed in that terrible winter, five were skippered by Gwynn Islanders. On April 10, vacationers at Jacksonville Beach, Florida, flocked to the shore to watch the tanker *Gulfamerica* burn and sink in broad daylight, a ghastly offshore drama that was repeated again and again. By May the raiders had spread their devastation into the Gulf of Mexico and the Passes of the Mississippi. In mid-June two freighters were torpedoed and sunk in full view of thousands of bathers at Virginia Beach, just twenty miles east of the Norfolk Naval Operating Base.

Because of a combination of ignorance, indifference, stubbornness, and scarcity of equipment, little was done to halt the invasion. Few commercial ves-

14-2. SS *Robin Moor,* torpedoed seven months before Germany's declaration of war against the United States. SSHSA COLLECTION, UNIVERSITY OF BALTIMORE LIBRARY

sels were armed, and the primitive radar equipment that existed at the time was the exclusive property of the navy. The desperate ships could count on little military support, yet there had been ample warning of impending trouble. Even while the United States remained neutral, the German undersea fleet had been bristling for action. In May 1941, the *Robin Moor,* displaying the American flag in open waters, had been sunk by a U-boat. The German penetration into British convoys was well known and in fact had been the catalyst for the shipbuilding program.

During the six months ending in July 1942, four hundred ships were lost in the western Atlantic. In *Operation Drumbeat,* Michael Gannon's terrifying litany of suffering sums up the tragedy:

> Most calamitous of all was the toll in human lives, which can be estimated at hardly fewer than 5,000 souls—U.S., British, Norwegian, and other merchant seamen; U.S. and Royal Navy officers and men; and civilian passengers. Whether shot, drowned, scalded, set on fire, frozen, smothered, crushed, starved, or maimed by sharks, they rested now on the bed of the sea.

The American response to the greatest ocean carnage in commercial maritime history was not defense but replacement. The authorities were slow— "reluctant" might be the word—to learn from the experience of their British counterparts. To attack an unseen enemy was difficult, but the nation knew how to build more ships. Surprisingly, most mariners returning from their individual disasters were willing to sign up for another voyage. The American merchant seaman, if he didn't get killed in the process, was a professional survivor.

Escorted convoys improved the delivery of goods along the American coast, but the routes through the Western Approaches and the Barents Sea were tougher because of their proximity to enemy ports. The odyssey of the SS *Carlton* illustrates the will to survive but is perhaps the worst episode in this period. The ship sailed from Philadelphia on Friday the thirteenth in March of 1942.

The *Carlton,* a 5,217-ton freighter built at Hog Island in 1920, got under way with a crew of forty-four and an armed guard of ten navy gunners and a reserve ensign. Steaming unaccompanied to Halifax, Nova Scotia, it was loaded with two hundred tons of TNT, sixteen tanks, and two hundred tons of tank ammunition. Navy men disliked assignments among merchant seamen on rusty old buckets like the *Carlton.* They found the pay differential disturbing, at least on first analysis, reasoning that they took the same seagoing risks as the others and even greater risks while under attack. A navy seaman drew a flat $450 a

14-3. Convoy. NATIONAL ARCHIVES

month; his merchant counterpart drew $100 for a forty-four-hour week plus overtime pay, which was assured at sea. The disparity in base pay was not great; bonuses made the difference. The National Maritime Union had negotiated a $100 monthly bonus for sailing in the Atlantic, plus another $100 for entering any combat area. The equalizers remained invisible: naval enlisted men received government-supplied uniforms, family allowances, life insurance, health care, retirement funding, and continued pay while ashore and on leave. The merchant mariner received no clothing, no insurance, and no pay when not under articles (although full employment was virtually assured in wartime—until the ship went down). Public Health Service hospitals rendered some health care for seamen in port, but medical attention at sea relied on textbook guidance; radio silence prevented any exchanges with shore authorities. Aboard ship, conversations between the uniformed contingent and their civilian counterparts were stilted.

As it traveled north the *Carlton* passed grim signs of the German presence: masts and upended blackened hulks of ships lost in the January attacks. After a period of idleness in Halifax, it departed on May 20 as part of the sixty-five-ship convoy PQ.16, headed for Murmansk, six thousand miles distant. Convoy speed was set at eight knots, the top speed of the slowest vessels. The fleet had a large British escort: five destroyers, four corvettes, four trawlers, a minesweeper, and an antiaircraft ship for a catapult-launched seaplane patrol. In open seas a lone German plane was sighted, circling to spot and report before it departed under a corvette's antiaircraft fire. Five days out of Halifax, eight low-level enemy bombers and nearly two-dozen dive-bombers converged on the convoy. In the confusion of the attack the *Carlton*'s armed guard shot down the convoy's sole aircraft. Three or four bombs were dropped close to the *Carlton*'s hull, on the quarters, midships, and aft, literally lifting the ship in the water. The crew, ordered to stand by the boats, had to make their way through scalding steam billowing from the engine room. The ship came to a halt. Reluctant to abandon, the captain asked for a damage assessment. After some urging, an oiler and a seaman went below to report on the broken steam pipes and take soundings in the leaking shaft alley. Two more detonations shook the ship,

14-4. SS *Tiger*, settled upright on bottom after torpedoing. Mobil Corporation

which now blocked the passage of the following ships in the column. A pair of destroyers approached the beleaguered freighter to sink it rather than delay the convoy. But the *Carlton's* chief engineer estimated that adequate repairs could be made in two hours, and a trawler took the ship in tow toward Iceland. More bickering ensued—there was concern about the state of the explosives in the cargo holds—until the captain forced the reluctant engine crew to go below. Protected by a carrier and a screen of three destroyers that had arrived on the scene, the ship nevertheless had a difficult five-day voyage to Iceland. Oil from a leaking line had become mixed with the potable water supply. Even with naval cover there remained the threat of further attack. Finally, the *Carlton* arrived in Reykjavik, completed its repairs, and waited to join PQ.17, the next convoy. That ill-fated group formed during the first week of June. Most positions had been filled in its nine columns and five ranks; the *Carlton* took the second position in the outboard starboard column, plodding behind the American Liberty *Samuel Chase.* Three rescue ships followed the fifth rank, making thirty-seven vessels in total.

Because the summer solstice was just a few days away, there was no darkness in the high latitudes and the convoy lived in continual exposure to observation and attack. On July 4, north of Bear Island, a blessedly thick sea fog hid the fleet. To avoid collision in near-zero visibility, the ships trailed fog buoys through calm waters. Then, near five o'clock in the morning, General Quarters sounded as a torpedo bomber emerged from a low cloud cover, soon to disappear in the fog. Lookouts on every vessel peered into the murk and waited. Later, gliding silently at thirty feet above the water, a plane approached the starboard flank from the convoy's quarter, aiming directly for the *Samuel Chase.* It released two torpedoes, then gunned its engines to climb out of range. The *Carlton's* chief mate called for a hard left rudder, engine full astern, pulling the bow ten feet short of the torpedo path. The *Carlton* sounded its warning siren as the bomb passed between it and the *Samuel Chase,* heading for the lead vessel in the second column. A gunner in that doomed ship's armed guard shot without effect at the speeding projectile before it blasted into the engine room and destroyed the steering gear, causing the ship to veer out of control. At this point the convoy scattered and the naval cover withdrew westward, leaving the *Carlton* and the other ships in the group utterly unprotected. Of the thirty-four cargo ships in PQ.17, only eleven would arrive at their Russian destination.

The *Carlton* was now without company. At a quarter to ten in the morning, a submerged U-boat aimed a torpedo directly at the solitary ship, and a violent explosion destroyed all but one of the thirty-two-foot lifeboats and four of the life rafts. The hull began shuddering and limping. As the crew abandoned ship they were enveloped in flames from burning fuel oil and a great black mushroom cloud. Another torpedo circled in a wobbly path around the ship, missing the rafts and lifeboat by an oar's length before it expired and sank. At ten-fifty the *Carlton* quietly went down by the bow. The U-boat surfaced to determine the ship's name before taking up the chase of the dispersed PQ.17 fleet. All but three of the freighter's crew survived the attack, some badly burned. The men in the lifeboat started rowing toward Russia with four rafts in tow. At five in the afternoon they gained hope as a German seaplane landed nearby to collect survivors. But the pilot would take only military men—the members of the armed guard. The civilians were left to continue their arduous journey. Five days later—it was now July 10—a British plane flew overhead to drop a rubber lifesaving suit, corned beef, and biscuits, and to promise a rescue. The rescue never came. Two weeks later, separated from its rafts, the lifeboat with seventeen aboard met another U-boat, which gave the men food, blankets, a compass, and directions. Later that day they landed in German-held Norway, not yet free of their curse. In mid-August those not under care for frostbite were put on a German troop-transport to sail with a thousand German troops from Oslo to Denmark.

On the way the transport hit a mine, and the troops, wearing heavy uniforms and fearful of the water, started to panic. The experienced Americans took charge of the evacuation, holding back those who foolishly attempted to jump overboard until rafts and flotation equipment could be put in place. The ship lost only six men in the accident, thanks to the heroic efforts of the American mariners. The worst of the ordeal was over for those who had sailed on Friday the thirteenth. They spent the rest of the war in a prison camp near Bremen, Germany.

The shipyard revival, started three years before the United States entered the war, was not strong enough to meet the initial wartime demands. The industry was torn between salvage, conversions, and new ship construction. Attempts were made to save most of the damaged vessels that had managed to stay afloat along the American and Canadian coasts and even those that had sunk in water no deeper than the height of their wreckage. But the cruel sea prevailed over some of the most valiant salvage efforts.

A large convoy left New York early in November 1942 and was attacked off the Newfoundland coast before dawn on its tenth day at sea. The twenty-one-year-old tanker *Brilliant* took a torpedo on the starboard side, just abaft the forward bridge. The cargo caught fire at once. The crew were forced to lower the boats even before the ship could slow down. Flames licked at their clothing and

14-5. Torpedoed and shelled, this tanker made it to port. NATIONAL ARCHIVES

14-6. Firefighting after a torpedoing. Note the ladder, railings, and steel plating, twisted and bent by the bomb's concussion. NATIONAL ARCHIVES

spread along the decks, and a wall of smoke and fire leapt higher than the top-mast. Junior Third Mate James Cameron was on duty on the bridge. The captain sent him to gather up cigarettes and equipment for the lifeboat. The remainder of the convoy continued to steam past the stricken ship while the young officer paused to secure the general alarm, respond to a call coming from the engine room, and collect the sextant and charts. Then he and others who had come to his aid rallied to put out the fire and succeeded. In the ensuing confusion the men got separated and the boats left without those who had quelled the fire. Before the *Brilliant* could rejoin the convoy, Cameron got orders from an escorting corvette to steer on a prescribed course for Saint John's. When things settled down, Cameron found that he was the only deck officer remaining aboard. By default he was in command of the severely crippled ship on this, his first voyage as an officer on the third mate's license he had recently acquired. Taking a head count he identified the men he could call upon as watch officers: the navy gunnery officer, the bosun, and the chief steward. It was perhaps the first time in history that a man who had signed articles as chief steward found himself as an officer in charge of a watch. The four had little idea how to handle the ship with its buckled plates and twisted catwalk, vibrating excessively as the seas began to rise; they had no choice but to push onward. Three days after separating from the convoy, with further direction from some navy ships they had encountered, they approached the coast of Newfoundland. The skipper of an auxiliary schooner carrying a load of hay, seeing their evident distress, took them under his guidance into Goose Bay. After a day at anchor they got the ship under way, and with an escort headed for Saint John's in search of a dockyard. There the shipowner, Standard Oil, replaced the *Brilliant*'s deck officers and promoted Cameron to third mate. But the ordeal had not ended.

The port lacked adequate facilities for repair, and after the debris was removed and some bulkhead braces welded in place, the owners arranged to send the ship to Halifax, six hundred miles distant, in a six-ship convoy. As the ships moved out, falling snow and gale-force winds surrounded them and the new captain wisely decided to return to port. Several weeks passed before conditions improved, and finally, two months after the torpedoing, the *Brilliant* once again headed out of Saint John's, accompanied by a Canadian destroyer and British naval tug. They had reached open, unprotected waters when the wind picked up and the seas ran high from the west and pounded at the tanker's damaged side. The torn bulkheads began to break, the forward section twisted into a new position, and the ship screeched in agony. Unable either to remain in the open sea or to reach the safety of port, the captain slowed the vessel and informed the escort that his ship was in danger of breaking in two. Several of the

14-7. Stern section, SS *Brilliant,* broken off in winter storm. MOBIL CORPORATION

men went aft along the contorted catwalk, gaining the safety of the poop before the main deck buckled in the middle and dropped into the sea. The captain, chief mate, and Third Mate Cameron were isolated on the forward section as it broke away and started to submerge. They and four others were last seen clinging to the gun turret on the port side of the bridge before the separated section slipped with them below the surface. The rest of the crew, thirty-two in number including two of Cameron's former watch officers, were marooned on the floating remains, which listed to starboard at 45 degrees. They were separated from the escort and had no radio contact, limited power, and a compass that operated with a large but unknown error. The one remaining lifeboat was swamped, hanging against the port side. Electricity failed and returned intermittently. The temperature dropped. Ice covered the decks and railings, and the lifeboat was filled with a solid cake of ice. For four days the hulk wallowed in the sea until a bomber, sent from Argentia in search of survivors, found it and signaled that aid would be sent. The next day a Canadian minesweeper and the tug that had originally accompanied them out of Saint John's came alongside and took off the *Brilliant's* weary and frozen crew. The abandoned hulk drifted for a hundred miles and sank when an attempt was made to take it in tow. Third Mate James Cameron, who had gone without sleep for four days in what was his first and only command, who was lost a month later with the bow of the *Brilliant,* was posthumously awarded the Merchant Marine Distinguished Service Medal.

Matson's flagship *Lurline,* which provided passenger service out of Hawaii, was three days from its San Francisco destination at the time of the attack on Pearl Harbor. Built in the Bethlehem Steel Yard at Quincy, Massachusetts, the *Lurline* would have returned there for refurbishing, had time permitted. Instead, after the debarkation of its last civilian passengers the army took it over for conversion in a Pacific yard. Before the year's end Matson also turned over the liners *Matsonia* and *Mariposa,* continuing to operate all three for the army. In Manhattan, the navy took the two-year-old *America* for similar duty. The navy also requisitioned the idle sixty-five-thousand-ton French liner *Normandie* and started work to convert it. The Matson vessels retained their names as army transports, but *America* and *Normandie* became, respectively, the USS *West Point* and the USS *Lafayette.* The *Lurline* did return to Quincy after the war.

The *Lafayette* (ex *Normandie*) caught fire on a wintry February day in 1942 while berthed on New York's North River at Pier 88, famous as the dock of the glamorous European liners. The New York Fire Department, afraid that the flames would spread into the city, insisted on pouring water on the vessel. Equally worried that the ship would capsize in its berth, naval officials pleaded with Mayor La Guardia to order the fire department to desist. But who would be responsible for any subsequent damage to the city? Feisty La Guardia called President Roosevelt and asked him to assign responsibility to the navy. The president refused. The mayor, a firefighting buff, backed his chief and told him to put the fire out. In the course of the firefighting effort tons of water filled the ship to its waterline, and the great liner rolled over in its berth nearly 80 degrees into icy water. The public witnessed it all—the squabbling, the firefighting, the loss of the famous liner, and the suspicion-charged inquiries that followed. The cause of the fire was never determined conclusively. In the hysteria of the war some suspected sabotage. A more likely cause was the conversion work under way aboard the ship.

The merchant fleet's rebirth was not without its birth pangs. The amended Neutrality Act gave inadequate lead time for arming the fleet before the U-boats arrived in the western Atlantic. Even when ships were armed, they carried nothing more powerful than single four- or six-inch guns mounted in tubs fore and aft, and perhaps a pair of antiaircraft guns on the bridge. Merchant mariners, fresh from training, climbed the gangways of new ships to find them sparsely equipped. Fire detection equipment, emergency diesel generators, radio direction finders, and lifeboat radios were all missing. The Liberty bridge structures included a wired gyro room—without gyrocompass. Mechanical lifeboat davits of older design required three or more men at cranks to lift and swing the boats over the side. Radar was rare on merchant ships throughout the war, installed toward the end on the newer C-2s and Victorys. There were a few improvements over older ships—running water in the officers' staterooms, steel plating in lieu of canvas dodgers on the bridge, access ladders into the holds separate from the hatches, an after emergency steering station. The replacement of chain railings on deck with steel bulwarks was a mixed blessing: decks remained dryer at sea, but it took longer to get rafts and crew over the side in an emergency. After a long struggle for approval that started in 1902, kapok became the officially sanctioned life jacket filler, replacing the sometimes deadly cork boards that had been in use for more than a century.

14-8. The Liberty *Valerie Chkalov*, bow snapped off in an Arctic storm. The two sections were towed to Canada and rejoined. The repaired ship was renamed *Alexander Baranoff* to sail for the American Mail Line out of Seattle. NATIONAL ARCHIVES

The Libertys had an early reputation for being slow; at eleven knots they were some five knots short of the theoretical standard speed of the deferred MarComm vessels. They were uncomfortable, having a tendency when light to roll violently in a seaway. More important, they were cheaply built and unsafe. The wooden booms on the first 122 ships split under moderate loads. Propellers often fell off, and the hulls were given to cracking. During a period of metal shortage some sailed with only one anchor. Marine engineers who had long since turned their backs on reciprocating steam engines had to relearn the operation of the older up-and-down drives because the engines were available, along with an ample supply of replacement parts. Most of the problems encountered in the Liberty ships were due to fixable design flaws and were quickly corrected. The wooden booms were replaced with lightweight, cold-rolled tubes; unstrengthened square hatch coamings, a common source of cracking, were stiffened, and the accommodation ladder opening in the sheer strake was closed. Light vessels were reballasted to lessen their crankiness without reduction of cargo space. It was determined that the propeller losses resulted from hasty mass-production methods: the bronze blades had been fitted too loosely to the steel shafts. A tighter fit eliminated the problem. Most troubling was the cracking of welded hull plates, a problem which persisted through much of the war. Some ships broke in two and sunk quickly. Some severed neatly at the forward engine-room bulkhead, the two sections eerily remaining afloat and upright as they drifted apart. Ships would ride a high wave with their ends quivering, then as cracks ran down the sides would break in two like a calving iceberg. Constance Tipper, a British metallurgist, identified the problem as metal fatigue from deep cold. The Kaiser-built vessels from his North Pacific yard were among the most affected. At issue was the modern technique of welding, which was faster and more economical than riveting. The plates of a riveted hull shift slightly in rough seas no matter how tight the seams. But properly welded plates function as a single piece, the seams stronger than the rest of the metal. In freezing temperatures, Tipper pointed out, some seams became as brittle as glass, with a similarly narrow range of elasticity, then broke under stress with a resounding crack. Nearly 10 percent of the Libertys built developed metal splits, one third of those showing major fractures. The use of tougher steel at the stress points, riveted strapping along decks and gunwales, reinforced hatches, and additional girders in the holds reduced the problem.

The preventive measures did not overcome a difficulty that stemmed from mass production. Riveting was a two- or three-man job: one man stood behind the plates buttressing the rivet, one faced him with a rivet gun, and usually a third passed hot rivets from a bucket. The same length of seam could be closed faster by one man with a welder's arc. The giant Bethlehem Steel Yard on Chesapeake Bay, producer of hundreds of Libertys, offered bonuses for fast work. One measure of the length of welds produced on a shift was the number of welding rods consumed. Workers found they could produce finished-looking seams faster by laying loose rods along them, then melting them with the torch to a superficial fuse. More rods were consumed and the resultant seams looked like normal welds, the surface of the plates' edges fused to the adjacent rod, while the seam itself had little strength. Upon discovery, faulty seams led to civil suits, and some workers were convicted of deliberately producing defective welding. The trials deterred the practice, a sad contingency when human lives hung in the balance.

Thousands upon thousands of shipyard workers—both men and women—gave heroic service. (A popular song at the time praised "Rosie, the Riveter.") Kaiser hired workers from the inland states. Twenty-five percent of them had never seen the ocean, and fewer than 1 percent had ever been in a shipyard. With a salute to the memory of Charles Schwab, ships again were built by the mile and at record-breaking speed. Sometimes they were assembled in dry basins to be flooded at "launch" time, the hulls floated to open water for fitting out. From the seven-month construction cycle of the first Ocean-class ships, Kaiser steadily reduced his delivery time by refining his mass-production techniques. It had taken him150 days to launch the first Liberty hull at the Bethlehem-Fairfield Yard, 95 more to fit it out, and 47 days from keel-laying to completion in Kaiser's yard at Portland, Oregon. A ship was launched after 10 days on the first anniversary of Liberty Fleet Day and delivered 5 days later. Following this by two months, while the nation was still at peace, Kaiser set an all-time record with the launching of the *Robert E. Peary:* 4 days, 15½ hours after keel-laying at the Permanente Metals Yard in Richmond, California. The *Peary* survived until 1963, scrapped in Baltimore after twenty-two years.

As structural problems were overcome, the later-built Liberty ships sustained tremendous punishment under most difficult conditions. Some civilian-manned Libertys inadvertently became fighting ships. One of the more spectacular examples of this was the *Stephen Hopkins.* In September 1942, the *Hopkins* encountered two apparently neutral ships in the South Atlantic, only to discover that one was the German raider *Stier,* armed with six 150-millimeter guns and two torpedo tubes, and accompanied by its escort *Tannenfels.* Captain Paul Buck, the Liberty's skipper, refused to strike the colors, and the Germans opened fire, ruthlessly shelling the poorly armed vessel. Raked by machine gun fire, the *Hopkins* gun crew managed to put thirty shells into the *Stier*'s waterline. As the freighter became engulfed in flames, its entire gun crew was killed. Edwin O'Hara, engine-room cadet on his sea tour from the U.S. Merchant Marine Academy, ran aft and took over the only gun, firing its last five 6-inch shells on the *Stier* and setting it afire. The *Stier* was so damaged that later its crew blew it up and sank it. The *Stephen Hopkins* went down, taking Captain Buck, the mortally wounded O'Hara, and thirty-nine others to the bottom. Nineteen survivors in a lifeboat headed for Brazil, two thousand miles to the west. Four died en route, and the fifteen remaining completed their ordeal thirty-one days later. Buck, O'Hara, and three other officers were honored posthumously with the Distinguished Service Award, and the *Stephen Hopkins* was named a Gallant Ship.

German claims of heavy destruction of Allied shipping in the western Atlantic were countered by exaggerated American claims of sunken subs, and denials or silence under wartime confidentiality concerning the known losses. While the public remained unaware of the extent of damage, maritime interests finally awakened from their lethargy to demand government action. Coastal blackouts were enforced, patrols increased, nets placed at harbor entrances, and nearby waters mined.

Merchant mariners were not accorded draft deferments until mid-1942. Early that year MarComm reduced its standards for seagoing billets and cut training time in half. In February it authorized a state maritime academy in Castene, Maine, and specified a reduced program of twenty-two months for state schools to develop licensed deck and engineering officers. Later in the year a Gulf Coast school was established in Pass Christian, Mississippi. The California school, operating on Treasure Island (man-made in San Francisco Bay for the 1939 World's Fair), was enlarged and relocated to San Mateo. In March President Roosevelt authorized the U.S. Merchant Marine Academy to serve the Merchant Marine "as West Point serves the Army and Annapolis the Navy." In April Captain J. Harvey Tomb, USN (Ret.), established the school on the former estate of Walter P. Chrysler in Kings Point, Long Island. (Tomb was famed in naval circles as commodore of the destroyer squadron that did not follow the example of the nine destroyers tragically run aground at Point Honda in 1923. He made few friends with his spectacular testimony at the inquiry, in which he criticized blind adherence to naval doctrine. He also faulted Congress for withholding funds for equipment that he said could have prevented the disaster.) The Coast Guard was assigned control of the five state nautical schools. It was also directed by the president to take over the Bureau of Marine Inspection and Navigation, which had been under MarComm. The bureau, a civilian agency, had garnered a reputation for dishonesty. The Coast Guard set out to recruit seventy thousand seamen and sixteen thousand merchant officers. Beset by the litter from the U-boat activity along the Atlantic and Gulf coasts, which it had to clean up, the Coast Guard found the additional work beyond its capacity. In July the massive training programs for nonrated sailors planned at Sheepshead Bay, New York, and the state academies for officers were turned over to a newly organized War Shipping Administration.

Two thousand, seven hundred and ten Libertys were delivered out of eighteen shipyards before the war's end. The ships were named for famous Americans—so many that eventually the names of merchant seamen, naval nurses, and other military people were added to the list. Hulls were compartmented, pumps and piping installed, and the ships were called tankers. Some were painted white, fitted with operating rooms, labs, and wards, and served as hospital ships. Others were painted haze grey and became navy-operated troopships, repair ships, or auxiliary cargo carriers bringing the first supplies to be landed in embattled territories. Later the Libertys carried war brides and military dependents. Thirteen became arks—they were used to transport animals. Old and beaten ones, at high risk to the skeleton crews manning them, made their last trips during the invasion of Normandy to serve as breakwaters. After the war, some were sent to nuclear test sites to collect fallout or to be vaporized as targets. The *George Calvert* was taken directly from its launching-ways for conversion to a wartime training ship, renamed *American Mariner.* It became a missile-tracking vessel, then was retired, given back its original name, and scuttled in the shallows of Chesapeake Bay for use as a target ship for naval flyers; its proud white hull still stands upright in humble service in the middle of the bay. The ships had varied superstructures but always the distinctive boxy hulls that marked them as Libertys. Designed for a life of five years and expected to be noncompetitive in the postwar world, they continued in operation, many surviving for twenty years. In the last months of the war, the Liberty class was supplanted by 527 new emergency-class Victory ships, which came closer to the goals envisioned by MarComm. Several other classes of vessels that had been planned for peacetime operations eventually were built, including 301 C-2 freighters and 163 cargo-passenger C-3s.

With navy support, the organized convoy program along the Atlantic and Gulf coasts improved the ratio of safe arrivals to losses at sea. Convoy duty, while enhancing security under attack, required unique ship-handling skills. Skippers accustomed to sailing alone had to learn to cruise in formation, turn on flank in unison with others, zigzag according to preordained plans. Watch officers had to react to visual signals from a fleet commodore, work out plots on a maneuvering board, and keep the ship on consistent course and speed with little tolerance for error. At night or in fog, mist, falling snow, or heavy rain, vessels steamed stem to stern, separated by little more than three ship-lengths, the eyes of the bow lookouts fixed on a single blue stern light of the vessel ahead. When the North Atlantic raged, safety dictated the widening of intership distances, and with it the risk of losing formation.

American shipbuilders replenished Allied tonnage faster than Germany could destroy it. When the United States entered the war, Congress approved a new initiative to produce twenty-four million tons of shipping in two years. By the end of the war, the nation had produced forty million deadweight tons, three quarters of it in the form of Liberty ships. The Battle of the Atlantic turned in favor of the Allies during the first quarter of 1943, the worst North Atlantic winter in living memory. By then Germany was feeling the effects of the endless stream of military equipment being delivered on the convoy route, and knew well that an invasion buildup was in progress. The German U-boats attempted once and for all to sever the supply lines between North America and Great Britain. Submarines surrounded the eastbound ships with relentless attacks. Convoy operations remained sloppy under poorly trained and uncoordinated skippers, and naval coverage remained thin. Casualties were enormous. But the replenishment strategy turned the tide. With the steady flow of men and materials behind them, it was not the Allies who had unacceptable casualties during that winter, but the German submarine fleet. In the first three months of 1943, the U-boats sank 174 Allied and neutral merchant ships. Germany lost 39 U-boats. As winter ended Germany broke off the attacks, never to recover its strength. The supply route survived.

The Pacific war was less threatening to the merchant service. Some losses occurred on the great circle routes to Australia, but these stretched the limits of Japanese submarine patrols. North Pacific cargoes were well protected by accompanying naval forces headed for the insular battle grounds—until the arrival of the kamikazes. Forty-four merchant ships were sunk in Pacific campaigns, many at the hands of the suicide pilots. The most devastating air attacks took place in November 1944, in Leyte Gulf after the battle for the Philippines. There, twenty anchored ships, loaded with troops and ammunition, fought off round-the-clock kamikaze attacks as "noncombatant" merchantmen assisted the gun crews and army doctors in the midst of the conflict.

14-9. Attack victim, survivors in lifeboat off port bow. NATIONAL ARCHIVES

In both oceans as ships came on soundings the U-boat threat was replaced by a different peril of war that would last long after the end of hostilities: mines, sewn like seeds from the sterns of minelayers or dropped from the air in sea lanes near harbors. Some drifted aimlessly, while others were moored to chains holding them a few feet below the surface. Ugly, horned contact mines, each protrusion a trigger of destruction; spider mines with long cables to reach for the contact that would set them off; proximity mines, signaled by a ship's magnetic field to explode as the hull passed overhead. Any one of these could send a ship to the bottom as swiftly as a torpedo. Some of the mines sank and became embedded in the muddy bottom, later to be stirred up by storm-tossed waters. In the shallow North Sea, old, unswept mines continued to destroy ships for a half dozen years after the war.

The United States had 55,000 merchant seamen before it entered World War II; by the end of the war it had 215,000. From the beginning of hostilities to V-J Day, 6,830 seamen were killed, about 11,000 wounded, and 604 taken prisoner, 10 percent of whom died in POW camps. The American merchant marine suffered a greater percentage of war-related deaths than the sum of the nation's military forces. The one federal academy authorized to carry the World War II Battle Standard Flag is the U.S. Merchant Marine Academy, which had 142 cadets killed in action. The surviving merchant sailors were accorded no recognition as veterans until fifty years after the war. The Veterans of Foreign Wars voted in December 1997 to allow merchant marine veterans to become members. In providing the greatest sea lift in world history, they became America's fourth arm of defense.

Chapter 15

REACHING FOR
LEADERSHIP: 1945–1970

W orld War II brought rapid improvement in the technology of commercial ship operation. Gone were the log lines towed astern, the standard tool for speed calculation in the 1930s. In their place appeared simple tables that converted engine revolutions to travel speed at any load. Gone, except on exploration vessels, were the deep-sea leads with their great reels of wire. Even the smaller hand leads got little use, many of them replaced by the circular flashing displays of sonar-based depth sounders. Soon to go was the engine-room telegraph, a striking brass pedestal with mechanically delivered engine orders emblazoned on the sides of its foot-wide drum, current status unmistakable under a long brass pointer: Full, Half, or Slow Ahead; Stop, Slow, or Full Astern; or Finished With Engines. Skippers had long wished for throttle controls directly at hand. Their wish was fulfilled when diesel engines replaced steam and engine-room crews were reduced. For the most part, ships no longer carried three chronometers, nor did captains feel pressed to take their timepieces ashore for rating. The U.S. Naval Observatory joined with Greenwich, Monaco, and other maritime centers around the world in support of a network of radio time signals, available around the clock for chronometer correlation. Accurate time, any time.

On deck, the old tall, stayed masts standing between hatches had been replaced by pairs of stubby, steel king posts. These lowered a ship's profile and center of gravity while still enabling the concurrent loading or discharge of cargo on both sides. Gone were the sputtering steam winches of the Hog Islanders and Libertys, supplanted by high-powered electric drives. The sturdy new cargo gear allowed ships to load giant locomotives, full grown elephants, and generators large enough to power a city. The airline carriers weren't up to that. The first all-new class of cargo ship to be delivered after the war was the MarComm-designed Mariner, intended as a replacement for the aging Victory ships. Between 1950 and 1955 twenty-nine of these fourteen-thousand-ton ships were delivered to support the Korean War. They were equipped with the most modern navigational and deck gear, and steam turbines that could drive them at an unprecedented twenty knots. United States Lines modernized its fleet of C-2s with nine Mariners; American President Lines took eight; Pacific Far East, seven. More than fifty Mariners were built. It looked as if the United States would continue to populate the sea lanes with these much-improved vessels. But three characteristics of the Mariners kept them from dominating the market. First, they were "stick ships," soon to be rendered obsolete by container-ships. Second, they were steam-powered. Although they carried the most efficient steam plants in the world, diesel power would soon provide equivalent speed with better fuel economy and safety, and with a smaller engine-room staff. Third, the Mariners were designed for a full crew of fifty-eight at a time when labor costs were escalating.

In 1955 with the growing demand for oil, a new type of vessel was introduced that shook the traditions of coastal navigation: the mobile offshore drilling unit (MODU). Designed to assemble and sink what became known as "Texas towers," the MODUs were high rigs with wide platforms for machinery and living quarters, positioned at sea to pump oil from deposits under the continental shelf. Even in stormy weather the sturdy structures were visible, brilliantly illuminated and often crowned with flaming gas at their tops. Within a few years the "towers" were found to be more reliable than light vessels. Given occasional maintenance, they could be left unmanned for extended periods.

Denmark and Germany used diesel machinery as early as 1910, and by the end of World War II, 25 percent of all seagoing vessels worldwide were diesel-driven motor ships. American shipbuilders were slow to recognize the trend, content with the more powerful steam turbines and turboelectric plants. Triple-expansion steam engines allowed the building of larger ships than could be driven by diesel-electrics, but this was a questionable advantage in a period of reduced trade. And there was no clear advantage in the steamships' standard speeds of eighteen knots or more, as compared with the motor ships' fourteen to sixteen. Of what good, one might ask, is a three- or four-knot edge in a race across the sea, when a third competitor flies overhead at over 250 miles per hour?

After the war, the Coast and Geodetic Survey (CGS) and the Hydrographic Office (HO) modernized their separate domains with updated charts and publications. The new HO charts of foreign waters reflected data culled from enemy and Allied sources during the two-ocean war. Both agencies published shoreline guides, sets of compact volumes bound in olive-green canvas: *Coast Pilots* (by CGS) for waters of the continental United States and Hawaii, and *Sailing Directions* (by HO) for foreign shores. These multivolume texts were the descendants of century-old logbooks, notes of whalers, and Maury's collections of Pilot Chart data. Some chapters contained more lore than actuality and made colorful if unreliable reading. Modern seafaring, especially in wartime, required more precision. Gradually, through the government-published *Notices to Mariners* the improved but duller data found its way to the bridges of commercial shipping.

The postwar period was one of innovation in navigation technology. A new use was found for Sperry's gyrocompass. An autopilot connecting a ship's steering mechanism with a gyrocompass repeater could keep the vessel on a straight course in open waters without human intervention; during the day the helmsman could be relieved at the wheel and put to work chipping paint. By midcentury, radar sets had become standard equipment. A masthead antenna circling five times per minute would feed reflected echoes to a cathode ray tube in the wheelhouse, and the screen would display a two-dimensional, monochromatic approximation of the surrounding vessels and landforms. Perhaps the crowning achievement in navigational technology to come out of the war was loran—long-range navigation. Loran enabled ships at sea to determine their positions on the basis of radio signals from the shore. It defeated the overcast skies of the North Atlantic in a great though imperfect navigational leap forward. One of its limitations was vacuum tubes subject to failure caused by vibrations or sudden temperature changes. The bulky shipboard receivers, far short on circuitry by later standards, required dialed adjustments, the use of conversion tables, and special charts overlaid with hyperbolic grids. Nevertheless, a ship equipped with appropriate gear and located anywhere within a thousand to fifteen hundred miles of three or more loran transmitters could fix a reliable position in minutes, at any time of day or night, and under nearly all weather conditions. Widely distributed transmitters made loran available to three quarters of the Atlantic, all of the Caribbean, and large portions of the Pacific.

Seasoned sea captains, long successful with binoculars, compass, sextant, and chronometer, were skeptical about most electronic innovations. Their suspicions were often justified. Radar, they felt, was better left off than on—the tubes wouldn't burn out. Loran, they insisted, should be verified with sextant observations, no matter how large a polygon of position the cloudy sky and murky horizon delivered. Further developments in technology were needed. Meanwhile, for many the fascination with technological change outweighed the shortcomings.

In 1941, with little notice, the United States started a supportive program to aid the British convoys by deploying Coast Guard cutters for search-and-rescue duty on ocean stations. The stations, identified alphabetically as Able, Baker, Charlie, etc., extended from west to east across the North Atlantic and later in the Gulf of Alaska. Each station consisted of a rectangular grid within defined coordinates of latitude and longitude. A cutter on duty would broadcast a regular signal, identifying its station and the cell within the grid where it was then located. The ships provided aircraft navigational beacons and served as emergency rescue vessels for both ships and aircraft. They also reported weather conditions, observed traffic, and collected oceanographic and fisheries information. Any passing ship could use the Coast Guard cutters' broadcast for positioning—one of the incidental benefits of the stations. (Ocean Station Charlie, the friendliest traffic cop in one of the more congested portions of the western Atlantic, marked the intersections of the east- and westbound transatlantic routes, a few miles apart, with the rhumb line to the Nantucket Shoals Light Vessel.) With the Cold War development of intercontinental ballistic missiles, the cutters were outfitted with advanced radar gear for missile tracking. The program reached a peak in the mid-1960s and lasted another decade, until satellites made the ocean stations obsolete. Ocean station duty was boring, risky, and immensely valuable.

The formation of the United Nations marked the end of five centuries of colonialism. The inhabitants of territories and protectorates were destined to seek independence in a new world of freedom. The continued existence of remote military bases depended no longer on capture and domination, but on successful negotiations between nations. Atomic weapons and the combination of undersea and air power blurred the well-worn tracks of trade routes. Traditional naval forces could no longer protect sea lanes, nor did they need traditional forms of support from their civilian counterparts. Alfred Mahan's long-revered doctrine on the interdependence of navy and merchant marine lost relevance. The American merchant marine was cast adrift from its naval alliances and left to float on its own, under the near-sighted vision of the federal bureaucracy.

One year after the war ended, when the functions of the War Shipping Administration were restored to the Maritime Commission, the United States maintained thirty-one foreign trade routes. Two events in the postwar decade served to keep the routes active and the government involved. The first, in 1948 under the Truman administration, was the implementation of the Marshall Plan to hasten European economic recovery and increase international trade. Not incidentally, the plan was also intended to contain the growing Soviet influence in Eastern Europe. The United States and fifteen free European nations signed an accord, and more than $12 billion was disbursed over four years. Much of that was loaded into the holds of American freighters in the form of steel, ore, grain, fertilizer, and chemicals. In time, it returned in the form of bicycles, crockery, marble, olives, Volkswagens, watches, and wine. The seaways were as busy as they had ever been in peacetime history. For the United States, with 3,644 American-flagged ships engaged in foreign trade, 1948 was a peak year.

After the war the U.S. Navy established its own support fleet of civilian-operated, noncombatant ships with little objection from shipowners or unions. The environment differed from that of 1917, the last time the government had tried to put the merchant marine under naval control. Then, the proposed takeover would have destroyed the unions and idled commercially owned vessels; it was blocked from the start. In 1949 the naval connection promised a buffer in the event of a decline in commercial activity. Instead of a naval fleet, however, the Military Sea Transportation Service (MSTS, later renamed Military Sealift Command) was formed in October in response to President Truman's insistence on "unification of the armed forces." The vision of overall unification was not fulfilled. The separate armed forces were unwilling to give up their specialized territories to join with each other in a much-reduced military organization. The effort for unification succeeded only in eliminating overlap of functions, as in the case of MSTS, which combined the activities of the Army Transportation Corps and the Naval Transportation Service. Except for the lack of armament and the presence of blue and gold stripes on the stacks, the haze gray tankers, passenger ships, and dry cargo carriers of MSTS could easily have been mistaken for the navy's regular auxiliary service fleet. Whatever the original objectives of its formation, the MSTS fleet grew rapidly with a sudden increase in demand for its services. This growth was a result of the second event that kept the merchant marine flourishing: the outbreak of war in Korea.

At the time, Truman's administration was dissatisfied with the independent Maritime Commission. MarComm's combined regulatory and administrative roles were ripe for reform. Vermont Senator George Aiken had been claiming since the middle of the war that MarComm was corrupt, that it was colluding with shipowners and wasting billions of dollars of government funds. His wartime charges were ignored. He launched a second investigation after the war and won support for the principle that the organization making the rules shouldn't be the one charged with carrying them out. MarComm's regulatory functions were transferred to a new Federal Maritime Board (FMB), and the Commerce Department's Maritime Administration (MarAd) was charged with overseeing any administrative activities of the merchant marine that fell within the federal government's purview. The arrangement was purely symbolic, and so it would remain for a decade, because the chairmanship of the FMB and the command of MarAd were vested in one and the same individual.

A disturbing trend faced MarAd, one it found difficult to counter and may have helped to sustain—the return of flags of convenience. This time, American-owned ships were registered not with well-known maritime nations, but under the flags of Panama and little-known Liberia. The reasons were obvious: bolstered revenues for those needy countries, avoidance of taxes, and fewer restrictions for American operators. Oil companies created the Liberian registry to introduce competition into the practice of flag conversion and thereby keep foreign accommodation generous. Faced with burdensome government regulations, the operators of unsubsidized vessels found it economical to move the paperwork offshore.

The not-so-cold war in Korea highlighted national concern about the spread of Communism and helped root Communist factions out of the unions. During the last years before World War II, the National Maritime Union was clearly under Communist control. The American wartime alliance with the Soviets helped Communists retain their grip. Six months after the war's end, seven maritime unions, including the NMU, set up the Committee for Maritime Unity, with Joe Curran and Harry Bridges acting as cochairmen. By then Harry Lundeberg and Bridges had split, after brawling publicly even to the point of fisticuffs over Bridges's radical views. Curran was uneasy about his affiliation with Bridges, and in January 1947, he and others withdrew from the committee, leaving Bridges to fight his own battles. By the summer of 1950, Curran's NMU had escaped the clutches of the red menace; no union wanted to face charges of Communist control.

A rejuvenated Europe and peace of a sort encouraged tourist travel, and American shipping companies eagerly went after the kinds of opportunities that had eluded them in 1940. No expense was spared—an approach made possible by government funding in construction differentials. United States Lines was first on the scene. It spent $6 million to restore the six-year-old *America* to its former glory after five years of carrying troops. On November 14, 1946, when *America* sailed again commercially from its old North River pier, the wartime rubble had hardly been swept from the French and English seaports at the other end of the route.

The Caribbean offered more for the tourist. Alcoa Steamship Company converted the Victory ship *Alcoa Cavalier* to a cargo-passenger carrier and sent it with tourists and general cargo to Jamaica and Suriname, where it was to pick up a return load of bauxite. The travelers were hustled from onboard air-conditioned comfort to palm-thatched bars beyond the dockside, where Calypso singers welcomed them with rum and Coca-Cola. They never saw the dusty mineral being loaded down chutes into the holds. The trip was economical, short, and cozy, with accommodations for fewer than sixty passengers. Bookings grew, and Alcoa soon added two more converted Victorys to its fleet. Mississippi Shipping's Delta Line put the splendid *Del Norte* into service at a cost of $7 million. The first of three newly designed cargo-passenger "coffee liners," the ship was roomy; it used space efficiently in a hull almost without sheer and included crew's quarters built into a broad, squat stack. Day or night under brilliant southern skies, one could inhale the invigorating scent of Brazilian coffee. Even the "banana boats" capitalized on the Calypso craze. The United Fruit Company increased tourism through the port of New Orleans with three large, white, passenger ships. Later, the company policy became "every banana a guest, every passenger a pest." But for the time being, tourism was booming from the Windward Passage to the Spanish Main.

In the Pacific, American President Lines came back to life in 1947 by establishing a route between the West Coast and the Orient for its flagship, the *President Cleveland.* Icy Alaska offered little attraction. Distance curtailed interest in Australia and the South Pacific—the trip from San Francisco to Sydney took three to four weeks. Even with a stopover at Tahiti, for most travelers this was too long to spend at sea. APL and Matson found better returns from their routes in the warm northern latitudes. United States Lines serviced Australia and the Orient from the East Coast with MarComm-furnished C-2s. The ships followed the old cargo routes of Kermit Roosevelt's American Pioneer Line.

Four attack transports that had seen little service in World War II—the USS *Duchess, Queens, Shelby,* and *Dauphin*—were delivered to American Export Lines for conversion to Mediterranean passenger-cargo service. They were redesigned as single-class vessels, new versions of the 1930s "Four Aces," with air-conditioned accommodations for 125 passengers and holds capable of carrying six thousand tons of general cargo. Export's *Excalibur* departed from a new terminal in Jersey City in September 1948; it was followed by the *Excambion, Exeter,* and *Exochorda,* all pursuing regular eight-week schedules. Their return cargoes were as interesting as their passengers: Israeli oranges; Italian wines, olive oil, and marble; baskets of live Moroccan snails; and barrels of Spanish sherry with cork for its future bottles.

The war made America conscious of the world. Tourism, once a pastime of the elite, drew people of all backgrounds. The "grand tour" of Europe, broken into segments, became a middle-class pursuit. Storefront travel offices opened on the toniest streets of major cities. Fifth Avenue, Boylston Street, State Street, Post Street, and Rodeo Drive were resplendent with the flags and posters of liners bound for England, France, Germany, Italy, Greece, Brazil, and the Orient. Colorful folders depicted luxuriantly furnished cabins, sumptuous dinners elegantly served by continental waiters, afterdeck swimming pools, exercise spas, and fetching after-hours night clubs in which one could mingle with the cream of society. Getting there was sure to be half the fun, and it needn't be on a Cunarder.

Bethlehem Steel's Fore River Yard in Quincy, the source of Matson's *Lurline* and *Mariposa,* was recognized for passenger liner production. American Export Line, enjoying success with its eight-week runs, contracted with Bethlehem for two larger, faster ships. The *Independence* and the *Constitution* both were launched in June 1950 and sent to Jersey City to be outfitted for a new service of three-week turnaround voyages to the Mediterranean. During the slow winters, the ships would take an occasional two-month cruise to the Black Sea. Originally designed with a passenger capacity of about 1,000, the accommodations could be expanded, as they were in 1959, to 1,110. Every first-class and cabin-class room had a private bath; tourist class offered shared baths between cabins. The two luxurious ships were the first truly new, full-sized American liners in the postwar period.

Competition for passengers crossing the Atlantic stiffened after North-German Lloyd, the French Line, and Cunard recovered from their wartime setbacks. The most formidable competitors were in the air—during 1958 and every year thereafter, the number of transatlantic passengers traveling by air exceeded those crossing on the ocean. But on the water, the United States was a strong contender. Three quarters of all first-class ocean passengers were Americans. People wanted either speed or Continental pampering. For the first time in a century, American operators sensed a chance to get a grip on the trade. American Export was making its mark in the Mediterranean. London, Paris, and Hamburg beckoned. United States Lines with its tired old *Manhattan* and *America* had fallen behind in the race, until doughty John Franklin, the company's second-generation leader, announced plans for a new liner that promised renewed fame. The *United States* was being built in the respected Newport News Shipbuilding Yard in Hampton Roads. In 1951 every aspect of the work suggested the ship would regain Atlantic superiority for its country. The reorganized United States Lines had never shaken off its dependency on government subsidies. Now it was partnered with the navy in producing what was expected to be the fastest passenger ship in the world, designed for elegant service but convertible to military use. The maiden voyage of the *United States* was not a disappointment. After the departure for Southampton in July 1952, the public waited expectantly to hear that the ship had recaptured the Blue Riband for America. In July the ship returned to New York with the coveted prize, to be welcomed by a parade of spouting fireboats. The record was in American hands for the first time since the *Baltic* captured it in 1850 and lost it the following year. The ship's success was the culmination of one man's lifetime of dedication. It was commanded by Captain Harry Manning, the most meticulous and demanding seaman in active service, a maritime hero. But Manning was no more than a silent partner to the ship's designer, the man who won it fame.

High in a Manhattan apartment complex a teacup clattered onto its saucer as a lanky man in a wrinkled suit pushed aside a crumb-speckled plate, folded *The New York Times,* and summoned his chauffeur. Within minutes he was riding through midtown traffic, headed for East River Drive and the Brooklyn shore. Seated in the rear of his Cadillac, William Francis Gibbs adjusted his black-rimmed spectacles to resume reading the *Shipping News*. Fog, rain, or shine, he traveled the route on a rigid schedule, two or three times every month. Then, parked on a point of land overlooking the Narrows he would wait, never for long, until he had sighted the two blue, white, and red stacks of the liner approaching from the sea. Today, he leaned through an open window, binoculars raised to his eyes, to study the ship's trim, examine the hawse-holes for hints of stain, search over the housing into vaporous air above the funnels for evidence of smoke or steam, assess the condition of the blue-eagled house flag flying from the foremast. The great ship entered the Narrows, eclipsing an outbound single-stacked freighter bearing similar colors. Gibbs failed to notice as the freighter dipped its ensign, so intent was he on the ocean liner. Then he nodded warmly, his eye caught by the return salute as the great black hull passed majestically beside the other ship. Given the opportunity, every United States Lines ship paid homage to the SS *United States.* If a captain failed to do so, within minutes he would learn of his oversight by radio from the skipper of the Blue Riband liner. Commodore Harry Manning insisted on the practice. An amateur flier, while captain of *America* Manning was known to glide over his ship as it stood idle in port and to radio the engineer with a complaint if he detected a wisp of smoke issuing from its stacks.

Gibbs examined the wake of the *United States,* pleased by the smoothness of the waters astern even as the ship held its fifteen-knot speed on entering the North River ("Hudson River" to the landbound). He rolled up the car window and sat back, headed now for Pier 86, one of the prestigious passenger piers on Hudson River Drive. Gibbs would be among the first to board the ship, there to continue his inspection in finer detail——instruments, logs, daily performance records at sea, fuel consumption, refrigerator temperatures. Nothing escaped him. Then, the passengers having debarked, cleaning crews at work, perhaps a private party continuing in one of the lounges, the abstemious designer of the fastest passenger liner afloat would relax in a corner with friends and chat about books, music, or his beloved New York Yankees.

Gibbs had thought about this ship since working on the plans of the *Leviathan.* Then, size attracted him. During the war he came to realize that speed would be essential in the competition with air transport. An optimized combination of capacity and speed on the water would be hard for a fleet of airliners to match. How often in 170 years had the cry been heard for combining capacity with speed? Gibbs planned the *United States* in 1943, working out the finest details in his mind before committing anything to paper. Name any portion of the ship and he could recite its specifications without reference to blueprints. His plans called for the lightest of materials, fireproof of course: aluminum and asbestos. He wanted "no oaken beams and plaster walls," in his own words, and no wood at all if it could be avoided. He questioned whether wood should be found even in the ballroom's grand piano. Aluminum rivets, railings, davits, and lifeboats; aluminum chairs and vases; aluminum coat hangers and picture frames. In the end the 990-foot hull was twenty-five hundred tons lighter than would customarily be expected. People wondered if the interior would have an *Art Deco* sleekness reminiscent of the lost *Normandie*—long, thin forms, rounded corners, minimal ornamentation, the emphasis on black, white, and gray. For the engine room Gibbs specified machinery built of new alloys. There would be eight boilers, six at work at any time, to build a steam pressure of a thousand pounds per square inch, the turbines driving four propellers to achieve a speed in excess of thirty-five knots. He envisioned accommodations for two thousand passengers: 870 first-class staterooms, 508 cabin-class, and 551 tourist-class. As a naval transport, the ship would be able to carry fifteen thousand troops.

The government approved Gibbs's work in 1945 and kept it under wraps until the keel was laid in February 1950. It took fifteen months to build the ship behind closely guarded fences and several months more to outfit it. The fifty-three-thousand-ton ship was floated from its drydock early in 1952 and sent on a shakedown cruise, keenly studied by the navy. During one run it reached a top speed of forty-four knots—a secret that was withheld for years. Commodore Harry Manning, hero of the spectacular rescue of the crew of the *Florida* in 1929 and current master of *America,* was named to command the *United States* on its maiden voyage. During the next three months, Gibbs made Manning a virtual partner, the two men going over the ship's finest details. With hundreds of celebrities on its passenger list, on July 3, 1952, the liner departed for Le Havre. Three days, ten hours, and forty minutes after passing Ambrose Light, as the president's daughter Margaret Truman pulled the ship's whistle, the *United States* passed Bishop Rock. It was the vessel's average eastbound speed of 35.5 knots that won it the Blue Riband. However, on its return it set a new westbound record of 34.4 knots. United States Lines, famed for its precise schedules, immediately announced a series of five-day crossings between New York and Southampton. Gibbs's wife frequently traveled on the ship, but after the maiden voyage Gibbs himself never made another trip aboard. He preferred to watch the ship's stately movements from the shore, where he had a better perspective. Even when it made the short voyage from New York to Newport News for its periodic overhaul, Gibbs would watch it depart from the North River, then take the train south to be on the pier at Hampton Roads in time for its arrival.

For United States Lines the winning of the Blue Riband was a Pyrrhic victory. The flawlessly maintained liner was found to be metallic in appearance, its decorations sparse to the point of bleakness and unimaginatively modern. When the novelty of sailing on the fastest passenger ship wore off, so did bookings.

15-1. SS *America* (foreground) outbound, SS *United States* arriving in Manhattan.
SSHSA COLLECTION, UNIVERSITY OF BALTIMORE LIBRARY

After its first five voyages the ship's passenger list rarely reached 1,800. The $78 million vessel, absorbing more than $9 million in annual operating subsidies, paid for itself for only two months of the year. In a replay of the company's experience with its first flagship, on some crossings the crew outnumbered the passengers. Within a few years, transatlantic jets offered eight-hour flights to London and Paris at fares lower than the liner's. Even the scant immigrant population took to the air. In 1954, after welcoming twelve million impoverished Europeans to American shores, Ellis Island closed, marking the end of that demoralizing but most profitable element of the passenger trade called "steerage."

In 1954 the diminished American merchant fleet was still the largest in the world, with 27,300,000 tons afloat as represented by 806 ships. American tankers carried 21 percent of the world's oil, seven million tons per year. Union leaders incorrectly saw this level of activity as indefinitely sustainable and shifted their demands from wage increases to longer vacations and pensions. The AFL and CIO merged in 1955 to become labor's single trade association. The AFL-CIO gave unified voice to 12.6 million workers, more than a third of the American work force, without lessening the frequency of contract negotiations between employers and individual trade unions. Workers' demands became harder to handle. Grievances, or "beefs" in the sailors' terminology, increased in frequency, often set up by petty union representatives. Under differing contract expiration dates, multiple shipboard unions could tie up a company for months with a rolling broadside of strikes and spiraling lists of requirements. Overseen by myopic government agencies, which after the war became more and more allied with union causes, labor-management disputes were apt to end with union victories. A Cargo Preference Act salved the troubled operators by granting subsidies as operating differentials. Shipping company management lost all imagination when it came to anticipating and meeting the seamen's real needs. With one exception, cost reduction through applied technology was untried; and it took management ten years to recognize that one attempt as a failure.

In July 1959 the first nuclear-powered merchant ship, appropriately named after the country's first transatlantic steamship, was launched in Camden, New Jersey. The NS *Savannah*, operated by the States Marine Line, traveled in both the Atlantic and Pacific amid much controversy. After being idled by a labor dispute in 1963, the ship was transferred to First Atomic Transport, a subsidiary of the merged American Export Isbrandtsen Company. In port the *Savannah* was as much tourist attraction as cargo carrier; with an annual operating cost of $3 million, it proved inefficient for general use. The vessel was

15-2. NS *Savannah*. SSHSA Collection, University of Baltimore Library

refueled for the first and only time in August 1968 before a Mediterranean voyage, one of its last. In 1969 it was retired, to join its namesake in the records of famous failed firsts.

A zealous antitrust witch-hunt was spawned in 1959 with the investigations of New York congressman Emmanuel Celler. The Celler Committee, responsible for oversight of regulated industries, exposed for public scrutiny the records of dozens of major shipping companies, domestic and foreign, in an attempt to show monopolistic collusion through the conference system. Since the first Atlantic Conference in 1908, maritime nations met periodically to stabilize ocean rates through negotiated mutual agreements. The revelations did nothing but raise suspicions of government manipulation by private businesses, inform foreign competitors of the internal doings of American operators, and tarnish the entire American shipping industry in the eyes of the public. Out of the hearings came one antitrust measure that split the MarAd functions. President Kennedy and his brother Robert, the U.S. attorney general, took note of the combined quasi-judicial, regulatory, and administrative functions still held by one person in the dual capacity of chairman of FMB and head of MarComm. The Kennedys, as it happened, were sons of the first maritime commissioner. In accordance with the 1961 reorganization plan, the FMB was replaced by the new Federal Maritime Commission, an independent agency that would handle regulatory activities. The Maritime Administration remained under the Commerce Department, with a Maritime Subsidy Board to oversee administrative matters. Thereafter the separated agencies wallowed in regulations and procedures, a boon only to the growing forces of admiralty and labor lawyers.

While the government maritime bureaucracy grew, the fleet diminished. The decline in foreign trade that had begun after the Korean War continued into the 1960s. In 1959 American Export sent two of its modest, single-class vessels, the *Excambion* and *Exochorda,* to the Hudson River Maritime Reserve fleet and increased the capacities of its popular *Independence* and *Constitution* by 10 percent. The change availed nothing. By 1962 the two larger ships, each able to carry more than 1,100 passengers, averaged 928 per trip. The Texas Maritime Academy took over the idle *Excambion* in 1965, renamed it the *Texas Clipper,* and put it to work as a training ship for maritime officers. In 1967, after these last two of the Four Aces were sent away, the average number of bookings on Export's big ships fell to 786; in 1968 it dropped to 694. In a striking contrast, the *United States* sailed in the summer of 1968 with a record 1,809 passengers. American Export's imaginative managers responded by entering into a joint venture with United States Lines, which was their chief American competitor: passengers would travel aboard Export's ships to Naples and return with United States Lines from ports in northern Europe. This was an enticing arrangement for travelers who had the time to take the grand tour. Airlines gave travelers their vacation time on the continent where they preferred to spend it.

Labor disputes added to American Export's problems. A European trip had to be canceled while American and Hispanic crew members wrangled over use of the toilet facilities. The troubled company turned to the Caribbean and put its big ships to work as cruise liners. The fare was $200 per week with full food service. An alternative—one that would have seemed almost sacrilegious in an earlier period—was "European" service: $98 for a one-week cruise, with food priced separately in shipboard restaurants and cafeterias. The voyagers weren't fooled; the cost of eating that way was greater than the $102 differential. In the late 1960s the staid old queens of the Med were repainted in bold psychedelic colors in an attempt to attract the hip, rebellious youth of that period. But the future yuppies didn't buy into the cosmetic change. Export then contracted with Fugazy Travel to operate the famous liners for convention cruises. Even the NMU booked a cruise for a seamen's working holiday, but the idea flopped. In 1968 the *Independence* and the *Constitution* were laid up in Baltimore, ending American Export's passenger operations. Later both ships were purchased by the American-Hawaiian Line for use as cruise ships within the island state. Still too costly even for that trade, the *Constitution* was laid up in 1996.

Two centuries of maritime history taught that money could be made by an astute investor with the right cargoes. One needed good timing and the willingness to break with tradition. The worldwide demand for oil brought one American into the oil barons' billionaire club dominated by Stavros Niarchos and Aristotle Onassis. Daniel K. Ludwig got an early start in maritime business. As a nine-year-old he found a sunken boat, which he bought for $75, repaired, and rented for $150. His grandfather had built Ludwig's Pier in South Haven, Michigan, the lakeside community where Daniel was born. His four uncles were Great Lakes ship captains. While his father drew a moderate income from real estate, the lad was attracted to the smell of the waterfront, leaving school after the eighth grade to work for a ship chandler and later for a manufacturer of marine engines.

At nineteen the independent Ludwig borrowed $5,000 on his father's signature to convert an old paddle-wheel steamboat into a barge for the transport of molasses and wood, essential distillery ingredients. That 1917 venture provided the pattern for a half century of credit-based fleet building. His investments in the shipping business grew livelier after he chartered a tanker. The pattern became clear: rent rather than buy, borrow rather than tie up capital, save rather than spend, use cash income for collateral on larger loans.

Ludwig was aboard a tanker in 1926 when an explosion permanently injured his back. He was tall and lean, and from the time of his injury he walked bent over in pain. The accident didn't deter his activities, but he became known as a cranky businessman, a miser, and a loner. He had an unassuming manner, and his wealth accumulated with little notice.

Six years into the Depression, Ludwig got a loan from the Chemical Bank of New York to buy several freighters. He converted the ships to tankers and started transporting other people's oil. When war broke out in Europe, a new opportunity emerged. Could Ludwig have read the history of privateering during the first decades of the republic? With government aid he added more tankers to the fleet and valiantly supported the war effort, with the understanding that after the war the ownership of the vessels reverted to him. By the end of World War II his company, National Bulk Carriers, was the fifth largest fleet operator in the nation. Except for single shares owned by each of the firm's officers, Daniel Ludwig was its only stockholder.

15-3. Supertanker *Manhattan,* largest merchant ship ever built in the United States

Ludwig owned a shipyard near the Norfolk Navy Base, where he developed labor-saving welding techniques and took the lead in constructing larger tankers. The MarComm T-2s of World War II were about 16,600 tons, and shortly after the war, ships of 25,000 tons were being produced. In 1950 the giant Bethlehem Steel pushed the limit with the world's largest tanker, the 114,000-ton *Manhattan,* which tested the capacity of its Quincy yard. Limited by the moderate size of his own drydocks, Ludwig looked to Japan. The Japanese were known to be building ever larger vessels, gaining a construction lead which they have never yielded. Labor costs in the Orient were half those in the United States. The Kure yard had the world's largest drydocks, where the biggest battleships in history had been built. Ludwig sent out his agents and leased the yard. By 1965 the Japanese at Kure yard had built several 200,000-ton tankers for Ludwig, the first of what came to be known as supertankers. The ships, without frills, were registered under Panamanian and Liberian flags and staffed with West Indian crews. When the tanker industry underwent startling financial changes in the mid-1970s, Daniel Ludwig branched into other fields. By that time he was stripping Amazonian rain forests for lumber. With holdings assessed at $3 billion to $5 billion, he ranked among the world's wealthiest shipowners.

Ludwig was neither an endearing nor a colorful individual. He dressed cheaply and was secretive, profane, and short-tempered. Often he was seen in Manhattan restaurants, alone at lunch. A longtime resident of New York, he counted as friends only a few well-known Californians—Clark Gable, Richard Nixon, Ronald Reagan. The oil baron died at ninety-five, described by his biographer as an "invisible billionaire." Soon the stream of giant tankers that grew from his pioneering investments would become all too visible.

The 1967 wreck of the *Torrey Canyon* off the English coast highlighted the increasing problem of oil spills and the issue of clouded responsibility. The ship, carrying thirty-five million gallons of oil, hit a reef eighteen miles west of Land's End, buckled, and during a week of stormy seas broke into three sections, pinioned on the rocks. The spill reached north along the Cornwall coast and east into the English Channel, resulting in 120 miles of oil-contaminated coastline. The ship was owned by the Union Oil Company of California, chartered to British Petroleum operating as Barracuda Tanker, and registered in Liberia. The captain was Italian. In such circumstances it was difficult to pin down responsibility. Oil transport had become a matter of high finance and spot-market commodity trading. Loaded vessels changed hands even while in transit. A Liberian or Panamanian tanker might be owned by a New York lawyer, financed by a bank in Hong Kong, and operated by a company in Monte Carlo. It might be classed by a tolerant Polish classification society and insured in the Singapore branch of a London underwriter. A Greek captain might be in charge of a Taiwanese crew. Meanwhile, in Chicago, options on the price of the cargo itself could be openly traded. To whom should the aggrieved turn for recompense when black sludge collects in the wetlands, petroleum-soaked birds die on the beaches, fish float in the miles-wide film of oil? The *Torrey Canyon* disaster was not the worst of the spills. It would be eclipsed in 1978 by the all-time record-breaker, when the *Amoco Cadiz* carrying sixty-eight million gallons of crude oil grounded off the French coast. Twenty-four million gallons were lost at once from its ruptured tanks, a fifteen-mile oil slick spread along the shore, and in the ensuing month the damage increased. But the *Torrey Canyon* spill was among the first to make political fodder of the supertankers. (Media reports on spillage often ignore the fact that the tanker rarely loses all of its cargo. Furthermore, cargo size can be expressed in deadweight tons, barrels, or gallons, and statistics sometimes confuse the units. And so many factors are involved that even spill size is not always useful in assessing the extent of devastation.) While scientists experimented with booms, burning, bulldozing, and detergents, private groups ranging from shoreside restaurateurs to shell fishermen to Audubon enthusiasts voiced their concerns. Pollution prevention became a top priority among the major maritime nations.

In the United States the task fell to the ever marginal Coast Guard. Responsibility for that energetic and dedicated organization was transferred in 1967 from the Treasury to the Department of Transportation (DOT). To establish a fresh image, DOT prescribed new officers' uniforms, closer in appearance to those of Greyhound bus drivers than to the dark blue outfits so long confused with the navy's. The familiar white cutters that cruised the nation's harbors and coasts now wore diagonal red stripes across their bows like ambassadors' chest ribbons. More important, DOT instituted modernization programs. It contracted with the Electric Boat Company to produce land-controlled buoys as replacements for the smaller light vessels, the new buoys incorporating automated lights, foghorns, and scientific devices. Gone were the friendly manned ships with their basketed lanterns, buff-colored houses, and seaworthy, tumble-home hulls. Texas towers supplanted the East Coast's well-known larger light-ships: Nantucket, Brenton Reef, Ambrose, Diamond Shoals, and Chesapeake. And, after three years of study, Congress assigned the rejuvenated Coast Guard the duty of protecting American shores from oil spills, a task it pursued with a tight purse and inspired passion.

The Dutch port of Rotterdam had developed a vessel transport center (VTC) for harbor traffic control, which the Coast Guard emulated in San Francisco in 1968. Primitive compared with air traffic control, the Coast Guard's system resembled that used on the Great Lakes as ships approached the Soo locks. At designated points ships were required to report to the Coast Guard by VHF (very high frequency) voice radio, which had a practical range across the water of ten to fifteen miles. Each ship would identify itself, its cargo and its destination. On shore, Coast Guard traffic coordinators observed the ships with radar, sliding tokens on an oversized chart to sort out the area's traffic. Radio talkers coached the bridge watches as their vessels moved along routes suited to current conditions, the skippers always in touch yet always responsible for their own actions. This was to be the Coast Guard's main bulwark against the risk of free-floating oil in American waters. The organization was like a high school team warming up to play a series in the major leagues.

Chapter 16

TANKERS AND
TECHNOLOGY: 1970–1996

With the collapse of the passenger trade, the focus of shipping companies moved to dry cargo. By 1970 there were only 37,600 berths on salt-water ships. Facing another strike in November 1969, United States Lines laid up its flagship, *United States,* in the port where it was first launched. The celebrated liner never sailed again under its own power, languishing instead against a pier in Newport News for a quarter of a century. Filthy with bird droppings and harbor soot, its flaking paint lost to rust, the ship was stripped, cannibalized, and finally auctioned in 1992 to a Turkish combine, which towed it to the Aegean. The new owners had its asbestos removed in a Russian yard near Istanbul with the thought of making it into an eastern-Mediterranean cruise liner. But they found the ship unsuited to their ambitious plans and in 1996 sent it back to its homeland. By then, all the davits and lifeboats had been removed and the four propellers lashed down on the afterdeck. Thoroughly gutted, even its plumbing torn out, the *United States* was towed by a Russian tug and sent across the Atlantic. For much of the trip the skipper was unsure of the final destination. Meanwhile, a dock had been reserved at Boston's army base, before the port authority objected on the grounds that the forlorn ship floated too high and would obstruct the Logan Airport flight paths. While tug and tow circled beyond the pilot station, an attempt was made to berth the ship in Quincy's former Fore River Shipyard. But the only adequate space there turned out to be silted up, too shallow to accommodate the liner's draft. Too tall, too deep, the ship was then dispatched to Philadelphia. At the Packer Marine Terminal the range light mast was removed and the radar mast cut down to enable the ship to slip under the Walt Whitman Bridge at low water with just five feet of clearance. It headed for Pier 96, but the Coast Guard interfered, concerned about its poorly rigged docking lines, there being no power on deck to adjust them. Dockage fees in Philadelphia are said to run at $1,000 per day. The ship was targeted for the Philadelphia Naval Shipyard before that famous yard ended operations on September 30, 1996. Wandering from pier to pier, the last holder of the Blue Riband is a modern-day *Flying Dutchman*. Its fate remains undetermined.

While American shippers had an oversupply of demanding and costly labor, labor shortages in Europe forced companies there to reduce crew sizes. The trend spread worldwide. In the early 1980s Japanese ships were operating experimentally with sixteen-person crews. By 1987 they were down to eleven persons, nearly all officers. American shipowners were forced to make similar economies. In 1961 American-flagged freighters typically carried a crew of forty-five, young people, their average age little more than thirty. By 1991 ships of similar size carried twenty-two, under union agreements four more than required by the Coast Guard. Maritime unions enjoyed their highest enrollments in the 1970s, but the need for seamen was in decline. For every battle won through collective bargaining, labor came closer to losing its war. Unions bargained for improvements in pay and benefits, and adopted some peculiar employment practices to spread jobs among dues-paying members. A union member's seagoing time may now be limited to half a year, the remainder shore-time off the union rolls: sixty days on, sixty off; six months on, six off. The result, theoretically, is that twice as many people get a shot at the available well-paid berths. After leaving a ship, the seaman reports to a union hall, where he is issued a date-time-stamped National Shipping Card. Like an option on a block of rising stock, the card grows in value as it ages, increasing the holder's chance of reemployment in any port where companies are hiring——until the card expires one year after issue. A licensed mate looking for work stows his dunnage in the trunk of a car and roams the seaports, checking for job postings at hiring halls where the few American-flagged ships are likely to need crew. His home may be in Maine, but he could find himself in Charleston or New Orleans when opportunity knocks. As posting time approaches, a half-dozen qualified people might be sitting in the hall, sleeping, watching television, scanning dog-eared magazines, clutching their shipping cards like hole cards in a high-stakes game of blackjack; the holder of the oldest unexpired card gets first option on the job. Seasoned mariners have acquired patience with the system in years of working within it. The typical age of seamen waiting in the hall creeps up toward fifty-five. It is virtually impossible for a young, newly licensed officer to join the Masters, Mates and Pilots because membership is limited to spread work among the current active enrollment.

After Lyndon Johnson signed the 1964 Civil Rights Act prohibiting discrimination in employment, Title VII specifically forbidding discrimination on the basis of sex, women were able to join the maritime labor force. But they had few opportunities to develop the requisite skills until 1972, when Richard Nixon signed the measure known as "Title IX" banning sex discrimination in higher education. Soon thereafter, federal academies opened their doors to women. Females were admitted to the U.S. Merchant Marine Academy in 1974, the Naval Academy in '75, the Coast Guard Academy in '76. The state academies also fell in line. Curiously, the International Organization of Masters, Mates and Pilots had admitted its first woman in 1967: Jean Bononcini, a thirty-eight-year-old grandmother, master of a thirty-four-foot charter boat licensed to operate up to ten miles from the mouth of the Columbia River. During the war years sailors had been amused to see Russian ships with women aboard as common seamen; now they had them as shipmates, in charge of watches, competing for the same jobs, even as skippers. The law gave unions an easy win when the customary practice of berthing unlicensed crew members in shared rooms by watch group was revised to provide private quarters for all. Reduce the space in an economy single-bed motel room by two thirds, replace the window opposite the door with a porthole, remove the television, put a shared shower and toilet between adjacent rooms, and you have an unlicensed seaman's cabin. Officers get a bit more space and a private bath.

The year 1968 brought a revolutionary change in cargo operations, the culmination of a decade of determined effort by a trucker named Malcolm McLean. In the mid-1950s, McLean, the operator of an overland trucking company, removed the piping and valves from a T-2 tanker and converted it to a metal box carrier, which he called a containership. The idea wasn't original; Seatrain had done something similar forty years earlier. It was McLean's concerted effort through ten years of conflict between shippers, stevedores, and port authorities that made it revolutionary. So confident was he in his scheme that he started Sea-Land Service with a fleet of containerships able to carry thirty-five-foot sealed boxes loaded from McLean Trucking Company's flatbed trailers. Freight forwarders saw merit in the system, which reduced pilferage, lowered cargo handling costs, and speeded up loading and discharge. The advantages extended to merchants, who benefited from quicker delivery of their goods and lower insurance rates. By permitting decentralization of bonded warehouses, the new system eased congestion at the piers. Pilferers were stopped by the sealed boxes, which bore no indication of their contents, whether gravel or gold. The only disadvantage from the shippers' point of view was that the containers made the work of pirates easier. The pirates found protection against traditional shipboard defenses in the vertical walls of the deck-load containers. They easily scaled the boxes with grappling hooks cast from boats running alongside, then invaded them with bolt cutters. On decks obstructed by the boxes, crews could no longer get a clear shot with fire hoses or flare guns—a risky practice in any case given the apparent collusion between pirates and many governments around the world. Injuring even an illegal boarder brings the risk of a fine or jail for the visiting captain, or at a minimum, increased expense and delay. Pirate attacks continue today as they have for centuries in the East Indies and the west coasts of South America and Africa, technology no match for determined looters.

Matson Navigation decided to use containers in the Hawaiian trade but disagreed with McLean about the length of the boxes. Twenty-four-foot containers were the easiest for Matson's trucks to handle on Hawaii's mountainous roads. In those days companies tailored container sizes to their own specialized requirements, until industry standards of twenty, thirty, and forty feet evolved. (For some years the basic unit has been the TEU [twenty-foot-equivalent], a box measuring 20'x 8'x 8'.) While shippers argued about a uniform container size, in 1968 McLean convinced the New York Port Authority to recondition the dock facilities in Port Elizabeth, New Jersey, and give his trucks marshaling space near the ships. That move inflamed port rivalries up and down the East Coast, even within the New York Port Authority. New Jersey had better access and more undeveloped land for expansion; Manhattan's docks couldn't provide adequate truck parking and turnaround space. Boston was reluctant to undergo the adjustment, blaming lack of space and concerns about reduced employment of longshoremen. The seaport feared that modern cargo movement would break its tenuous hold on the transatlantic trade, while across the harbor air freight carriers routinely took off for Europe with boxed freight. The stevedores' unspoken concern was that they could no longer see what was available for plunder. Philadelphia, Baltimore, and Norfolk voiced similar objections. All of these cities needed only to exercise a little imagination; there was ample waterfront space, as time would prove.

The longshoremen got involved, first because of the relocation of ILA workers from the North River piers to Port Elizabeth, then because of the workload reduction that resulted as containerization replaced traditional break-bulk cargo handling. Cargo hooks went idle and with them their owners, the number of jobs cut in half according to ILA president Thomas Gleason. Palletizing survived only in smaller ports. A conventional ten-thousand-ton dry cargo freighter required sixteen thousand man-hours to unload and reload using forklifts, pallets, and cargo nets. Cases could spill their contents when dropped or split down the side with a slyly wielded hook. Thousands of dollars worth of goods went into holds in exposed cartons and crates and came out in lunchpails or strapped inside a stevedore's trousers. To handle the same amount of cargo in locked metal boxes took only 1,100 man-hours. Truckload shippers were ecstatic. A containership might carry 1,240 twenty-foot containers, some in its holds and some stacked three-high on deck, exceeding by far the load a comparable break-bulk freighter could stow below decks. Shipping companies hastily redesigned traditional vessels, retaining the bridge and housing aft in the classic oil-tanker profile. Bridge crews with tanker experience had no trouble handling the modified ships. Some Matson ships carried the bridge fully forward with engine room and stack near the stern as on the Great Lakes ore carriers. Either way, containerization brought a fresh venue for merchant deck officers.

The donnybrook exploded when a union walkout delayed the maiden voyage of *American Lancer,* United States Lines' first containership and the test case for all companies dealing with the union. Labor won concessions, but the weary shipping companies strengthened their resolve to push for further manpower reductions. They would achieve this through containerization, the use of less costly shore labor, and improved technologies. American Export Line, ever ready to make alliances, joined first with Isbrandtsen, then with Farrell Lines, to put a new series of containerships afloat. A major change in dry-cargo shipping was under way.

Technology gave the American merchant fleets a new lease on life. Crew reduction was often achieved through small technological improvements. Better metal coatings, which could be maintained by contracted in-port labor, eliminated the century-old practice of assigning deck hands to bang at rusty decks and bulkheads with chipping hammers. Prepackaged frozen food, prepared ashore by maritime caterers and cooked aboard under radiant heat or, later, in microwave ovens, could be delivered hot to crew and officer messes by a single cook. Simple facility remodeling also helped reduce the size of crews. One less relief seaman was needed in each deck watch after a toilet was installed aft of the bridge. Ordinaries were the first to be dropped from the crews. The overall result was reduced need for all unlicensed personnel and less training of newer sailors, a trend that shifted the average age of dedicated seamen higher.

The 1980s brought more dramatic improvements in electronics. The "iron-mike" steering system was augmented with computer-controlled tracking: any course could be selected and steered automatically, point-to-point on a great circle without human interference, barring obstructions. Solid-state circuitry made radar both more reliable and more informative and reduced installation and maintenance costs. Ships began carrying multiple independent radar sets with different levels of function: head-up or north-up display, close or distant range. Position-plotting radar displays became collision-avoidance systems. (The equipment combines surface plotting with a computer-controlled maneuvering board: the user selects with a cursor any object observed on the screen, say, a "blip" thought to be another ship at some distance. In seconds a table of current data associated with the object's apparent motion is projected beside it on the screen and is constantly updated to give the object's true course, speed, and closest point of approach. Alarms sound before the closest point becomes too close.) Loran sets shrank, their computation and digital readout units no larger than a stack of navigation tables. They gave a continuous display of the receiver's latitude, longitude, course, and distance covered over a specified period. If the user entered the location of a series of targeted way-points, the loran could compute the proper course and distance to each from any named position. Thus the error-prone drudgery of dead reckoning was practically eliminated. Like the desktop computers that preceded them, shipboard electronic instruments got better every year.

Nowhere were such advances more appreciated than on the Great Lakes and their tributaries. The inland shipping industry is often taken for granted in maritime affairs. Its grain, steel, and ore carriers plod predictably over well-trafficked routes. Its history has involved little conflict between labor and management because the Lakes Carriers' Association has been more considerate of shipboard manpower than its counterparts on either coast. But the challenges of the inland waterways require a special breed of seaman. The weather can be ruthless. Ice obstructs operations for three to four months every year, and shipping traffic routinely clogs the waterways during the remaining period. Inland shippers were the first to switch to diesel power and hire diesel engineers in great numbers: 80 percent of Great Lakes ships were diesel-powered in 1970, as compared with 20 percent on the coasts. The inland rules of the road differ from those of international waters, and the lakes themselves are divided between Canadian and U.S. jurisdictions. Bridge watches require capable pilots, familiar with the locks and narrow waterways. Navigational reference points include not only the customary buoys and range lights, but shoreside shopping malls, church steeples, and grassy knolls. In 1969 the need for specialized officer training was recognized with the opening of the Great Lakes Maritime Academy under MarAd sponsorship. The former USS *Alleghany*, renamed the USTS *Northwestern*, became its schoolship. The smallest of the six state academies, Great Lakes Maritime is probably the best equipped. Some 150 cadets pursue a Coast Guard/MarAd-specified curriculum tailored to the lakes. They soon learn that midcontinent weather can be more threatening to ships than that encountered in midocean.

In November 1975, during one of the heaviest storms to strike Lake Superior in thirty years, the ore carrier *Edmund Fitzgerald*, steering for the eastern end of the lake with both of its radars disabled, sank after giving no more than a hint that it faced trouble. The radio beacon and light on Whitefish Point, seventeen miles distant, were both out. The ship was north of the customary course to the Soo locks, loaded with twenty-six thousand tons of taconite destined for the Detroit steel mills. There had been radio communication about the *Fitzgerald*'s situation but without specifics. The cargo holds may have taken in water through the hatches. A satisfactory explanation may never be found as no one from the crew of twenty-nine lived to tell the story. In recent years divers have returned to the broken hull, hovering over it like the mystery that hovers around its sudden loss. The subject of a popular folk song, the wreck of the *Edmund Fitzgerald* is a chilling reminder to Lakes mariners of the fallibility of modern equipment.

MarAd put muscle on the manpower squeeze by pressing the administration to relax its restrictions on construction differentials. The 1970 Merchant Marine Act, signed by President Nixon in October, was costly legislation aimed at rejuvenating shipbuilding by authorizing a ten-year subsidized fleet modernization program. A provision in the law specified that the Coast Guard and the designated operating company must agree on crew size before construction of any subsidized vessel could begin. In seeking agreement, the operators stressed economy; the Coast Guard, safety; the top maritime unions put their oars in for full employment. Deck and engineering officers were represented by the Masters,

Mates, and Pilots union and the Marine Engineers Beneficial Association, respectively. The NMU represented the unlicensed crews. Through their hiring halls the unions controlled the hiring of all but captains and chief engineers; in effect the crews worked for the unions that placed them. Among adversaries with diverse goals, there was little consolidation of purpose. By 1984 union strikes lost them their last contracts with the oil companies as those shippers entered into contracts with more cooperative organizations. The newly formed American Maritime Officers union and the long-established SIU took up representation of crews on unsubsidized ships and a growing share of the total seagoing labor force.

What was reputed to be the world's largest oil supply was discovered in January 1968 on Alaska's North Slope, one of the most forbidding areas of the planet. Located between the Brooks Range and the Arctic Ocean, the North Slope is difficult to reach by land or sea. Storm systems from Siberia rage with violence across the Bering Sea and up into the Arctic Ocean, freezing the Beaufort Sea through ten months of the year. Even in late summer, sea ice extends close to Alaska's northern coastline. Winter temperatures can drop to 45 below; winds are regularly clocked in excess of a hundred miles an hour. Mankind's intense thirst for oil revived interest in the legendary Northwest Passage, the route connecting the Atlantic's Baffin Bay to the Beaufort Sea, and now, to the Alaskan oil fields. Humble Oil contracted for a specially modified tanker in a gamble to be the first company to haul Arctic oil into the temperate zones. Seatrain, the innovative shipper of truck and rail containers, had expanded its activities to include tankers, and using the newly developed technique of computer simulation, it proposed that a large, well-fortified tanker could accomplish the task.

In August 1969 the ice-breaking supertanker *Manhattan* left Philadelphia for Point Barrow, by way of Baffin Bay. It was accompanied above the Arctic Circle by a Coast Guard icebreaker, which was forced by hull damage to withdraw before entering the most grueling part of the passage. Ice damaged the *Manhattan*'s propellers, but it pushed on, and on September 15 it became the first commercial vessel in history to negotiate the Prince of Wales Strait. Battle-weary, the tanker proved two things: that before the onset of winter a vessel could get through, and that given the difficulties, the voyage wasn't worth it.

The search for another transport route resulted in a controversial proposal before Congress to construct an above-ground pipeline, running eight hundred miles from Prudhoe Bay to Valdez, a fishing port in Prince William Sound, east of Anchorage. Some considered the idea preposterous. The cost of building the line and conveying the oil might far exceed the unknown value of the supply. Emotions were high from the beginning. Environmentalists anticipated ill effects at the pipeline's proposed southern terminal, the *Torrey Canyon* and *Amoco Cadiz* disasters still fresh in memory. In an evenly divided Senate, the bill passed in July 1973 with the swing vote of Vice President Spiro Agnew. Oil from Prudhoe Bay, reserved by law for U.S. consumption, started flowing through the Trans-Alaskan Pipeline to Port Valdez late in 1977, and the parade of supertankers began.

Oil became king in the ever dwindling fleet of American-flagged ships, crowned by default as the nation's other shipping enterprises struggled to survive. In 1982 United States Lines, reduced to freighter operations, absorbed the failing Moore-McCormack Lines. Four years later, unable to manage overseas containership operations at a profit, it went bankrupt. Sea-Land took over some of its ships. By 1983 container shipping was second only to oil in international trade, and Sea-Land had the majority of vessels; but it, too, suffered financial strain. Only three major American freighter companies remained under the American flag in 1995, operating digitized cargo pipelines in the form of containership fleets: Sea-Land, trading worldwide; Lykes Brothers, connecting the nation's southern ports to Central and South America; and American President, retaining its presence in the Pacific. All three companies applied for reflagging, driven to foreign registry by taxes, insurance costs, the curtailment of construction subsidies, and more than anything else, the cost of labor. American wages are four times those of foreign crews.

In 1988 the MEBA and NMU joined forces to cut overhead costs, attempting to strengthen their bargaining positions in the face of dwindling memberships. Meanwhile, only freighter efficiency and the expedience of coastal transport kept the American flag aloft. The industry continued to change through improvements in technology. Since 1960 fuel fleets included liquefied natural gas (LNG) carriers with their unique spreads of white-domed, refrigerated tanks. "Stick ships" with their complex arrays of masts, king posts, and cargo booms were replaced by containerships, as seaports tore down covered piers and acquired nearby property to provide acres of truck parking. Shipping in the last quarter of this century has become the bulk transport of goods in hoppers, tanks, and containers. The same ship that carries oil on one voyage can quickly be converted for the transport of grain on the next. Seagoing parking garages receive truck and rail cars aboard roll-on, roll-off (Ro-Ro) ships that can be unloaded and reloaded in the course of a single well-disciplined day. An attempt to avoid dockage fees and achieve fast turnaround produced the minimally successful LASH (lighter-aboard-ship) design. Preloaded barges were brought by tugs to the moored LASH vessel, then lifted and stowed by gantry cranes, and the ship was soon under way. Well suited to the waterways of Vietnam and used successfully during the war there, the technique attracted several Pacific operators, especially those still wary of containers. But there were difficulties with inefficient stowage, and the LASH vessels proved to be economic failures, driving the Prudential Line and Pacific Far East Line into bankruptcy. Break-bulk, a decade or two earlier a major source of commercial shipping's revenue, fell to a handful of small companies, eclipsed by the conglomerates' containerships, Ro-Ro, LNG transports, and the ever bigger tankers.

It was the Ro-Ro trade that first put Malcolm McLean and tanker king Daniel Ludwig head-to-head in competition, and later joined them in partnership. During the 1960s Ludwig had taken over the nearly defunct American-Hawaiian Steamship Company, divested it of its obsolete cargo carriers, and set about to enter the intercoastal trade with Ro-Ro ships. At the same time, McLean was planning to include Ro-Ro in his buildup of a worldwide Sea-Land fleet. (By then he had been divested of his trucking company under antitrust regulations.) The Pacific wasn't big enough for both of them. McLean was thinly financed for expansion but knew his way around the maritime administrators, and he succeeded in holding off Ludwig's efforts. Ludwig had the money and decided that if he couldn't fight McLean, he would join him by buying up some 11 percent of McLean Industries stock. The two tycoons had more interest in power and finance than in ocean shipping. The conflict was resolved in 1969 when the R. J. Reynolds tobacco conglomerate, seeking diversification, bought out McLean Industries. Both Ludwig and McLean pocketed enormous profits, and the Sea-Land ships sailed on.

These were thrilling times for people who could adapt to changing technologies. Motivated by ratification of the 1974 Safety of Life at Sea (SOLAS) conventions, the shipping industry took a fresh look at ocean communications. After three satellites were sent into geosynchronous orbits around the equator in 1976, the Marisat system established wireless voice communications around the world. Radiograms became obsolete when a captain could pick up a handset and call home or office from anywhere in the world. (Some skippers asked with concern, "Can home or office call me as easily?") Radio operators found themselves in a dying job and quickly redefined their role. They developed expertise in setting up, maintaining, and operating computer network servers for the bridge, cargo office, and engine-room data collection systems. "Sparks" the radio operator became a computer-savvy Maintenance Radio Electronics Officer.

The 1970s brought advances in weather forecasting. During a period of government reorganization in 1970, the Hydrographic Office (HO), its charting function then part of the Defense Mapping Agency, was combined with emerging programs to study weather and oceanography. The National Oceanographic and Atmospheric Administration (NOAA) was formed, taking over the HO's longstanding function of charting the oceans and merging the HO with the National Ocean Survey, National Weather Services, and National Marine Fisheries Services. Bureaucracy was reduced, but the prices of the exquisitely crafted HO charts soared. Weather forecasts, on the other hand, became cheaper and more accurate. By the 1980s it was possible to receive reliable, NOAA-mapped weather status reports by fax at any time of day or night, on land or sea.

The cumbersome SatNav positioning system developed by the Department of Defense (DoD) in the 1960s, which used five military satellites, led to the design of a much-improved global positioning system (GPS) in the '70s, held tightly within the DoD domain. Civilian engineers soon recognized the tremendous potential of GPS in hundreds of applications, ship positioning being just one. Their challenge was to pry GPS out of the hands of the military so that commercial users could achieve the same remarkable accuracy. In 1980 DoD offered a compromise—a modified GPS less accurate than the military system. In 1996 the federal government took the wraps off entirely. Now, civilians too can use the small, inexpensive, battery-powered device to define their position on the globe in three dimensions with a precision of a few meters. Aircraft can use GPS to guide a landing, taxis to find a street. Shipboard navigators have set aside their sextants and replaced the hallowed noon position slips with hourly position plots gathered at the push of a button. Only prudence and the rare event of GPS failure keep mates working with chronometer, sextant, and almanacs.

The training of cadets has had to keep pace with technological change. Selected Kings Point cadets, trained in both deck and engine-room disciplines, can now sit for both mate and engineer Coast Guard licenses, and become what the academy optimistically calls "officers of the future." Million-dollar ship simulators have enhanced the training methods in the officer schools as well as in navy-sponsored commercial "hawse-pipe" programs for training less academic mariners.

The United States has lagged behind Europe in the use of diesel engines, despite European improvements that long ago made them cheaper and more fuel-efficient than steam turbines. When the advantages of diesel became clear, American engineers were held back by a combination of construction differential subsidies, low-cost oil, and their own skill in producing the most powerful and efficient steam plants in the world. Subsidized ships were required to use equipment built in the United States by American labor. But the first American-made diesels were slow and unsafe. Because of the shrinking market for big-ship diesels, European companies had no incentive to set up plants near American yards. Progress came only after the rising oil prices of the 1970s forced American manufacturers to achieve the necessary technology transfer. Today, only the expensive supertanker fleet still faces the conversion to diesel. The chief obstacle seems to be the public demand for full gas tanks, which keeps the ships too busy to go to the drydock for the time it would take to convert them.

At the time that the *Manhattan* was being modified for icebreaking, the maximum tanker size was about 300,000 deadweight tons. Tankers exceeding 150,000 tons were classified as very large crude carriers (VLCCs). The Suez and Panama canals were limiting factors (large vessels barely able to pass through the canal's locks became known as Panamax ships). But the canals' importance diminished as oil supplies and refinery ports multiplied around the world. American tanker ports in New York, Philadelphia, and Houston, limited by their upriver approaches, did what they could to accommodate larger ships. Perhaps the most bizarre effort to keep the oil flowing can be seen on the Houston Ship Canal. The Port of Houston was founded in 1836 on a bayou that ran forty-five miles to Galveston on the Gulf Coast. In 1914, after a disastrous hurricane that almost obliterated Galveston Island, a sea-level canal with a greater controlling depth was built to open the upstream port to large passenger vessels. After World War I, oil refineries appeared nearby, which brought even larger tankers into the canal. As ships got wider, the canal pilots developed an unusual passing maneuver for the narrow stretches of the waterway, which they swear is safer than having one ship linger on the side to yield passage. Morgan's Point is a good spot to observe what the locals call "Texas Chicken." Two ships meeting head-to-head will be seen to steer directly for each other and increase speed, building their bow waves like foam on the mouths of attacking dogs. At the critical moment both dodge to starboard, little more than half a ship's width from the center of the channel. The resulting surge of water trapped between the hulls cushions them as they pass, preventing the condition whereby reduced pressure between moving bodies draws them uncontrollably together. Pilots are a close-mouthed lot, not apt to share their secrets. How two pilots on approaching vessels can trust each other to execute the Texas Chicken, how they know when to turn, and how they remain calm during the exercise are mysteries left for the observer to ponder.

Long Beach, San Francisco, and the ports at the approach to Puget Sound were better equipped to welcome supertankers. Shipbuilding and port expansion went into an upward spiral of accommodation to which there seemed no limit. In protected bays, receiving terminals were built in deep water, man-made islands connected by pipelines and a roadway to the mainland. Shipbuilders used new alloys of high-tensile steel, specified in computer-aided designs, to produce ships larger than the VLCCs. Before the oil started flowing across Alaska, the Norwegians and Japanese built ultra-large crude carriers (ULCCs) exceeding 300,000 deadweight tons. The long hulls of the supertankers were designed to be flexible and to provide the maximum cargo space per unit of enclosure weight. The foil wrapper on a potato chip bag is thicker in relation to its contents than the plating of a supertanker is to its load of oil.

Environmentalists familiar with Prince William Sound's pristine waters spoke out. So, too, did responsible Coast Guard authorities. A requirement of double-bottomed construction was proposed for all oil carriers entering the Sound, but fleet operators dismissed it as too costly. The modernization of navigational aids continued. Lighthouse automation was completed by 1986, and a new buoyage system conforming to world standards was scheduled for completion by 1990. All of the black buoys were replaced by green, perhaps less confusing for foreign visitors. By 1989 the Coast Guard had eight radar-equipped VTCs in place to monitor supertanker movements in oil ports from New Jersey to Alaska. Eight thousand tankers had passed in and out of Port Valdez without incident in a twelve-year period——except for one or two near misses and some

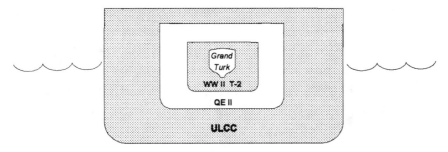

16-1. Relative hull sizes in cross-section, eighteenth to twentieth centuries

small spills—testimony, it seemed, to the caution exercised in the long stretch of water in Prince William Sound. In fact, the record reinforced the complacency that resulted in the most destructive oil spill in history.

A few minutes after midnight on Good Friday, March 24, 1989, the loaded supertanker *Exxon Valdez* ground its hull into the rocks off Bligh Island in Prince William Sound. (The island is named for its discoverer, William Bligh, who was Captain Cook's navigator and later was deposed as captain of the HMS *Bounty.*) Within hours, 11 million gallons of petroleum surged over the waters and nearby shore. Springtime never arrived for the area's waterfowl, fish, and flora, grimy with cold, black oil. When the investigation was complete, the event became a metaphor for the troubled times. Indifferent, rule-bound authorities; callous, cost-cutting shippers; bored traffic controllers; overworked mariners inattentive to duty; alcohol, drugs, and greed all joined in a sordid litany of contributing causes.

The reader is welcome to join hundreds of others—Alaskan natives, bartenders, columnists, environmentalists, reporters, tankermen, and television commentators—in assessing the extent of Joseph Hazelwood's culpability. These

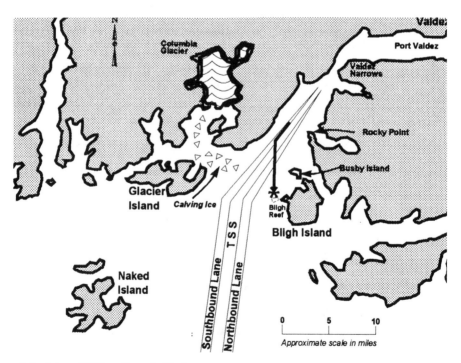

16-2. Prince William Sound, Alaska. ARTWORK BY JEFFREY PETERS, ADAPTED FROM *ANCHORAGE DAILY NEWS*

are the facts: the main source of this account is Appendix N ("Chronology") of the Oil Spill Commission Report.

23 MARCH 1989

2112   The 211,000-ton *Exxon Valdez,* loaded with 54 million gallons of crude oil, clears Berth 5 in Port Valdez, aided by two tugs. On the bridge are Captain Joseph Hazelwood, chief mate and undocking watch officer James Kunkel, local pilot William Murphy (an employee of Alyeska Pipeline Service Company), and A-B Paul Radtke at the helm. To Hazelwood's surprise upon his return aboard at 2030, the port authorities have advanced the scheduled departure by one hour.

2125   With a single tug astern escorting the ship through the Valdez Narrows, an unidentified speaker, not Hazelwood, calls the USCG Vessel Traffic Center (VTC) to report *Valdez* under way.

2135   Hazelwood turns navigational command (the "conn") over to Kunkel and goes below to his cabin.

2150   Third Mate Gregory Cousins arrives on the bridge to relieve Kunkel for the remainder of his customary eight-to-twelve watch. Cousins holds a second mate's license and has made thirteen to fifteen trips through Prince William Sound on the bridge of other ships, three on the *Valdez.* Although his license does not have a Coast Guard pilotage endorsement for the Sound, it is possible he conforms to current requirements, so frequently altered is the standard. No one is checking. His experience with pack ice is minimal, but Cousins is regarded by Chief Mate Kunkel as an "exceptional" officer. The fatigued Kunkel, having worked loading cargo for more than fourteen hours with little respite, retires. Cousins has agreed to remain on watch after midnight to allow Second Mate Lloyd LeCain more time to sleep; LeCain has also worked extra hours with little time off. Captain Hazelwood has agreed to stand Kunkel's next watch (0400–0800 on Friday morning) so that the mate can rest. Pilot Murphy gives helm orders and directs the watch officer to make necessary changes in engine speed.

2200   Radars are in use to investigate the slot between islands and reefs to port and a field of icebergs calving from the Columbia Glacier far to starboard.

2217   Preparing to pass Entrance Island, the *Valdez* slows to required speed of six knots.

2220   With Entrance Island abeam to port, 0.36 miles distant, the *Valdez* turns into Valdez Narrows, where Middle Rock limits the practical width of the strait to nine hundred yards. The ship is operating at half speed (55 rpm). Visibility about four miles in drizzle; sea calm, wind light, tide rising. Reports have been received of ice in the channel ahead. Chevron and Arco tankers are both about one hour ahead of the *Valdez,* both taking a diversionary course eastward (to the left) of the ice.

2249   *Valdez* requests traffic and ice report from the VTC. It states that it is increasing speed and passing Potato Point at the southern end of the Narrows. The VTC reports small pieces of ice from Freemantle to Glacier Island to starboard of *Valdez's* planned path, which deviates into the northbound (left) lane; traffic is reported by the VTC as clear.

2253   The *Valdez* passes Potato Point to starboard. Visibility is improved to eight miles as the ship enters Valdez Arm, moving slow ahead as it approaches Rocky Point pilot station, fourteen miles from Port Valdez. Duties shift on the hour; at the pilot's request, A-B Radtke is posted on the bow as lookout when A-B Harry Claar relieves him on the helm.

2305   Pilot Murphy asks the third mate to call the captain to the bridge, anticipating arrival at the pilot station.

2310   Hazelwood returns to the bridge for the pilot's disembarking. Murphy detects the smell of alcohol on his breath (which he had also noted earlier when the two first met before getting under way), but he judges the captain to be fit and focused. Hazelwood assumes the conn, directs the third mate to escort the pilot to the Jacob's ladder on the port side of the main deck, and by hand-held radio instructs the bow lookout to assist in disembarking the pilot.

2315   The engine reduced from half ahead (45 rpm) to slow ahead (31 rpm).

2324   Pilot off. Hazelwood sets the engine to full ahead (56 rpm) and the course to 218°; he calls the VTC (addressed as "Valdez Traffic"), identifying himself as *Exxon Valdez*. Alone with the helmsman on the bridge, overseeing the departure of the pilot boat to port and studying the radar, in his opening conversation with the VTC he starts to reference his ship by the name of his previous command, *Exxon Baton Rouge* but corrects himself ("Valdez Traffic? Ah, Exxon Bata, ah, Valdez"). He pauses, then reports the pilot's departure. He then states that he is increasing to "sea speed," with the estimated time of arrival 0100 at Naked Island, a location where ships report their positions to the VTC.

2325   The VTC confirms the *Valdez* report and requests an updated ice report "when you get down through there." Hazelwood responds that judging from the radar he probably will divert from the traffic separation scheme (TSS) and end up in the inbound lane if there is no conflicting traffic. Hazelwood: "We may end up over in the inbound lane, outbound transit. We'll notify you when we leave the, ah, TSS and, ah, cross over the Separation Zone. Over." The VTC states that there is no reported traffic, indicating concurrence with the plan. [Ice calving from the Columbia Glacier was being massed together by the current and pushed west-to-east across the TSS. Bergs vary from chunks the size of tree trunks, of little concern to a tanker, to "growlers" the size of small craft. The latter must be avoided or approached slowly, with possible loss of steerage; hence the diversionary route. To shift lanes the *Valdez* needed a run of about ten minutes on a course 20° to the left of the normal 200°, i.e., 180°.]

2331   The *Valdez* turns left to a course of 200°, about midway between the Narrows and Bligh Reef. Hazelwood calls the VTC: "At the present time, ah, I'm going to alter my course to two-zero-zero and reduce speed about twelve knots to, ah, wind my way through the ice, and Naked Island ETA might be a little out of whack, but, once we are clear of the ice out of Columbia Bay, we'll give you another shout. Over."

2335   (approximate time)
The captain calls Radtke by hand-held radio and tells him to inform the A-B relieving him as lookout to go to the bridge to stand her watch.

2339   The third mate plots a fix, placing the ship in the middle of the TSS.

2340   At the VTC, radarman Gordon Taylor is preparing to be relieved by radarman Bruce Blandford. Taylor sees the *Valdez* blinking on and off the screen, and tells his relief that the ship is crossing into the separation zone and possibly into the northbound lane to avoid ice. Meanwhile, the *Valdez* has changed course to 180° and Hazelwood has put the ship on automatic steering (the "iron mike"). Third Mate Cousins is aware of the changes, and the captain gives him spoken instructions about changing the course back to the right; this includes identification of a position 1.4 miles from Busby Light when it bears 235° where the course change is to be made. Ice, not yet visible, appears on the radar two miles dead ahead on the former 200° course, to the right of the new course. [Conflicting testimonies about instructions given by the captain on the turning point raise doubts as to what was said and understood. This is the more likely position to have been specified, but also the more dangerous one.]

2345   In the control center Blandford relieves Taylor and devotes several minutes to changing audio tapes of radio conversations, getting coffee, and rearranging the traffic data sheets. (Because he is left-handed, he must reorganize them from their customary layout.)

2349 or
2350   The *Valdez*'s recording fathometer puts the ship outside the hundred-fathom curve.

2350   The watches change aboard ship. A-B Robert Kagan relieves Harry Claar at the wheel; A-B Maureen Jones relieves Paul Radtke and takes the lookout station on the starboard bridge wing. Third Mate Cousins continues on watch, standing in as agreed for Second Mate LeCain, but having no experience with the sailors on LeCain's watch. (Kagan is known by others to be easily confused and is not regarded as a good helmsman, being inclined to swing the ship about the mark.) Kagan acknowledges the course of 180° as he takes over from Radtke, and Cousins takes the ship off the mike with Kagan now at the wheel.

2352   A "load program up" command is given, apparently by the captain, placing the engine under computer control. Within forty-three minutes this should increase the speed from 55 rpm to a sea speed of full ahead, or 78.7 rpm. Hazelwood instructs Cousins to "start coming back into the lanes" once the ship is abeam Busby Island Light. ["Ship . . .abeam . . .light" is commonly used terminology but is potentially confusing because it leaves the compass bearing in doubt, as lights have no "beam." "Light abeam ship" leaves no doubt that the light should bear at a right angle to the ship's designated course. There is no record of what Hazelwood actually said. The words used here are from the National Transportation Safety Board (NTSB) report.] After the discussion Hazelwood leaves the bridge to get out messages.

2355   Busby Island Light is abeam to port, about 1.1 miles distant. [The transcription from the *Exxon Valdez*'s deck log to the Commission Report states this as "abeam to starboard," clearly an error. Various testimonies agreed within 0.2 mile as to the accuracy of the fix, placing the light properly to port.] At about this time Jones, the lookout on the starboard wing, warns the bridge that Bligh Reef Light is sighted ahead, off to the ship's right. Within a minute she gives a second report confirming her first observation. Cousins acknowledges it.

2356   (approximate time)
Cousins orders right 10° rudder, then orders the rudder angle increased to 20°. With the ship swinging to the right, the helmsman may have given some counter rudder to slow the swing. Cousins calls the captain to inform him that there is a problem.

24 MARCH 1989
0001   The ship is east of the deep shipping channel and moving into the leading edge of the ice.

0003   (approximate time)
Cousins and Hazelwood are on the phone when they feel the ship ground, and both hang up. Cousins issues an order for hard right rudder. From first impact the ship travels six hundred feet before coming to a stop.

0004   Captain Hazelwood is on the bridge and gives a number of rudder orders in an attempt to free the vessel. Third Mate Cousins logs the grounding.

0026/27   Hazelwood reports the grounding and some leakage to the VTC. Blandford switches on his radar and sees a display of the *Exxon Valdez* quite evidently on the reef.

0310   (approximate time)
Chief Warrant Officer Mark Delozier, USCG, is among others boarding the *Exxon Valdez*. He finds Hazelwood near a bridge window, drinking coffee, smoking, hand over his mouth. Delozier smells alcohol and asks what caused the accident. Hazelwood replies, "You are looking at it."

Ten hours after the incident Hazelwood's blood alcohol level was found to be about half that permitted by the Alaska drunk-driving standard, but 50 percent higher than the Coast Guard limit for seamen operating a ship. Later, CWO Delozier found two empty bottles of 0.5 percent "nonalcoholic" beer (standard Exxon issue), which in testimony Hazelwood said he had consumed after returning aboard. Did Hazelwood keep alcohol aboard? It was not proven. Did he have a history of alcohol problems? Yes, he was known to be a heavy drinker from his days as a cadet in the New York State Maritime College. He was still under a New York DWI (driving-while-intoxicated) constraint. He had been warned earlier about his drinking problem, and at the suggestion of his Exxon supervisor he had undergone treatment for addiction.

Was his ability impaired on the night of the accident? That remains undetermined. His crew members did not think so, having observed him for months. The Coast Guard found that his actions after the grounding were exemplary. Many people, from stevedores and common seamen to battlefield generals and U.S. presidents, have performed quite well with a few ounces of alcohol under their belt. Ship captains require less eye-hand coordination than a person driving in normal automobile traffic. In commanding a ship, experience and judgment are paramount.

Was Hazelwood known to be a capable seaman? Yes. Several instances from his cadet days onward support this. Pilot Murphy gave testimony to that effect. The *Exxon Valdez* was Exxon's newest and most advanced tanker, and Hazelwood's assignment to it was indirect evidence of his abilities.

In later testimony before the NTSB Hazelwood said of his absence from the bridge, "I should have been up there." In the State of Alaska court, Hazelwood pleaded no contest to the charge of violating the Coast Guard policy against drinking liquor less than four hours before taking command of a vessel.

He also pleaded no contest to the charge of improperly leaving the bridge while the ship was headed for Bligh Reef. He was found guilty of negligent discharge of oil, and the finding was appealed, reversed, and counter-appealed. Through all of the accusations, castigations, and commentary, he remained resolutely silent about what had occurred on the *Exxon Valdez*.

The investigations revealed unforeseen shortcomings in the operations of the Alyeska Pipeline Company, Exxon, and the Coast Guard, and in the security precautions in Port Valdez. Evidence was reported that VTC civilian radarman Blandford had used alcohol shortly before but not necessarily while he was on watch, and Taylor was known to have been a marijuana user sometime before his duty period. Because of that, the NTSB relieved the Coast Guard of its role as an investigator in the case.

Along with a $2 billion bill for the cleanup, the accident brought several reforms. The authorities issued new regulations concerning speed limits in Prince William Sound, the employment of a pilot in the iceberg area, the use of escort tugs and security guards. Crew members about to go on duty were required to submit to a breath-analyzer test witnessed by a mate before sailing. The American Bureau of Shipping reviewed the requirements for steel hulls, and the Coast Guard called for more thorough inspections. The Alaskan environmentalists may have been somewhat mollified by the measures, which nevertheless amounted to turning up the heat after the pipes had burst.

Five months after the accident the Coast Guard extended its study of the accident to review tanker operations in all U.S. waters. Among its findings: Construction standards and maintenance of American ships had declined despite an increasing number of vessels more than seven hundred feet long, which were more likely than shorter vessels to suffer wear and tear, develop cracks, and lose oil at sea; shipping companies were increasing the pressure on shipmasters to meet tough schedules and strive for maximum speed even in rough seas; standards for manning ships overlooked the duties that officers and crew are required to perform when not on watch; excessive reliance was placed on technical systems and on the ability of crews to solve problems on the spot. The Coast Guard also came down hard on itself. Its summary report found that the organization had cooperated with owners and operators by allowing tankers to be unprepared for inspections, and had excused failures as "facilitating commerce." The report found Coast Guard inspection teams to be undermanned, undertrained, underequipped, and demoralized.

Public reactions to the findings and to the destruction in Prince William Sound and elsewhere in the world led to the federal Oil Pollution Act of 1990

(OPA 90). The act requires tankers to have double hulls, but allows existing single-hulled vessels to continue in operation through 2015. Unlicensed seamen are no longer permitted to hold documents for life; like officers, they must renew with the Coast Guard every five years. As part of the renewal, drug tests are administered and driver's license records are checked for alcohol-related violations. Renewal candidates are also tested for job-related knowledge. This test is less stringent than in the past. Before the advent of computer testing, license examinations were administered by Coast Guard officers and petty officers, who could observe the candidate at work, albeit in a classroom environment. Now the exams consist of multiple-choice questions presented by computer in an interactive sequence called adaptive testing: the more correct answers the candidate gives, the more difficult the subsequent questions become. On such a test there is a high probability that the candidates' scores will represent accurately the extent of their knowledge. But the test measures only memory; unlike tests for comparable skills such as flying an airplane, it does not measure on-the-job performance.

OPA 90 provided for the establishment within ten years of a modern Vessel Traffic Service, known as VTS 2000. This would extend the aged VTCs to serve seventeen ports around the nation. Progress has been slow because of controversy about distribution of the costs—the tug and barge industries don't need the service and want nothing to do with assessment. Five ports—New York, Galveston-Houston, San Francisco, Seattle, and Valdez—have systems that do not assess fees.

After the accident, oil companies attempted to reduce negative publicity by removing their corporate names from their tankers. Some changed the names of their shipping subsidiaries. The *Exxon Valdez,* prohibited from entering Prince William Sound under any name, became *Seariver Mediterranean,* a Seariver Shipping tanker delivering Exxon oil from the Persian Gulf to ports in the Mediterranean. Amoco and Texaco have reduced the size of their shipping divisions, preferring to let independent companies do the work and take the risk. Chevron and Mobil, on the other hand, have modernized their fleets. They have commissioned the construction of double-hulled tankers conforming to OPA 90 standards, but are not averse to shipping under foreign flags to foreign ports to reap the benefits of fewer regulations and cheaper labor.

A refreshing departure from the general decline of break-bulk carriers—history-making in a small way, with a hint of future potential for American shipping—came about in 1992 through the efforts of the fifth African-American owned shipping company in the nation's history. The first was that of Paul Cuffe, born in Cuttyhunk, Massachusetts, to a Pequot Indian mother and a freed black father. During the Madison administration, around 1815, Cuffe petitioned the president to have the Norfolk customs collector clear one of his vessels for New Bedford; clearance had been denied because the owner-captain was black. By then Cuffe had been a successful shipbuilder, master, owner of multiple vessels, foreign trader, and merchant. Madison moved accordingly and Cuffe continued in operation. The second African-American shipping company was Marcus Garvey's Black Star Line. A black leader of Jamaican origin, Garvey tried twice during the 1920s to create a profitable shipping line. The Black Star Line operated the *Yarmouth* under Canadian registry for three years, sending it on three ocean voyages before Garvey was convicted and jailed for mail fraud and forced to sell all of his ships at auction. He formed another business even before his sentence was commuted—the Black Cross Navigation & Trading Company, which operated the *General G. W. Goethals* for the U.S. Shipping Board and the Panama Railroad for about a year. Black Cross was an intermediary between shippers and ship operators, the type of business that would be known later as a non-vessel-owning common carrier (NVOCC). As ocean carriers, NVOCCs are classified as shipping companies. Around 1985 the Eagle Shipping Lines became an NVOCC, the fourth black-owned ocean carrier.

Arizona law professor and admiralty lawyer John P. Morris II took a long chance when he founded the Red River Shipping Corporation. With $100,000 in equity capital, he purchased an option on an old tanker, the *Red River,* for carrying grain to the Far East. The cargo didn't materialize, but having established at least the name of a company, Morris pushed on. Under a Small Business Administration program that enables small, disadvantaged businesses to compete for sole-source government contracts, Morris arranged to carry soybean oil to Pakistan and bulk wheat to South Africa for AID (Agency for International Development). He chartered the Japanese-built, Peruvian-flagged MV *Advantage* from a ship management company called American Automar, which undertook to reflag it. By 1988 Red River Shipping had turned over its first profit. Morris, now joined by his business-trained son, John III, learned the process of reflagging, and made two military supply runs during the Persian Gulf War. He then entered into competitive bidding for part of the Military Sealift Command's thirteen-vessel Afloat Prepositioned Force, and won by taking a 51 percent ownership of the *Advantage.* He later acquired a second vessel, purchased from a French firm, which he reflagged and renamed *Buffalo Soldier.* Both ships were 21,900-ton, multipurpose, double-'tween-deck general cargo carriers. They were uniquely designed, part stick-ship, part containership, and part Ro-Ro. In 1992, with the acquisition of the *Advantage,* Red River Shipping became the first black-owned shipping company to operate powered vessels under the stars and stripes.

During the last forty years the number of oceangoing vessels flying the American flag has declined steadily from its peak of 3,500 ships to fewer than 300, most of them tankers. American ocean trading continues and ample cargo continues to move around the world. But the cargo travels under the flags of the Bahamas, Liberia, Cyprus, Panama, the Marshall Islands—rarely under the stars and stripes. The U.S. flag flies only from the trucks of coastal carriers and from vessels under government preferential cargo contracts. Cruise liners are almost exclusively foreign and have gained a reputation for a cavalier approach to safety. For low-risk adventure on an American ship try the Hudson River Day Line or the Nantucket Steamship Authority, or take the three-day inland passage between Seattle and Skagway, Alaska.

Many of the remaining American-flagged ships are falling into disrepair. ULCCs are being sold abroad, retired, and sent to the breakers. VLCCs and smaller tankers continue to threaten the shorelines while feeding the largest per capita demand for energy in the world. When subsidized ships, the property of American taxpayers, are deactivated they are not necessarily scrapped. Those in good condition go to the reserve fleet, moored or docked in protected waters, held for possible reactivation. Incidentally, those that are scrapped are not "converted to razor blades"—an expression based on a rumor started in 1936, which the Gillette Company has been denying ever since. (Razor blades are made from high-quality surgical steel, not scrapped steamships.) In 1990–91 several reserve-fleet ships were restored to active service in support of Desert Storm, the only major use of retired vessels that has been made since World War II. Even the old ships were supplemented by more suitable, newer, foreign-built vessels. Operation Sealift to the Persian Gulf provided essential supplies in time for a quick completion of that affair, using companies like Red River Shipping.

The last working sail-powered pilot vessel, the *Roseway,* was withdrawn from its Boston harbor station in 1972. Sailing pilot boats had plied the waters of Boston, Mobile, San Francisco, and Portland, Maine, through war and peace during most of the century. But VHF, high-speed launches, and helicopters finally made the faithful old guides obsolete. The schooner *Roseway* with its famous black sails remained in active service the longest.

Dipping the ensign to the memory of Samuel F. B. Morse and "CQD"

16-3. MV *Buffalo Soldier*. Courtesy Red River Shipping Company

Binns, in 1995 the Coast Guard discontinued its use of Morse code. Spoken English does the job. Thus ended a technology that from Morse's early work spanned a hundred and seventeen years of American use of his invention. Is the voyage of the American merchant marine, for all its promising sunrises, triumphant and turbulent crossings, midcourse changes and masterful landfalls, near its end? Is it time for "finished with engines"? After a year of wrangling in both houses, Congress passed the Maritime Security Act of 1995, amending the 1936 Merchant Marine Act. Signed by President Clinton on October 8, 1996, the new act mandates a U.S. presence in international commercial shipping by extending operating differential subsidies to privately owned vessels that can be militarily useful. This gesture of support calls up an echo from the nation's earliest days, when the Derby fleet was formed. The story of Red River Shipping parallels that of the Derby fleet in important ways: the father-son relationship, the background of the chief officer in business, not seafaring, the modest start, and the auspicious use of government aid coupled with a large measure of individual financial courage. Perhaps it marks a new beginning.

Epilogue

Their pictures hang in a dimly lit corner of the museum, old monochromes placed at a remove from the imposing, gilt-framed oils of eighteenth-century sea captains. These small, rigidly posed photographs of merchant crews from the 1860s tell a different story. Sailmakers, foretopmen, stokers, firemen, oilers, and wipers; a mate standing stiffly beside a great, spoked wheel; three mustachioed engineers, looking uncomfortable in brass-buttoned, double-breasted jackets, hands behind their backs as if to hide their blackened nails. The twentieth-century photographs are less formal: a watch-capped lookout somberly scans the forward horizon; two enginemen, tails of their soot-stained shirts hung out, lean against the chain railing of a Hog Islander. There is one grim picture of men in the water with gaunt, oil-soaked faces, desperation in their eyes as they cling to the remains of a wrecked lifeboat. In a publicity photo, an officer in dress whites stands on the promenade deck of a liner, smiling at a bevy of bob-haired ladies. A more credible shot shows a stevedore signaling directions to a winchman, who lifts netted cargo over a hatch. Last, a hard-hatted seaman struggles with a pipe fitting in the midst of a clutter of valves and oil supply lines.

These mariners answered no siren call to the sea. They learned a trade that gave them an ordered life, a taste of adventure, a collection of memories to be embellished and retold, and in recent decades a good living, at least while it lasted. In the process they learned to love the life at sea. They are the men who have made the merchant marine. Today, many are out of work. Joining them in the idle ranks are carpenters, bosuns, electricians, pursers, and radiomen, mariners with skills no longer needed on shipboard. Can we learn from these men, living or dead, about the causes of the decline of a great maritime power? Can we find hope for revival? Or will the final change be without challenge as the last American flag is lowered from an active ocean trader, to be preserved perhaps for display beside the framed oils and old monochromes?

Today the active unlicensed seaman on ocean waters typically is about fifty-five years old and can claim more than thirty-five years spent at sea. He sailed for adventure when he started. He does it now for the money, tolerant of the demands of unique working conditions. It costs $3 million a year to staff a typical American-flagged tanker with two captains and double crews of twenty-four (four more than the Coast Guard requires).

Excluding those in land-based work or employed by the government, seven thousand to eight thousand seamen make up today's merchant service. They ship thirty-five million tons of cargo per year. This is in striking contrast with the figures half a century ago, when sixty thousand oceangoing mariners shipped fifty million tons a year. Tonnage has dropped, and the man-hours needed per ton have dropped even more. The modern ships with their greater capacity are more efficient and spend less turnaround time in port, while crew size is half what it was at midcentury. Three watch-standing mates with collateral duties do the work once done by four. A bosun and five A-Bs—two men per watch—cover the unlicensed duties on deck. Among these nine men, more than half are likely to be licensed as officers, some as second or chief mates. The chief mate may hold an unlimited master's certificate, any tonnage, any ocean.

Pay scales do not reflect the drop in demand, however. Containership chief engineers and captains earn $132,000 to $150,000 annually, for six months aboard, six ashore, not all of the latter considered paid vacation. (Seamen are entitled to unemployment compensation during their period ashore.) A newly licensed officer at entry level can earn $7,000 a month. Add medical insurance and retirement funding, and it's not a bad living. A-Bs get $30,000 per year plus overtime with similar benefits and perhaps a small severe-weather clothing allowance. That's the same wage as a messman in the steward's department; a cook can earn $45,000. It's possible to ship with an oil company for seventy-five days, then take fifty paid vacation days with company-funded travel between home and ship (home can be anywhere in the continental United States). Terms and conditions vary with the unions. The American Maritime Officers union, once representing only licensed personnel on unsubsidized ships, now puts its members on most of the government-owned vessels used in prepositioning and other Department of Defense operations. So, too, the SIU in its representation of unlicensed seamen. Members of both unions sail at wages that are some one-third less than those paid to Masters, Mates, and Pilots, and National Maritime Union members. AFL-CIO membership is at its lowest level since 1969, although the benefits of decades of tough bargaining have accumulated. Shipping subsidies, whatever form they take, follow circuitous routes into the pay envelopes of American seamen.

Mates often carry pilotage endorsements for the waters they sail (a requirement, in some waters, of the company or Coast Guard), although oceangoing ships rarely enter or leave port without a local pilot aboard, the extra cost more than offset by reduced insurance premiums. The predominant ambition of many active deck officers upon retirement is to become a pilot. It's a job that will continue to exist as long as ships come into port. Eleven hundred pilots are employed in twenty-four maritime territories, needed as much by foreign-flagged ships as American. Except in the Panama Canal they act only as advisers, their advice not always sought or followed. They take none of the captain's legal risk, although they share the blame and can lose their jobs when things go awry. Pilot qualifications vary. In some states a pilot need never have commanded a large ship—tugboat experience is enough. State regulators are often guided in their formulations by the pilots' associations they oversee. The associations are tight groups locked together like law firms, and their members answer to no one but each other. Piloting is an attractive way to spend one's last years at sea, but before anyone seriously aspires to it, let him (or her) climb a forty-foot Jacob's ladder in a howling wintry wind to clamber over the gunwale of a rolling ship, nothing but the waves below. Let him stand beside a skipper in a thick fog as the ship under them loses power, or guide a vessel in a cross-wind into a narrow slip, unable to understand the foreign chatter taking place in the wheelhouse around him. Let him sit in an admiralty courtroom listening to insurance lawyers quibble over the quality of his nautical skills. Not without justification, a pilot's annual earnings can hit six figures.

A chief engineer heads a department probably smaller than the chief mate's. Each of three watch-standing assistant engineers is accompanied by an unlicensed engineman during the day and is likely to be alone at night. Computers exercise much of the engine control—people are no longer needed to attend to steam pressure gauges. Engine-room maintenance is often handled by shore-based contractors, who may travel aboard on short voyages to complete their work. Engineers find more opportunities ashore than do their deck counterparts—in shipyards, public utilities, and manufacturing plants. Their retirement goals are more realistic.

The ordinary seaman has been replaced by the utility worker, who divides his time between the deck and engine room. Also eliminated is the purser/ hospitalman, whose duties now fall to the captain's computer and to the youngest officer as dispenser of bandages, drugs, and sympathy. In the event of a serious illness far from port, telephones and helicopters sometimes help.

The radio officer is next to be expended. His is a dying job, already discontinued in other countries. No radio officer is required aboard an American ship that remains within 150 miles of land. With training the captain or any licensed officer can become the designated radioman. When needed for brief periods, radio officers come aboard as independent contractors, for $300 a day.

Most seamen are happy to work double shifts and seven-day weeks, resigned to the union limitation of a half-year under articles. They are loyal to their unions because it was union leadership that got them where they are; they are blind to escalating labor costs as contributors to sparse employment. Blame the shipowners, blame the government, blame the American standard of living. The higher turnover rate among unlicensed seamen than among officers—on average, 25 percent of the crew leaves at the end of a voyage—may be as indicative of age, waning health, and skill in playing the shipping card as it is of dissatisfaction. Aboard or on the beach, those who work at sea think of themselves as seamen.

The captain sits in his suite, fifteen seconds and one deck away from the bridge. He has a bedroom, lounge, and office equipped with computer, weather-fax, pager, Marisat phone, shipboard phone, and portable phone. In his lounge he has a CD player, a VCR, and a bookcase of paperbacks, all little used. He has file cabinets and shelves full of bound books of regulations. Ask him what troubles him most about life at sea. His ship could be in the eye of a hurricane, low in fuel. A plague of pox could be permeating the crew. The cook could have been trained in the kitchen of a Cuban jail. His answer is predictable: paperwork. He'll tell you the paperwork—imposed by governments and shipowners—is driving him to the edge of toleration. But visit him ashore, after six months off, and you'll find him edgy. He may be blessed with a loving family—if so, he is fortunate, broken homes being endemic to the profession— yet you'll find him checking weather charts in eager anticipation of his next voyage. The seaman is never far from the sea, mentally and often geographically. The skipper of a ferryboat lives on an island so that he can commute by ferry to his departure port. A tanker's mate lives in a yachting town so that he can work on the waterfront while at home. For them, it matters not the job, it's the sea that's in their blood.

Few today can claim to have seen the full spectrum of maritime life in this century. Bob Scott of Oxnard, California, can—at least from the perspective of the engine room. In four wartime years he sailed on the Great Lakes and along every American seacoast; he sailed to Pearl Harbor, the Philippines, Belgium, the Persian Gulf, and Japan. He sailed on an ore carrier, a railcar ferry, tankers, freighters, and a troopship. One of his ships was so new that not all the paint was dry, and the dishware and mattresses were still wrapped in paper. One old Liberty, partially converted to an oiler, rolled, clanked, and groaned under an added deck cargo of locomotives. He sailed for a week on a Victory and for two months on a rusty, wheezing old C-1. Nine ships in all carried him over the world. He sailed as a coal-passer, fireman, water-tender, and oiler and advanced during his last year at sea to junior engineer and third assistant. After the war he put his savings toward a mechanical engineering degree at the University of Michigan, and watched as hundreds of veteran classmates cashed their monthly green checks under the benefits of the G.I. Bill. After graduating he went to General Electric's plant in San Jose to work on the control rod drives for the NS *Savannah,* and thence to install them at the Camden Yard of New York Shipbuilding. His name might still be found where he carved it under the seat of a *Savannah* bar stool. Reflecting on his time at sea, and contrasting it to the seagoing life of those he knows today as "youngsters," Scott notes one thing that hasn't changed: the brevity of the adventure for those who want a family life. He is concerned about other factors that may further shrink the merchant marine. The money is good, shipboard living is comfortable, but he wonders if highly trained American officers are prepared to man foreign-owned ships, as he feels soon they must. "Maritime subsidies or B-2 bombers?" he asks. He has little compassion for those who mourn the end of the era. One last commentary wraps up his recollections, words his father left with him when as a lad he was anxious to head beyond the horizon: "In wartime you're a hero and in peacetime, you're a bum."

It's been ten years since Todd Barr graduated from the U.S. Merchant Marine Academy. He shipped out for a short while as an A-B, spent three and a half years as a licensed officer with the tanker company he had sailed with as a cadet, then found his way to Arco Marine. At graduation he determined that he would get his master's license before he was thirty, a goal he achieved with only days to spare. Barr takes high technology for granted but demands that cadets sailing with him continue to work the maneuvering board and take daily sun lines. "How would you respond," he asks them, "if after an accident the examining officer asked whether you had used every means at your disposal? Don't depend on electronics. Stay in practice." As chief mate of the SS *Arco Anchorage,* Barr has recently received his full pilotage endorsement for Prince William Sound, qualifying him to become a captain. In his view, although American-flagged merchant ships are not likely to increase beyond their present bleak number, there always will be an American fleet—the Jones Act and the nation's military needs guarantee that. Meanwhile, he says there are too many schools producing licensed officers. Either the state schools on the East Coast or the federal academy (his alma mater) should be shut down; to him the choice is clear, and he reels off the sequence in which the state academies should be closed. He speaks favorably of his own experience and looks on Arco as a progressive shipping company and good employer, but wonders whether he really wants to command a tanker. The desire to get settled and start a family nags at him, making each departure tougher. He wants to do something else with his life soon. But in a few weeks he'll be packing to ship out on the *Anchorage.*

Erin Fitzgerald, a cadet at the U.S. Merchant Marine Academy, looks forward to her first sea term, having recently completed her year as plebe and fourth classman. She'll be leaving soon to join an American-flagged ship in New York for a six-month cruise, probably to the Caribbean and South America. Less than two years ago, after attending a college fair, she surprised her parents by stating in no uncertain terms that Kings Point was where she wanted to go after high school, there and no place else. It was a curious choice for a young woman with no maritime background, descended from two generations of Irish-American railroad workers. Erin's father and grandfather both worked for the Chesapeake and Ohio; her mother teaches in a vocational school. She hears no distinct call to the sea, but clearly, after completing what should be the toughest of her four years, she is imbued with the spirit of Kings Point. She has chosen an engineering curriculum with associated courses in business. Sixty percent of her classmates have selected the path to deck officer. All are confident that there will be ample opportunity for them upon graduation, as the skills they acquire at Kings Point are suitable for navy and Coast Guard jobs as well as for the merchant service. In return for their government-funded education, Kings Point graduates assume a five-year obligation to work in the maritime trades. Under the terms of the agreement, these trades now include various components of intermodal transportation—trucking, railroads, even airlines—as long as they are associated with the traditional merchant marine. Erin has her eye on CSX

Transportation, an outgrowth of several middle-Atlantic railroads, including the Seaboard Coast Line and the Chessie System. (Both Sea-Land and American Commercial Lines, one of the largest American-flagged barge companies, are parts of this international transportation company.) Like her parents, she is much in favor of unions—a view confirmed by what she hears from experienced instructors at the academy. However, she reports that because of membership limitations, no recent graduates have been able to join the major maritime unions. She is firm in her conviction that there will always be an American merchant marine—the nation needs it to maintain independence from foreign support and as a source of well-trained military leaders. Kings Point, she says in as spirited a manner as she can muster, offers an ideal balance of hands-on training and tough academics—the best way to learn marine trades. As for being a female in a still predominantly male environment—fewer than 10 percent of her classmates are women—Erin is unfazed. She of the early ballet classes, once and still a capable musician, Erin has proved herself on the drill field and in an otherwise all-male machine shop. In 1999 the officer corps of the American maritime world will gain a Renaissance woman.

The common thread in the views of these three, whose experience spans more than a half century, is that survival of the merchant marine is a military necessity. Congress agrees, as is apparent in the 1995 Maritime Security Act. Mahan lives. The unhampered delivery of battlefield supplies anywhere in the world depends on the availability of civilian ships and personnel.

In the latter half of the nineteenth century, when the American maritime presence was in disarray, people saw four reasons for redevelopment of a robust merchant fleet. First, they looked to Great Britain and concluded that a sound merchant service goes with being a major nation. That romantic and simplistic belief was clearly contradicted by the examples of Spain, Imperial Russia, and China, all major nations without significant maritime forces. Second, again looking to Great Britain, people thought a large fleet was needed to guarantee access to raw materials and markets. Yet flags of convenience could just as easily provide access to foreign trade, and trade helped keep the peace however ships were registered. Third, some people saw business opportunities in the nation's growing seaports, dockyards, and shipping companies. But more regarded those ventures as high-stakes gambles with unfavorable odds; in their view, a country as vast as the United States afforded better investment opportunities inland. Finally, people cited the utility of liners as potential naval auxiliaries. From the time of the privateers to the present, this has been the best case for federal subsidies. But it carries an inherent weakness: if you progressively deplete the merchant fleet to build a navy (for instance, by converting civilian ships to the Military Sealift Command), at some point the diminished civilian fleet will have less need for naval protection. That is exactly what happened in both world wars. It was American shipyard productivity that twice reversed the situation. The nation regained its maritime power when the buildup was driven by wartime need and backed by ample capital. The money was borrowed from future peacetime taxes.

Five elements are needed to sustain a strong merchant marine: seaports, capital, ships, trading partners, and labor; only the first of which comes free to the United States. No other nation has better natural harbors. Industry abounds in seaports such as New York, Hampton Roads, San Francisco, and Puget Sound, and there is room to spare for development. The country is also blessed with splendid inland waterfronts on the Great Lakes and the Mississippi River.

Maritime capital can't easily be eked from private enterprise in the United States, given the adverse odds borne out by history. It must come from taxes, allocated funds that do little more than restore security lost through warfare. It is questionable whether funding in anticipation of military needs is still appropriate, that being the major bone of contention every time subsidy programs come up for review.

Rarely has this country been innovative in its ships, and never was the timing favorable. The glory of the clipper ships, the most exquisite sailing vessels in world history—eclipsed by steam; steam turbines, the best ever engineered, when European diesel engines exceeded them in economy, efficiency, and safety; nuclear power, its shipboard price out of all proportion to performance; the fastest passenger liner ever built, setting records as air transport became cheaper. Highways, air, and outer space are the territories for America's transportation potential.

Trading partners we can find, but not necessarily to the benefit of our own merchant fleet. As a nation of consumers, we have always faced trade imbalances; without imposed controls, imports would far exceed exports, and the rest of the world would own our gold. From this point of view it is in our interest to function as a come-and-get-it economy. America's future trading routes are those where our grain, cotton, coal, and oil will be carried away under the flags of those who need the commodities and are willing to transport them inexpensively. Foreign flags are raised by cheaper labor—hungry sailors, who care little about safety and less about comfort, willing to work for one fourth the wages earned by American seamen.

Perhaps labor is the key. No one goes to sea for community service. We can't expect American seamen to work for the same wages or under the same conditions as their overseas counterparts. We need to take a broader view of the American maritime industry, one that offers new forms of employment for skilled American mariners. Technology presents as much opportunity for development today as it did with the advent of steam or steel. New initiatives and fresh insights are needed for all kinds of maritime endeavors: sea-bottom exploration, ocean mining, offshore drilling, clean oil delivery, the laying of fiber-optic cable. And coastwise and intercoastal shipping still offer economies of scale over land transport, particularly if the costs of controlling highway pollution are factored in. Intermodal transport offers a new set of challenges. Private enterprise must set the course, as it did in the nation's earliest years. It needs courageous spokesmen like Joseph Peabody and Edward Knight Collins. Look back on two centuries of clumsy government regulation, and ask if the industry can regulate itself. The American Bureau of Shipping proved the feasibility of self-regulation. Minimize dependency on government, and profit-motivated conduct must still consider the larger community. Industrialists Schwab and Kaiser did, to their own advantage and the country's benefit. If this nation can't again produce dedicated leaders in the maritime industry, what nation can? History tells us hope remains for a rebuilt maritime service. Look to the museums, for there is preserved a heritage of free enterprise pursued with courage and civic pride. Let us keep the history alive.

Chronology

1803   Louisiana Purchase opens coastline to Gulf of Mexico

1805   U.S. Weather Service adapts British Beaufort scale
American ice trade begins

1807   Jefferson's embargo
Coast Survey established
Fulton's *North River Steamboat* begins Hudson River service

1811   *New Orleans* first steamboat on Mississippi

1812   War with Great Britain

1818   Black Ball Line begins first scheduled transatlantic runs

1819   Acquisition of Florida
Savannah makes first steam-assisted transatlantic crossing
Congress legislates against steerage overcrowding

1825   Erie Canal opens

1835   Physical punishment aboard ship forbidden "without justifiable cause"

1837   Ericsson demonstrates screw propeller
First use of steam whistle
Sumner proposes new method for finding position at sea

1838   Steamship Inspection Act sets operational standards for passenger-
carrying steam vessels
Morse demonstrates telegraph
Blue Riband instituted, inspired by practice of recording steamship
passages
Lighthouse Service assigned to Treasury Department

1841   Forbes invents double topsail

1845   Annexation of Texas completes Gulf Coast of United States
U.S. Naval Academy opens

1847   Discovery of gold in California starts gold rush

1848   *California* departs New York; in 1849 is first steamer through Golden
Gate
Maury introduces pilot charts

1849   Vanderbilt founds Accessory Transit Company to provide steamship
            service to West Coast via Nicaragua
        California gold rush attracts East Coast ships

1850   Collins Line's subsidized *Atlantic* begins service between New York and
            Liverpool; *Baltic* wins Blue Riband
        Clipper ship *Surprise* breaks speed record from Boston to San Fran-
            cisco via Cape Horn
        McKay builds clipper in sixty days, launches *Stag Hound*
        Flogging abolished
        Ballot states law of storms
        First international electric telegraph system

1851   McKay launches *Flying Cloud,* best-known clipper

1852   McKay launches *Sovereign of the Seas*
        Steamboat Inspection Service established
        Lighthouse Board established; initiates annual publication of *Light List*
            and *Notices to Mariners*

1853   McKay's *Great Republic* burns at dock before maiden voyage
        Perry opens Japan to trade

1854   Collins's *Arctic* lost after collision in fog
        Trains lose McKay's *Staffordshire*
        Western river engineers form fraternal organization, predecessor of
            Marine Engineers' Beneficial Association

1855   Two thousand pilots and twenty-five hundred engineers licensed
        Sault Ste. Marie locks open

1856   Declaration of Paris outlaws privateering
        Collins's *Pacific* lost with all hands

1857   British compile list of seventy thousand signals, basis for International
            Code of Signals
        Panic of 1857 ruins Collins Line, White Diamond Line, Cope Line,
            and Ocean Line

1858   *Western World,* pride of Great Lakes, halts operation
        Failure of first Atlantic cable

1859   *Dreadnought* crosses Atlantic in less than fourteen days

1861   America's merchant marine emerges as world's largest
        Civil War

1864   USS *Kearsarge* sinks CSS *Alabama*
        Merritt begins salvage work

1865   Explosion of Mississippi steamboat *Sultana*

1866   *Great Eastern* completes laying of first two successful Atlantic cables

1867   Alaska purchased from Russia

1869   Suez Canal opens for powered vessels

1870   *Robt. E. Lee* wins Mississippi River race with *Natchez*

1872   Shipping Commissioner's Act reinforces desertion laws

1873   Mandatory licensing examinations for captains and mates

1874   New York State starts first merchant marine officers' school
        Desertion Act of 1874 replaces that of 1872

1875   Marine Engineers' Beneficial Association formalized as labor union

1876   Coast Survey becomes Coast and Geodetic Survey
        British Plimsoll mark to curtail overloading required for Lloyd's classi-
            fication

1877   Weather Service established

1883   McKay elected to lead Lake Carriers' Association

1884   International Meridian Conference
        Bureau of Navigation assigned to oversee shipping commissioner

1886   England launches thirty-five-hundred-ton riveted steel tanker

1887   Congressional Merchant Marine and Fisheries Committee established

1889   *City of New York* and *City of Paris* introduce flags of convenience
        Philadelphia sail training schoolship established

1891   Pacific unions combine as Sailors' Union of the Pacific
        Founding of Massachusetts Nautical Training School, first schoolship
            to train licensed engineers
        Ocean Mail Act passed to subsidize overseas mail carriers

1892   Dollar Line founded
       National Seamen's Union of America is formed and affiliates with American Federation of Labor (AFL)

1894   Fall River Line begins Boston–New York passenger service

1895   Maguire Act abolishes imprisonment for desertion from coastwise vessels

1897   Supreme Court's *Arago* decision denies Thirteenth Amendment protection to seamen under articles
       White Act abolishes imprisonment of U.S. citizens for desertion in American or nearby waters and ends corporal punishment

1898   Annexation of Hawaii and Puerto Rico

1899   Goodwin Sands light vessel (English Channel) sends first wireless distress call

1901   Amendments to 1857 International Code of Signals
       San Francisco City Front Federation strikes against open shop

1902   *Thomas W. Lawson,* seven-masted sailing vessel, is launched

1904   Marconi Company leases radio equipment and places its operators aboard ships

1906   International Radio Telegraphic Conventions established

1907   Metropolitan Steamship's *Yale* and *Harvard,* world's fastest commercial ships, offer regularly scheduled fifteen-hour passage between New York and Boston

1908   Sperry demonstrates gyrocompass
       First Atlantic Conference regulates shipping rates
       International agreement on SOS signal
       Matson starts Hawaiian service; Moore-McCormack starts Scandinavian service

1909   Furuseth and La Follette establish friendship to benefit seamen
       Binns, radio operator of *Republic,* sends first Atlantic CQD

1910   Denmark and Germany introduce diesel engines

1911   Gyrocompass tested on Old Dominion Line's *Princess Anne*

1912 Sinking of British-built *Titanic*

1913 Most destructive storm in Great Lakes history

1914 Cape Cod and Panama Canals open
World War I
U-boat activities disrupt British trade
SOLAS established, its resolutions unratified by United States

1915 Wilson signs La Follette Seamen's Act, defining seamen's rights
Coast Guard established through merger of Revenue and Lifesaving
   Services
Bureau of Standards develops RDF
Sinking of *Lusitania*
International Mercantile Marine (IMM) in receivership

1916 Shipping Act creates Shipping Board
Emergency Fleet Corporation (EFC) established
Hog Island Shipyard built

1917 United States joins World War I
Rice, of *Mongolia,* fires first American shot in the war
Charles Schwab named head of EFC

1918 *Vaterland* converted to troopship *Leviathan*
EFC launches one hundred ships on July 4

1919 Five Hog Islanders launched in forty-eight minutes, ten seconds, on
   May 30
Morgan revives IMM

1920 Merchant Marine (Jones) Act increases Shipping Board's control and
   reaffirms cabotage

1921 Shipping Board establishes union lockout on government ships
United States Lines formed from IMM's American Line and made
   managing operators for U.S. Shipping Board

1923 *Leviathan* returns to commercial service on July 4

1924 Dollar Line offers around-the-world service on *President Harrison*
Federal subsidies inaugurate several new shipping lines

1927 C & D Canal becomes sea-level waterway

1928   Merchant Marine Act extends mail contract subsidies

1929   Daring sea rescue by *America*'s Manning
United States Lines reorganized as private corporation
Launch of *Seatrain,* world's first containership
California Maritime Academy founded

1931   *Mariposa,* first fully air-conditioned ship, begins West Coast service to Hawaii

1932   Bureau of Marine Inspection takes over Steamboat Inspection Service and Bureau of Navigation
Lurline becomes Matson Line's flagship

1933   EFC abolished

1934   *Morro Castle* burns off New Jersey coast
Riots connected with maritime strike shut down San Francisco

1935   Lundeberg takes over Sailors' Union of the Pacific
Wagner Act establishes NLRB (National Labor Relations Board)
Rex and *Normandie* win Blue Riband silver cup

1936   Merchant Marine Act abolishes Shipping Board and establishes Maritime Commission
United States ratifies 1929 SOLAS convention

1937   Kennedy becomes first head of Maritime Commission
National Maritime Union formed
First commercial transatlantic passenger flights
Maritime Commission proposes C-class freighters

1938   Radar introduced
Maritime Commission authorizes large merchant fleet

1939   C & D Canal widened for full operation
Amended Neutrality Act extends limit of Atlantic sea frontier

1940   *America* replaces *Leviathan* as flagship of United States Lines
Maritime Commission agrees to build sixty Ocean-class ships for Great Britain

1941   Because of U-boat attacks, merchant vessels begin traveling in convoys
Kaiser delivers first Ocean-class ships

September 27 is named Liberty Fleet Day with launching of fourteen new ships

Coast Guard introduces ocean station vessels

1942   Coast Guard takes over Bureau of Marine Inspection and Navigation

War Shipping Administration assumes functions of Maritime Commission

Federal Merchant Marine Academy and Maine Maritime Academy open

Normandie burns at New York City pier

Liberty ship *Stephen Hopkins* sinks German raider

1943   German subs withdraw from Battle of the Atlantic

1944   Kamikazes attack twenty merchant ships in Philippines

1946   War Shipping Administration returns control to Maritime Commission

America returns as United States Lines flagship

Cargo-passenger ships introduced to Caribbean

Ship Sales Act establishes National Defense Reserve Fleet

Reorganization abolishes Bureau of Marine Inspection and Navigation

1947   Curran withdraws National Maritime Union from (Communist) Committee for Maritime Unity

President Cleveland begins service to Orient

1948   Marshall Plan

American Export introduces single-class passenger ships for Mediterranean service

1949   Military Sea Transportation Service (later, Military Sealift Command) established

1950   Functions of Maritime Commission transferred to Department of Commerce, Federal Maritime Board, and Maritime Administration

Korean War

Independence launched for Mediterranean service

1952   *United States* wins Blue Riband

1954   Cargo Preference Act provides subsidies for ships carrying government cargoes

1955 MODUs introduce Texas towers
AFL and CIO merge

1959 NS *Savannah* launched

1961 Federal Maritime Commission assigned regulatory role

1962 Texas A&M University establishes Texas Maritime Academy

1965 Supertankers of 200,000 tons are introduced

1967 *Torrey Canyon* wreck highlights problem of hidden ownership
Coast Guard transferred to Department of Transportation

1968 American Export Lines ends passenger operations
Sea-Land introduces containerships

1969 *United States* laid up
Great Lakes Maritime Academy opens
Manhattan clears Northwest Passage

1970 Merchant Marine Act authorizes ten-year subsidized shipbuilding
program

1973 Department of Defense develops GPS

1975 *Edmund Fitzgerald* sinks in Lake Superior

1976 Women admitted to U.S. Merchant Marine Academy; state maritime
academies and Coast Guard Academy follow within a few years
Marisat communications link initiated

1977 Trans-Alaskan Pipeline begins operation

1978 *Amoco Cadiz* record oil spill

1980 GPS becomes available for civilian use

1982 Moore-McCormack taken over by United States Lines

1986 United States Lines in bankruptcy

1988 Merchant seamen of World War II are granted veterans' status
Marine Engineers' Beneficial Association and National Maritime
Union join forces

1989 *Exxon Valdez* spill illustrates risks of supertankers

1990   Oil Pollution Act regulates American tanker operations
Standardization of buoyage system completed in U.S. waters

1992   Red River Shipping, first modern African-American shipper to operate
its own vessels under U.S. registry

1994   House Merchant Marine Committee dissolved

1995   Coast Guard discontinues use of Morse code

1996   *United States* towed home to United States
Maritime Security Act extends preferential cargo subsidies for militarily useful, privately owned vessels

1997   Veterans of Foreign Wars votes to allow merchant marine veterans of
World War II to become members

Bibliography

Albion, R. G. *The Rise of New York Port, 1815–1860.* New York: C. Scribner's, 1939. A study in economics; not maritime-oriented.

Albion, R. G., W. A. Baker, and B. W. Larabee. *New England and the Sea.* Mystic, Conn.: Mystic Seaport Museum, 1972.

Bailey, Thomas Andrew, and Paul B. Ryan. *The* Lusitania *Disaster: An Episode in Modern War and Diplomacy.* New York: Free Press, 1975.

Ballard, Robert D., with Spencer Dunmore. *Exploring the* Lusitania. Toronto: Madison Press Books, 1995.

Bartholomew, C. A. *Mud, Muscle, and Miracles: Marine Salvage in the United States Navy.* Washington, D.C.: Government Printing Office, 1990.

Bass, George F., ed. *A History of Seafaring Based on Underwater Archeology.* New York: Walker, 1972.

Bauer, K. Jack. *A Maritime History of the United States: The Role of America's Seas and Waterways.* Studies in Maritime History Series, ed. William N. Still, Jr. Columbia: University of South Carolina Press, 1988.

Baughman, James P. *The Mallorys of Mystic: Six Generations in American Enterprise.* Middletown, Conn.: Wesleyan University Press for Marine Historical Association, 1972.

Behar, Richard, and Scott Brown. "Joe's Bad Trip." *Time,* 24 July 1989, 42–47.

Berwick, Arnold. *The Abraham Lincoln of the Sea: The Life of Andrew Furuseth.* Santa Cruz, Calif.: Odin Press, 1993.

Blume, Kenneth John. "The Hairy Ape Reconsidered: The American Merchant Seaman and the Transition from Sail to Steam in the Late Nineteenth Century." *American Neptune* 44 (Winter 1984): 33–47.

Boorstin, Daniel J. *The Discoverers.* New York: Random House, 1983.

Botting, Douglas, ed. *The U-Boats.* Seafarers Series. Alexandria, Va.: Time-Life Books, 1979.

Bourne, Russell. *Floating West: The Erie and Other Canals.* New York: W. W. Norton, 1992.

Braynard, Frank Osborn. *Famous American Ships: A Historical Sketch of the United States as Told Through Its Maritime Life.* New York: Hastings House, 1956.

Braynard, Frank Osborn, and William H. Miller. *Fifty Famous Liners.* 3 vols. New York: W. W. Norton, 1987–88.

Braynard, Frank O. *S.S. Savannah: The Elegant Steam Ship,* New York: Dover Publications, 1988.

Brinnin, John Malcolm. *The Sway of the Grand Saloon: A Social History of the North Atlantic.* New York: Delacorte Press, 1971. This descriptive source has only a minimal nautical perspective and contains factual errors, but is pleasant to read.

Canfield, H. S. "Aboard a Semmes Prize." *Magazine of History 1908* (1908): 137 included in Library of Congress collection: *Americana: Catalog of the Famous Abbat Reprints. . . .* Geneva, N.Y.: W. F. Humphrey Press, 1936.

Carse, Robert. *The Long Haul.* New York: W. W. Norton, 1965.

Collinder, Per Arne. *History of Marine Navigation.* Translated by Maurice Michael. New York: St. Martin's Press, 1955. The age of this book makes it hard to find. Bowditch's *Practical Navigator* (H.O. 9) is still published.

Cutler, Carl C. *Greyhounds of the Sea: The Story of the American Clipper Ships.* 1930. Reprint, Annapolis: Naval Institute Press, 1984. Well illustrated with good details.

———. *Queens of the Western Ocean: The Story of America's Mail and Passenger Sailing Lines.* Annapolis: Naval Institute Press, 1961.

Dalzell, George. *The Flight from the Flag.* Chapel Hill: University of North Carolina Press, 1940. Strout's story can be found here.

Dana, Richard Henry. *Two Years Before the Mast.* 1840. Reprint, with Dana's "Twenty-four Years After," Modern Library, 1936.

Davidson, Art. *In the Wake of the* Exxon Valdez: *The Devastating Impact of the Alaska Oil Spill.* San Francisco: Sierra Club Books, 1990.

De La Pedraja, René. *A Historical Dictionary of the U.S. Merchant Marine and*

Shipping Industry: Since the Introduction of Steam. Westport, Conn.: Greenwood Press, 1994. Contains excellent articles on marine propulsion.

———. *The Rise and Decline of United States Merchant Shipping in the Twentieth Century.* New York: Twayne Publishers, 1992. This splendidly researched study focuses on the machinations within the shipping lines' executive suites.

Delgado, James P. *To California by Sea.* Columbia: University of South Carolina Press, 1990.

Delgado, James P., and J. Candace Clifford. *Great American Ships.* Washington, D.C.: Preservation Press, 1991. A guide for travelers, organized in geographic segments.

De Pauw, Linda Grant. *Seafaring Women.* Boston: Houghton Mifflin, 1982.

Derby, Elias Hasket. "The Life of Elias Hasket Derby, 1739–1799." *Hunt's Merchants' Magazine,* 1900.

Devereux, Tony. *Messenger Gods of Battle.* London: Brassey's, 1991.

Dickens, Charles. *American Notes.* 1842. Reprint, New York: Fromm International Publishing, 1985.

Farnquist, Thomas L. "Requiem for the *Edmund Fitzgerald*." *National Geographic,* January 1996, 36–47.

Ferguson, David L. *Cleopatra's Barge: The Crowninshield Story.* Boston: Little Brown, 1976.

Freuchen, Peter, with David Loth. *Peter Freuchen's Book of the Seven Seas.* New York: Julian Messner, 1957.

Gannon, Michael. *Operation Drumbeat: The Dramatic True Story of Germany's First U-Boat Attacks Along the American Coast in World War II.* New York: Harper & Row, 1990.

Gibson, Charles Dana. *The Ordeal of Convoy N.Y.119.* New York: South Street Seaport Museum, 1973.

Gilchrist, David T., ed. *The Growth of the Seaport Cities, 1790–1825.* Charlottesville: The University Press of Virginia, 1967. Proceedings of a conference sponsored by the Eleutherian Mills–Hagley Foundation, March 17–19, 1966.

Goldberg, Mark. *American Merchant Marine History Series.* Vol. 1, *The "Hog Islanders";* vol. 2, *Caviar and Cargo;* vol. 3, *Going Bananas.* New York: American Merchant Marine Museum, n.d. *Caviar and Cargo* covers the C-3 passenger ships and *Going Bananas* discusses one hundred years of American fruit ships.

Gordon, Arthur. *The Years of Peril: The World War II Story of Mobil Men and*

Ships. Fairfax, Va.: Mobil Shipping and Transportation Company, 1994. Based on Gordon's 1954 compilation for Mobil Marine.

Gray, Ralph D. *The National Waterway: A History of the Chesapeake and Delaware Canal, 1769–1965.* Urbana: University of Illinois Press, 1967.

Guérout, Max. "The Wreck of the C.S.S. *Alabama:* Avenging Angel of the Confederacy." *National Geographic.* December 1994, 67–83.

Harlow, Frederick Pease. *The Making of a Sailor; or, Sea Life Aboard a Yankee Square-Rigger.* 1928. Reprint, with corrections, Mineola, N.Y.: Dover, 1988.

Harris, Sheldon. *Paul Cuffe, Black America and the African Return.* New York: Simon & Schuster, 1972. Biography of a free black man and entrepreneur who lived in the early nineteenth century.

Herring, Thomas A. "The Global Positioning System." *Scientific American,* February 1996, 44–50.

Hodgson, Bryan. "Alaska's Big Spill: Can the Wilderness Heal?" *National Geographic,* January 1990, 5–43.

Holland, Francis Ross, Jr. *America's Lighthouses: Their Illustrated History Since 1716.* Brattleboro, Vt.: Stephen Greene Press, 1972.

Hughes, Thomas Parke. *Elmer Sperry: Inventor and Engineer.* Baltimore: Johns Hopkins University Press, 1971.

Infield, Glen. *Disaster at Bari.* New York: Macmillan, 1971.

Irving, David. *The Destruction of Convoy PQ.17.* New York: Simon & Schuster, 1968.

Jobé, Joseph, ed. *The Great Age of Sail.* Translated by Michael Kelly. New York: Viking Press, 1967.

Jones, Howard Mumford, and Bessie Zaban Jones, comps. *The Many Voices of Boston: A Historical Anthology, 1630–1975.* Boston: Little Brown, 1975.

Keeble, John. *Out of the Channel: The* Exxon Valdez *Oil Spill in Prince William Sound.* New York: HarperCollins, 1991.

King, Dean with John B. Hattendorf and J. Worth Estes. *A Sea of Words: A Lexicon and Companion for Patrick O'Brian's Seafaring Tales.* New York: Henry Holt, 1995.

Labaree, Benjamin Woods. *The Boston Tea Party.* New York: Oxford University Press, 1964.

Land, Emory S. *U.S. Merchant Marine at War: Report to the President.* Washington, D.C.: War Shipping Administration, 1946.

Lane, Carl D. *What You Should Know About the Merchant Marine.* New York: W. W. Norton, 1943.

Leckie, Robert. *George Washington's War.* New York: HarperCollins, 1992.

Lobley, Douglas. *Ships Through the Ages.* London: Octopus Books, 1972.

MacGregor, David R. *Merchant Sailing Ships, 1815–1850.* Annapolis: Naval Institute Press, 1984.

Maddocks, Melvin, ed. *The Great Liners.* Seafarers Series. Alexandria, Va.: Time-Life Books, 1978.

Mahan, Alfred Thayer. *The Influence of Sea Power upon History, 1660–1783.* 1890. Reprint, New York: Hill & Wang, 1957.

Marshall, Michael W. *Ocean Traders.* New York: Facts on File, 1990.

Marvin, W. L. *The American Merchant Marine: Its History and Romance from 1620 to 1902.* New York: Charles Scribner & Sons, 1902.

Matthews, Frederick C. *American Merchant Ships, 1850–1900.* 2 vols. 1930. Reprint, Mineola, N.Y.: Dover, 1987.

Maxtone-Graham, John. *The Only Way to Cross.* New York: Macmillan, 1972.

McCullough, David. *The Path Between the Seas: The Creation of the Panama Canal, 1870–1914.* New York: Simon & Schuster, 1977.

McDougall, Walter A. *Let the Sea Make a Noise . . .: A History of the North Pacific from Magellan to MacArthur.* New York: Basic Books, 1993.

McElwaine, Robert. *The Great Depression,* New York: Times Books, 1984.

McKay, Richard C. *Donald McKay and His Famous Sailing Ships.* New York: Dover Publications, Inc., 1995.

McPhee, John. *Looking for a Ship.* New York: Farrar Straus Giroux, 1990. An account of the author's travels aboard a Lykes containership with long-time mariners.

McPherson, James M. *Battle Cry of Freedom: The Civil War Era.* New York: Oxford University Press, 1988.

Middlebank, Martin. *Convoy.* New York: Morrow & Co., 1976.

Middlekauf, Robert. *The Glorious Cause: The American Revolution, 1763–1789.* New York: Oxford University Press, 1982. This classic history of the Revolution has a wealth of detail, but contains little about seaborne commerce.

Miller, Theodore R. *Graphic History of the Americas.* New York: Robert E. Krieger Publishing, 1969.

Miller, William H. *The Last Atlantic Liners.* London: Conway Maritime Press, 1985.

Monroe, Jeffrey W. "A Disaster in Dispute: the *Morro Castle* Fire." *Sea Classics,* November 1995, 14–19, 66–68.

Moore, Arthur R. *A Careless Word . . . A Needless Sinking.* Kings Point, N.Y.: U.S. Merchant Marine Museum, 1984.

Morison, Samuel Eliot. *The Maritime History of Massachusetts, 1783–1860.* Cambridge, Mass.: Riverside Press, 1961. A thoroughly researched and detailed history.

———. *The Two-Ocean War.* Boston: Atlantic Monthly Press, 1963.

Morris, James M. *Our Maritime Heritage: Maritime Developments and Their Impact on American Life.* Newport News: University Press of America, 1979.

Morris, Roger. *Atlantic Seafaring.* Auckland, New Zealand: David Bateman; International Marine, 1992.

Nalder, Eric. *Tankers Full of Trouble.* New York: Grove Press, 1994. A journalist's report from on board.

Neill, Peter, ed. *Maritime America: Art and Artifacts from America's Great Nautical Collections.* New York: Balsam Press, 1988.

Nelson, Bruce. *Workers on the Waterfront: Seamen, Longshoremen, and Unionism in the 1930s.* Chicago: University of Illinois Press, 1990.

O'Neil, David. "America's Orphan: the U.S. Flag Merchant Marine." *Sea History,* (Spring 1996): 6–9.

Parry, J. H. *Romance of the Sea.* Washington, D.C.: National Geographic Society, n.d.

Putney, Martha S. *Black Sailors: Afro-American Merchant Seamen and Whalemen Prior to the Civil War.* New York: Greenwood Press, 1987.

Quartel, Rob. "The American Flag at Sea: A Shipper's Perspective." *Sea History* (Summer 1996): 6–7.

Rantoul, Robert S. *The Cruise of the "Quero": Captain John Derby, 1741–1812.* Salem, Mass.: Essex Institute, 1900.

Riesenberg, Felix. *Standard Seamanship for the Merchant Service.* New York: D. Van Nostrand, 1927. A textbook for merchant seamen.

Riesenberg, Felix, Jr. *Sea War.* New York: Rinehart, 1956.

Saddler, Jean. "Small Firm Making Waves in Military-Cargo Business." *The Wall Street Journal,* 25 September 1992.

Salecker, Gene Eric. *Disaster on the Mississippi.* Annapolis: Naval Institute Press, 1996.

Samuels, Samuel. *From the Forecastle to the Cabin.* 1862. Reprint, with a critical foreword by R. D. Paine, Boston: Charles E. Lauriat Co. The book is hard to find; Carl C. Cutler has drawn on Samuels's work in *Greyhounds of the Sea* (q.v.), in his coverage of the *Dreadnought.*

Sawyer, Leonard Arthur. *The Liberty Ships: History of the "Emergency" Type Cargo Ships Constructed in the United States During World War II.* Cambridge, Md.: Cornell Maritime Press, 1970.

Sawyer, Leonard Arthur, and W. H. Mitchell. *The Liberty Ships.* Cambridge, Md.: Cornell Maritime Press, 1970.

Semmes, Raphael. *The Confederate Raider* Alabama. Bloomington: Indiana University Press, 1962. Semmes published his autobiography in two volumes; this one covers his climactic cruise on the *Alabama* and his subsequent retirement from the Confederate Navy.

Shields, Jerry. *The Invisible Billionaire: Daniel Ludwig.* Boston: Houghton Mifflin, 1968.

Shipley, Robert, and Fred Addis. *Paddle Wheelers.* St. Catharines, Ontario: Vanwell Publishing, 1991.

————. *Propellers.* St. Catharines, Ontario: Vanwell Publishing, 1992.

Simpson, Colin. *Lusitania.* London: Longman, 1972.

Sobel, Dava. *Longitude: The True Story of a Lone Genius Who Solved the Greatest Scientific Problem of His Time.* New York: Walker, 1995. This beautifully written book tells in detail the story of the Harrison chronometers.

Spectorsky, A. C., ed. *The Book of the Sea.* New York: Appleton-Century-Crofts, 1954.

Starbuck, Alexander. *The History of Nantucket: County, Island, and Town, Including Genealogies of the First Settlers.* Rutland, Vt.: Charles E. Tuttle, 1969.

Swerdlow, Joel L. "Erie Canal: Living Link to Our Past." *National Geographic,* November 1990, 39–65.

Syrett, David. "World War II: The Battle of the Atlantic." *American Neptune* 44 (Winter 1984): 48–60.

Taft, Philip. *Organized Labor in American History.* New York: Harper & Row, 1964.

Taylor, John M. *Confederate Raider: Raphael Semmes of the* Alabama. Washington, D.C.: Brassey's, 1994.

Thompson, Mark L. *Steamboats and Sailors of the Great Lakes.* Detroit: Wayne State University Press, 1991.

Tute, Warren. *Atlantic Conquest: The Men and Ships of the Glorious Age of Steam.* Boston: Little, Brown, 1962.

Villiers, Alan, ed. *Men, Ships, and the Sea.* Washington, D.C.: National Geographic Society, 1962.

Wall, Robert. *Ocean Liners.* New York: Quarto, 1977.

Wood, Virginia Steele. *Live Oaking: Southern Timbers for Tall Ships.* 1981. Reprint, Annapolis, Md.: Naval Institute Press. 1985.

Wright, Esmond. *Franklin of Philadelphia.* Cambridge: Harvard University Press, 1986.

Yergin, Daniel. *The Prize: The Epic Quest for Oil, Money, and Power.* New York: Simon & Schuster, 1992.

Alaska Oil Spill Commission Report. Anchorage: *Exxon Valdez* Oil Spill Trustee Council, 1990. The account of the *Exxon Valdez* accident given in Chapter 16 of the present work draws heavily on Appendix N ("Chronology") of the commission's report.

American Maritime Documents, 1776–1860. Mystic, Conn.: Mystic Seaport Museum, 1992. Early documents reproduced in facsimile.

Americans Who Have Contributed to the History and Traditions of the United States Merchant Marine. Kings Point, N.Y.: U.S. Merchant Marine Academy, 1943.

The History of American Bureau of Shipping. New York: American Bureau of Shipping, 1995. This history is updated frequently by ABS.

Salem: Maritime Salem in the Age of Sail. Washington, D.C.: National Park Service, U.S. Department of the Interior, 1987. A colorfully illustrated handbook for the visitor to Salem.

U.S. Coast Guard Marine Casualty Report: SS Edmund Fitzgerald *Sinking in Lake Superior.* Report No. USCG 16732/64216, Springfield, Va.: National Technical Information Service, 1977.

Notes on Sources

The author's sources were many: journals, old books, magazines and newspapers, biographies, obituaries, classic texts and textbooks, microfilms of logbooks, ship manifests, old letters, and direct correspondence with maritime experts. Among writers heavily drawn upon are Samuel Eliot Morison, for his detailed research on Massachusetts maritime affairs through 1860; K. Jack Bauer, author of a scholarly history organized by trade, explaining why many developments took place; Michael Marshall, whose extended history of ocean trade contains useful diagrams and photographs; Frank Braynard, who relates history through pictures and his own drawings of famous American ships; Eric Nalder, for his journalist's insight into life on modern oil tankers; and John McPhee, whose writing seemed to have captured the author's own experience on freighters thirty years earlier. Unless otherwise noted, biographical information was drawn from the *Dictionary of American Biography*.

The maritime museums of America are rich sources of information. Among the most useful to this work were the Peabody Essex Museum in Salem, Massachusetts; the Mariners' Museum in Newport News, Virginia; the Museum of America and the Sea (Mystic Seaport Museum) in Mystic, Connecticut; and the Smithsonian Museum of History and Technology in Washington, D.C.

The growth of the American coastlines is based on Theodore Miller's *Graphic History of the Americas,* a book useful in studying trade routes. Details concerning federal legislation have been extracted from documents in the

National Archives and the Library of Congress. Photographs, prints, and other pictures in the collections of the Library of Congress and the Naval Historical Center in Washington, D.C., gave accuracy and color to sparsely documented events. The quarterly journals of the Steamship Historical Society of America, the National Maritime Historic Society, and the Peabody Essex Museum have also proved helpful for background information; those cited below have been direct sources. An invaluable reference was René De La Pedraja's *Historical Dictionary of the U.S. Merchant Marine and Shipping Industry* (hereafter, *Historical Dictionary*), an encyclopedia spanning the chronology from Fulton's steamboat (1807) to the 1993 deflagging of American President Lines ships. Descriptions of recent policy changes were drawn from *The New York Times* and the *Journal of Commerce*.

The Bibliography preceding this section provides complete citations of books referenced below.

CHAPTER 1

A posthumous portrait of Elias Hasket Derby hangs in the Peabody Essex Museum and appears in Peter Neill's *Maritime America: Art and Artifacts from America's Great Nautical Collections* (hereafter, *Maritime America*). The same portrait, reversed in reproduction, appears in *Salem: Maritime Salem in the Age of Sail* (hereafter, *Salem*), a handbook of the National Park Service. For early maritime history, see Samuel Morison's *Maritime History of Massachusetts* (hereafter, Morison's *Massachusetts*); for the Boston Tea Party, see Benjamin Labaree's *Boston Tea Party;* Ben Franklin is covered in Esmond Wright's *Franklin of Philadelphia*. Salem's ships are discussed in several books, including Morison's *Massachusetts* and Jack Bauer's *Maritime History of the United States: The Role of America's Seas and Waterways* (hereafter, Bauer); a painting of the *Mount Vernon* is shown in *Maritime America;* the travels of the *Grand Turk* are outlined in Elias Derby's biography "Life of Elias Hasket Derby, 1739–1799." The *Grand Turk* illustration is from a woodcut engraving in *Hutchinson's Navigation, 1777,* later copied by the Chinese to decorate a soup tureen, which became the Peabody Essex Museum's earliest acquisition. *American Maritime Documents, 1776–1860* contains facsimiles of letters of marque and other early shipping documents; see also the reference to a letter of marque under "Chapter 3," below.

CHAPTER 2

Shipboard health and the Customs Service are covered in *Salem.* A portrait of George Crowninshield Jr., painted by Samuel F. B. Morse, hangs in the Peabody

Essex Museum, where a model of *Cleopatra's Barge* is also on display. Morison, Bauer, and several American histories discuss the impact of Jefferson's embargo. Frank Braynard's *Famous American Ships: An Historical Sketch of the United States as Told Through Its Maritime Life* (hereafter, Braynard) contains Braynard's drawings and descriptions of several important vessels, including Fulton's original steamboat. A newer source for well-known American ships is *Great American Ships* by James Delgado and Candace Clifford (hereafter, Delgado). The ice trade is discussed both in Bauer and in Morison's *Massachusetts*. Daniel Boorstin, in *The Discoverers*, goes into some detail on the art of taking lunars.

CHAPTER 3

Tensions leading to the War of 1812 are covered in most American histories. For information about Gray and the *Constitution*, see Morison's *Massachusetts*. The *New Orleans* is depicted in Braynard. For more about Peabody and the *George*, see *Salem*. The letter of marque was issued by James Madison to commission the ship *Alexander*, which was owned by George Crowninshield Jr. among others.

CHAPTER 4

The development of the Erie Canal is covered in Russell Bourne's *Floating West: The Erie and Other Canals;* Joel Swerdlow's "Erie Canal: Living Link to Our Past," in the *National Geographic,* is illustrative. The Erie's effect on the port of New York is discussed in R. G. Albion's *Rise of New York Port (1815–1860).* Braynard includes illustrations of the *Walk-in-the Water,* the Black Ball's *Pacific,* and Savannah Steamship's *Savannah.* Douglas Lobley, in *Ships Through the Ages,* describes the *Pacific's* interior, and attributes ownership of the *Savannah* to the Dutch. Virginia Steele Wood's *Live Oaking: Southern Timbers for Tall Ships* describes the use of wood from Sea Island, Georgia. Per Arne Collinder's 1955 book *History of Marine Navigation* details the work of Thomas Sumner. Richard Henry Dana's classic, *Two Years Before the Mast,* abstracted here, belongs in every nautical library. It is the original American source on the geography and history of Spanish California. Morison mentions Sturgis, of Bryant & Sturgis. *America's Lighthouses: Their Illustrated History Since 1716,* by Francis Holland Jr. (hereafter, Holland), explains the Fresnel lens and covers in detail the travails of the Lighthouse Service. Warren Tute's *Atlantic Conquest: The Men and Ships of the Glorious Age of Steam* (hereafter, Tute) recounts the introduction of packet ships. His perspective is British, but the book contains many American details. A facsimile restoration of the Thompsons' New York office can be seen in Mystic Seaport. The first news of the scheduled packets appeared in the New York *Evening Post,* on October 27, 1817. John Brinnin conveys a vivid impression of life in the passenger quarters and stokeholds of early packet ships in his *Sway of the Grand Saloon: A Social History of the North Atlantic.*

CHAPTER 5

Tute is an authority on Cunard. Michael Marshall's *Ocean Traders* (hereafter, Marshall), like Tute, has a British perspective; it gives a broad survey of world-wide ocean transport and a good explanation of composite ships. Morse's work with the telegraph is described in most encyclopedias. Charles Dickens gives a humorous, satirical, and sincere description of his visit to the United States in *American Notes,* extracted in the present work. Braynard includes pictures of the *Washington* and the *California.* Tute and Delgado are parallel sources for the history of this period, the latter covering the western trade in more detail. Bauer explains the role of the federal government.

CHAPTER 6

The National Archives contain thousands of logs that Maury used in his work. Delgado's *To California by Sea* tells the story of the gold rush and Vanderbilt's part in it. The description of clipper ship rigging in Chapter 6 of the present work was drawn from several sources: Carl Cutler's *Greyhounds of the Sea: The Story of the American Clipper Ships,* which remains definitive, Felix Riesenberg's *Standard Seamanship for the Merchant Service,* Joseph Jobé's *Great Age of Sail,* and J. H. Parry's *Romance of the Sea.* A good source of terminology is *A Sea of Words* by Dean King, with John Hattendorf and J. Worth Estes, which also contains useful illustrations of eighteenth-century British warships. In *The Making of a Sailor; or, Sea Life Aboard a Yankee Square-Rigger,* Frederick Harlow includes several sea chanteys, from which the short excerpt was taken. The words of the chanteys were as varied as the men who sang them, quite removed from the verses of a prayer meeting. Linda Grant De Pauw's *Seafaring Women,* classified as a book for juveniles, provides well-researched and readable tales of women at sea.

CHAPTER 7

The story of Samuel Samuels is based on his autobiography, *From the Forecastle to the Cabin.* Tute gives more detail on the *Dreadnought,* several grim facts about steerage conditions, the losses and decline of the American merchant fleet; Marshall has statistics of the period. Tute discusses the *Great Eastern* and the laying of the Atlantic cable. See any good encyclopedia for the Declaration of Paris. Braynard has several drawings of ships of the period. The number of passengers lost in the sinking of the *Arctic* was given by the *New York Daily Times* on March 21, 1856, after all hope had expired for any further details arriving from England. Both Jack Bauer, in *A Maritime History of the United States,* and René De La Pedraja, in the chronology of his *Historical Dictionary of the U.S. Merchant Marine and Shipping Industry,* mention a crew of 141.

CHAPTER 8

From the middle of the nineteenth century, and certainly after the Civil War, newspapers become an increasingly valuable source. Few specific articles are cited here, but the *New York Times Index* is the best source, together with microfilms of the identified editions. Bartholomew's *Mud, Muscle and Miracles: Marine Salvage in the United States Navy* (hereafter, Bartholomew), while navy-oriented, has a rare description of the founding of the Merritt salvage company; Merritt is also mentioned in the privately published *History of American Bureau of Shipping* (hereafter, ABS). John Taylor's *Confederate Raider: Raphael Semmes of the Alabama* is based on Semmes's long autobiography, half of which is a separate book, *The Confederate Raider Alabama.* Taylor also covers the voyage of the *Sumter,* more objectively than Semmes does. Max Guérout's article in the *National Geographic,* "The Wreck of the C.S.S. *Alabama:* Avenging Angel of the Confederacy," maps the raider's voyage. In "Aboard a Semmes Prize," historian H. S. Canfield records Strout's own words on the recapture of the *Cuba* in the *Magazine of History, 1908* (cited in George Dalzell's *Flight From the Flag*). Gene Salecker's *Disaster on the Mississippi* reveals new details of the *Sultana* tragedy. Alan Villiers, editor of *Men, Ships, and the Sea* (hereafter Villiers), tells the colorful story of the *Natchez* and the *Robt. E. Lee.* Braynard and Tute discuss the Keystone Line and associated American efforts to regain Atlantic trade. Marshall notes the extent of the shipwrecks in this period.

CHAPTER 9

Arnold Berwick's *Abraham Lincoln of the Sea* (hereafter, Berwick) is the source of much of the labor history in this and subsequent chapters. Alfred Thayer Mahan's classic text, *The Influence of Sea Power upon History, 1660–1783,* is cited because of its political importance to maritime affairs; it contains little pertinent history. ABS tells of the origin of the Plimsoll mark and the story of Edison's illumination of the *Columbia.* Each maritime academy has recorded its own history; De La Pedraja's *Historical Dictionary* includes a thorough and fair history of the founding of the state schools. Marshall and Tute, with help from Braynard, again are good sources on Atlantic trade. *Ocean Liners* by Robert Wall (herafter, Wall) covers IMM and J. P. Morgan.

CHAPTER 10

See Berwick and *Historical Dictionary* for more about Furuseth and La Follette. The sources of labor statistics in this chapter are Marshall and *Organized Labor in American History,* by Philip Taft. Braynard, Tute, and Wall supply more detail on the Atlantic and East Coast trade. In "The Hairy Ape Reconsidered," an article in *American Neptune,* John Blume discusses the transition from sail to steam. Multiple editions of *The New York Times* (hereafter, *NYT*) tell the story of the sinking of the *Republic.* Bauer describes the funding of the Cape Cod Canal, and David McCullough tells the full story of its creation in *The Path Between the Seas: The Creation of the Panama Canal, 1870–1914.* The *Thomas W. Lawson* is well documented with photographs in Villiers; in *Our Maritime Heritage,* by James Morris; and in *Ships Through the Ages,* by Douglas Lobley.

CHAPTER 11

Berwick, Braynard, Tute, and Wall describe developments prior to World War I; Berwick and Wall have more detail on the Pacific trade. For the *Lusitania* advertisements and details of the ship's departure and sinking, see contemporary editions of *NYT* and other New York papers; Colin Simpson's *Lusitania* is the first history published since the opening of the cargo manifests during the 1960s. *The Lusitania Disaster,* by Thomas Bailey and Paul Ryan, tells the full story, including the revelations of cargo content; the authors take issue with some of Simpson's conjectures and refute others; photographs of the hulk captured by Robert D. Ballard do little to resolve the dispute. Emery Rice wrote his own story of the *Mongolia* in an International Mercantile Marine publication; contemporary newspapers also documented the confrontation.

CHAPTER 12

Tute and Bauer touch on the significant Jones Act; more details on its passage can be found in *NYT* articles; and De La Pedraja tells of its effect in *The Rise and Decline of U. S. Merchant Shipping in the Twentieth Century* (hereafter, *Rise and Decline*). Philip Taft's *Organized Labor in American History* is authoritive but has little on maritime labor. The story of the *Leviathan* is well documented in the National Archives, as well as by Braynard, Wall, and Tute. Gibbs is mentioned in conjunction with several of his works; an obituary in *NYT* provides many details of his life. Ralph Gray's *National Waterway: A History of the Chesapeake and Delaware Canal, 1769–1965* is a detailed account with photographs. Fried, Manning, and their adventure on *America* are well covered in contemporary editions of *NYT.* Peter Neill touches on the ghost fleets in his *Maritime America: Art and Artifacts from America's Great Nautical Collections.*

CHAPTER 13

Braynard discusses the *Seatrain* and the Pacific ships of this period. Berwick provides information on seamen's wages. Bruce Nelson covers the labor strife of the period in *Workers on the Waterfront: Seamen, Longshoremen, and Unionism in the 1930s.* Tute gives details on the prewar Blue Riband winners. Leonard Sawyer and W. H. Mitchell, authors of *The Liberty Ships* (hereafter, Sawyer and Mitchell), are recognized authorities on the subject and give a nearly complete account of the construction and histories of those vessels. Several details in the present work concerning the War Shipping Administration are from Emory Land's *U.S. Merchant Marine at War: Report to the President. NYT* has coverage of the *Morro Castle* tragedy, even as late as 1988.

CHAPTER 14

Bauer describes the state of the merchant marine during the Depression. Morison's *Two-Ocean War* (hereafter, Morison's *War*) touches on the rise of the NMU and personnel disparities between the navy and the merchant marine. Kaiser's biography appears in a contemporary issue of *Time,* and in a *NYT* obituary. The Battle of the Atlantic is told through German diaries and from interviews with surviving seamen in Michael Gannon's *Operation Drumbeat, The Dramatic True Story of Germany's First U-Boat Attacks Along the American Coast in World War II* (hereafter, Gannon). Gannon and Morison's *War* differ in their views of Rear Admiral King's response; this author sides with Gannon. David Irving tells the *Carlton's* story in *The Destruction of Convoy PQ.17* in which he recalls interviews with naval and merchant seamen who were aboard several of the ships. See also, Martin Middlebank's *Convoy* and Gibson's *Ordeal of Convoy N.Y.119.* Morison's *War* and Gannon cover the early German penetration of the convoys; Gannon also covers the affair of the *Robin Moor.* Arthur Gordon's privately published *Years of Peril* tells the story of Cameron and the *Brilliant.* Morison's *War* plots the extent of the 1942 shipping losses. The little-known story of Gwynn Island is recounted in Stone, William T., and Fessenden S. Blanchard, *A Cruising Guide to the Chesapeake* (New York: Dodd, Mead, 1978); this yachtsman's book is not included in the bibliography. Bartholomew and *NYT* give details of the loss of the *Normandie.* Sawyer and Mitchell's *Liberty Ships* and Sawyer's *Liberty Ships: History of the "Emergency" Type Cargo Ships Constructed in the United States During World War II* are definitive. Bauer gives a lower figure for the number of Libertys (he may have excluded those converted to tankers); Sawyer is considered to be correct. Morison's *War* describes kamikaze attacks. David Syrett's article "World War II: The Battle of the Atlantic," in *American Neptune,* references the Admiralty Historical Section, "The Defeat of the Enemy Attack on

Shipping, 1939–1945," appendix 2, in describing the turning point in the ocean war. Braynard tracks the *Lurline.* The American Merchant Marine Veterans are the source of the statistics in the present work on merchant mariner casualties.

CHAPTER 15

The development of radar and loran is recounted in Tony Devereux's *Messenger Gods of Battle.* Bauer treats the postwar reorganization of federal agencies; *Historical Dictionary* charts the bureaucracies in detail. The information in the present work on later developments in the U.S. Coast Guard, the Military Sea Transportation Service (Military Sealift Command), the Hydrographic Office (later part of NOAA), and other agencies is from the author's direct research within those organizations or their replacements (Military Sealift Command, NOAA, and so forth). Wall, Melvin Maddocks' *Great Liners,* John Maxtone-Graham's *Only Way to Cross,* and Braynard and William Miller's *Fifty Famous Liners* are illustrative sources for the rise of Atlantic liners. In *Rise and Decline* De La Pedraja gives a business-oriented perspective on the development of the big shipping companies. Braynard has pictures of the well-known ships. Several articles in *NYT* tracked the *Savannah.* The *Congressional Record* carries details of Aiken's investigations of the Maritime Commission. Jerry Shields tells the Ludwig story in *The Invisible Billionaire: Daniel Ludwig.* An obituary of William Francis Gibbs in *NYT* gives a substantial account of the *United States.* The author's own recollections of life in the United States Lines, coupled with those of Commodore Alexanderson, are also incorporated in the discussion in the present work.

CHAPTER 16

The Maritime Administration is the source of shipping statistics for the postwar years through 1995. John McPhee's *Looking for a Ship* describes life aboard a containership, and the state of maritime unions in the last quarter of the twentieth century. William Miller's *Last Atlantic Liners* covers the demise of the passenger trade. Contemporary *NYT* articles describe the introduction of McLean's containerships. The Great Lakes Maritime Academy is the source of the details of its founding and of information about life on the lakers. Thomas Farnquist's "Requiem for the *Edmund Fitzgerald,*" in the *National Geographic,* has photographs and the route of the ship's final voyage. A letter to the editor after the publication of Farnquist's article (Tom Burk, *National Geographic,* May 1996) reports that the freighter *Manitoulin* heard a safety call from the *Fitzgerald*—a signal less urgent than an SOS. The *U.S. Coast Guard Marine Casualty Report*

No. USCG 16732/64216 leaves a strong impression that leaking hatches contributed to the foundering. Eric Nalder's *Tankers Full of Trouble* (hereafter, Nalder) gives an overview of the tanker trade and sheds light on stresses within the oil-shipping world. Navigational details of the *Exxon Valdez* accident are from the *Alaska Oil Spill Commission Report;* the map was adapted from the *Anchorage Daily News.* John Keeble's *Out of the Channel: The* Exxon Valdez *Oil Spill in Prince William Sound* goes beyond official reports, supports Nalder, and provides an earlier history of oil spills. It is also the source of the author's statistics in the present work. A *Wall Street Journal* article and the author's interview of John Morris are the sources of details of the founding of Red River Shipping. (For a history of Afro-American seamen before the Civil War, see Martha Putney's *Black Sailors: Afro-American Merchant Seamen and Whalemen Prior to the Civil War,* and for more on Paul Cuffe, see Sheldon Harris's biography, *Paul Cuffe: Black America and the African Return.*) For contrasting views on the current and future state of the American-flagged merchant marine, see David O'Neil's "America's Orphan: The U.S. Flag Merchant Marine" and Rob Quartel's "American Flag at Sea: A Shipper's Perspective" in consecutive issues of *Sea History.*

Index

About the Author

John A. Butler is a graduate of the Massachusetts Maritime Academy and Holy Cross College. He served as a licensed deck officer for American Export and United States Lines, and as a line officer on a U.S. Navy (MSTS) tanker and troopship, and has skippered a variety of cruising sailboats. He was employed by IBM for more than thirty years, holding positions in marketing, management development, and technical education.

His articles on computer technology and maritime affairs have been published by *LAN Technology*, Science Research Associates, and *Professional Mariner*. He is a member of the National Maritime Historical Society, the Steamship Historical Society of America, and Washington Independent Writers, and is the author of *Strike Able-Peter: The Stranding and Salvage of the USS* Missouri. In his spare time he edits the World Wide Web site of the Massachusetts Maritime Academy Alumni Association.

He and his wife of thirty-six years live in Potomac, Maryland, and are the parents of five children.